NICHOLAS C BROWN

BETTER THAN RICH AND FAMOUS

My Papua New Guinea days

Mereo Books

2nd Floor, 6-8 Dyer Street, Cirencester, Gloucestershire, GL7 2PF
An imprint of Memoirs Book Ltd. www.mereobooks.com

Better than rich and famous: 978-1-86151-964-1

First published in Great Britain in 2020
by Mereo Books, an imprint of Memoirs Books Ltd.

Copyright ©2020

Nicholas C Brown has asserted his right under the Copyright Designs and
Patents Act 1988 to be identified as the author of this work.

The address for Memoirs Books Ltd. can be
found at www.memoirspublishing.com

Memoirs Books Ltd. Reg. No. 7834348

Typeset in 13/20pt Century Schoolbook
by Wiltshire Associates Ltd.
Printed and bound in Great Britain

CONTENTS

About the Author
Dedication
Foreword
Introduction

PART ONE

1   A bit of a surprise.. 1
2   How on earth did I get here?............................... 5
3   Traveller's genes 9
4   So, the journey begins…...................................... 14
5   The reality of the sea 22
6   Kuraio at last 45
7   Getting on with it 65
8   Apprehension 93

PART TWO

9   Incredible fortune 125
10   Travel for business 149
11   Climb every mountain... 174
12   We nearly didn't make it 209
13   On the Sepik 216
14   Work and pleasure 234
15   So many goings on 252
16   Back to Bougainville... 267
17   What's next? 279

Postscripts
- The fate of the MV *Kiriaka Aro* 300
- Mining Bougainville 303
- Cargo cult revisited 306

Bibliography.. 308
Other Books.. 310
Acknowledgements 311
E&OE and note on terms used.................................... 312
Endnotes 314

ABOUT THE AUTHOR

Nicholas Brown was born on the 24th of December in 1946 in Ealing, London, a Christmas gift for Mum and Dad! He grew up in the West Country, studied in the Midlands, and worked for a few years in Buckinghamshire. Determined to travel further and see more of the world, he left Britain in 1972.

After living and working for several years in Papua New Guinea, he travelled through Asia and took a posting in the Caribbean before finally settling, as much as he ever would, in Australia.

Along with great enthusiasm for experiencing new and unusual places, Nicholas spent much of his career to helping others develop their businesses, undertaking occasional voluntary work and having a great time in doing both.

Nearly fifty years on he decided it was time for a change and retired to enjoy writing, raging about politics, listening to music, watching Formula One motor racing and – travelling!

Nicholas is married with one daughter.

DEDICATION

I dedicate this book to my mother, Dorothy Helen Cowper, who enjoyed adventures of her own in her childhood. She travelled twice by ship between the UK and the Antipodes in the 1920s, quite an undertaking in those days.

With her father passing away far too soon on her last visit to Australia, she returned to Britain with her mother and sisters, leaving him, my grandfather, buried in Fawkner Cemetery, in Melbourne.

Helen, as she was known, was a practical, unpretentious and attractive woman who stood no nonsense, had no qualms about telling me right from wrong and, amongst many other things, how to look out for myself.

The stories that follow are of events which I could never have experienced without her encouragement. They are an expression of my deep gratitude for being so wonderfully supportive and understanding in all my endeavours.

FOREWORD

By Margaret Ryan RSM AO
(PNG 1977-1980, revisited 2014, 2016, 2017, 2019)

Papua New Guinea achieved independence in 1975. The 1970s, pre and post-Independence were exciting times for Papua New Guineans and expatriates alike. 'Rich and Famous' is a fascinating reflection of the time Nick enjoyed there. It is an honest and forthright tale of the adventures of a young English VSO volunteer that began in 1972 with an assignment to Bougainville Island as a "boat captain" on the Solomon Sea and ended as a Technical Officer in the Public Service, travelling for one of the newest governments on the planet. It is a tale of his time spent in helping in a country on its way to independence, and in the process, enjoying all the challenges and adventures (and a few misadventures) one could imagine.

His story rings so true for me. The VSOs, as with most other volunteers, were thrown into foreign lands with little political, social, lingual or cultural briefing. Often there loomed a substantial gap between professional experience and the magnitude of the task at hand. Almost always, the resources for the task were sadly lacking. "Boat captain" indeed – more like boat in need! This tale of adventures, from the coastal islands to the Western Province, from the developing capital of Port Moresby to the languid, crocodile-infested Sepik River, gives the fascinating observations of the young foreigner to the awakening PNG nation. It makes great reading.

Eventually, after Nick had completed his stint as a volunteer, he faced the prospect of returning to England with its ongoing struggling economy or returning to PNG to continue the adventure. The problem was that the years away had been so formative (for young workers especially) that the notion of returning was now viewed through eyes that were "half PNG, half Anglo". Britain had diminished in meaningfulness, but the decision to stay or leave had to be made, and that is a part of the story.

By some happy coincidence, some forty years after our time in Papua New Guinea, Nick and I ended up as neighbours and friends in Australia. We had worked there, unknown to each other, for some of the same period, at opposite ends of the nation.

As members of an Australian relief team we were up before dawn, worked flat-out in the hospital or went out on medical patrols through the swamps or up the steep sides of the Torricelli Mountains; our social life was the hospitality shown in each other's homes or those of the villagers. Yet we shared the same zest for adventure, the same willingness to give our all and the same propensity for misguided strategies as did Nick. We tried with all our strength to help this young nation forward. We had much to learn, and the learning makes for good reading.

INTRODUCTION

"I wanted real adventures to happen to myself. But real adventures, I reflected, do not happen to people who remain at home: they must be sought abroad." – James Joyce

I came to realise that there are countless activities of significance standing tall beside the pinnacles of making a fortune or winning a Nobel Prize. Travelling through foreign lands, sailing the open sea, climbing a mountain or simply admiring nature's beauty… for those who choose to dare, the list is long. But little accrues from sitting in an office and dreaming, one must get out there and do it!

Being quite realistic about my prospects of ever achieving fame and fortune, I decided to move away from my predictable world and do something quite different. Essentially, the impetus came down to affairs of the heart, a mundane job and, above all, a burning desire to see the world.

My ensuing adventures occurred during the decade of the 1970s, an era of great importance for humanity. There was the 'hippy' movement that carried over from the 1960s, morphed into 'Flower Power' and then gained leverage against the war in

Vietnam. There was economic recession in the West, increasing violence in the Middle East, genocide in Cambodia and some form of closure in Mao's Cultural Revolution in the Far East. There was a lot going on.

The kind of turmoil I experienced however was of a different nature. The wars and violence passed me by as I went from adolescence to young adulthood, but many other, lower-order things affected my generation (sex, drugs and rock and roll spring to mind). We had survived the swinging '60s, and were now rocking through the '70s. And I ended up enjoying it all in a part of the world that was as remote as one could imagine from my original home of Britain.

My story comprises anecdotes woven together as a memoir of my time in what was originally the UN Mandated Australian Territory of Papua and New Guinea. The narrative includes stories of the years before my departure from Britain in 1972 but focuses mainly on the time I lived and worked in that tropical paradise. Significant events played out for the people there, and for me also, as the country quietly transitioned through self-government to eventually become an independent nation.

This is a story of travel and adventure, about living and working in the tropics, well before the advent of mobile phones and the Internet. It is about the good and the exciting, the bad and sometimes the quite frightening; and, to a certain extent, about enlightenment.

PART ONE

CHAPTER 1

A BIT OF A SURPRISE

One evening in London, in 1972, I joined forty-nine other adventurous 'do-gooders' at a Voluntary Service Overseas (VSO) orientation night. As we reached the door, we were each given a lapel badge stating our first name, the title of a job and the name of the country where we were going. Glancing at the badges being handed out ahead of me, I saw 'David – Doctor – Botswana', 'Alison – Teacher – Trinidad' etc., the sorts of jobs and places that I thought overseas volunteering was all about. Taking my badge, I looked, and looked again; it read 'Nick – Boat Captain – PNG'.

I stared in amazement. This is surely a mistake? I loved sailing and I recalled how I had told the Selection Panel about my messing around in a dinghy on Taplow Lake, but to captain a boat? This was a little more serious, and in somewhere called 'PNG'. Where on earth was that anyway?

After a few seconds of shock, I played along as if I knew exactly what I was in for and chatted nonchalantly to others, who looked equally surprised when they saw my badge. I was not going to complain at the eleventh hour, even if I had no idea what the job might entail.

An excited-looking guy with a moustache and a wild head of hair appeared from out of the crowd. "Hi Nick, I'm Martin, I'm going to Papua New Guinea as well," he said.

Peering at my badge, he exclaimed, "Boat Captain. Wow! That's pretty cool. What's your background?"

With an intense, in-your-face, animated manner, Martin did not beat about the bush. We were all very excited at going overseas and, to a certain extent just a little nervous, although we would never admit to it.

"Hi Martin. All pretty exciting isn't it, but where are we going?" I said, avoiding the tricky bit about the boat. "Where exactly is Papua New Guinea?"

"Oh, its north of Australia somewhere, Pacific Ocean, I think. Not sure really, but it's not Africa. We'll soon see!"

"Can't wait. When do you fly out?"

By this stage everyone in the group was talking at the tops of their voices, shouting excitedly about their postings to make themselves heard.

"Week tomorrow, via New York and Honolulu. I guess we'd be on the same flight?"

Amazing. Everyone else was going to Africa or the Caribbean and here I was going to a place I had never even heard of.

Immediately after the orientation, I raced home to find out where PNG was. My lack of awareness was reasonable, as I discovered my old atlas called the place 'The Australian Trust

Territory of Papua and New Guinea'. Then, from the VSO notes, I found the name had just been changed to Papua New Guinea this very year. There again, it was often known as "New Guinea," or "TPNG" or simply "PNG". All rather confusing! My uncertainty continued when I found that this was only the eastern half of the island. The western half was part of Indonesia and that had its own choice of names, Dutch New Guinea, Irian Jaya or West Papua – depending on one's political persuasion, I imagined.

Reading up the British Council notes and what little I could find on the place, it appeared that PNG was mainly known for the writings of anthropologists who, it seemed, had a particular interest in cannibalism, savages and 'free love'. I wasn't too sure about the first two, but I certainly liked the sound of the last!

Before I left England, I made it clear to VSO that I was not sure I was able to captain a boat. The response was, essentially, "Don't worry, there is much more to the job than that. They need someone to look after the mechanical equipment, manage a business, that sort of thing. You'll be working with the West Coast Development Society on Bougainville."

And, to make sure I would at least be up to the job of dealing with the machinery (and assuming I could handle the management), VSO enrolled me on a tractor maintenance course. I travelled up to Massey Ferguson near Coventry and, as one would expect of a manufacturer, everything was professional, the machinery, the tools and equipment were comprehensive and the workshop facilities clinical. There were some parallels with the place where I had studied automobile engineering a few years earlier, but Massey's equipment was far better than that of the Technical College at Bromsgrove, despite it being one of its kind for the British motor industry.

CHAPTER 2

HOW ON EARTH DID I GET HERE?

"It's better to own a little and see the world than to own the world and see little" – Alexander Sattler

At last it looked like I really was going to travel and I reflected on my good fortune and how I had managed to get thus far. It was only a year or so back that my employer had told me they had shelved their plans for expansion into Germany and I would be stuck in Slough forever!

My emotions were in a mess for other reasons, even before that. After a long and somewhat tumultuous relationship, I had been jilted. I had to escape. That was how I had found this job a hundred miles away from the pain, a challenge to occupy my mind and get over it all.

Now, having concentrated on my work and enjoying fun with friends for a couple of years, I had recovered from the emotional turmoil; I was sharing a flat in Maidenhead, partying and having a ball. I'd survived the swinging '60s and was just getting into the 1970s, horse riding on Dorney Common, racing an autocross car I'd built, sailing a dinghy on Taplow Lake and all too often drinking with friends at a pub of an evening.

Sometimes a few of us flatmates would paddle across the Thames to Skindles Hotel in a little clinker-built rowing boat and, after a few beers, testing our sobriety, we'd struggle back against the current to save ourselves from being swept downstream. It was a time of partying and life was good, but something was missing, something fundamental. I was not getting anywhere, career-wise or physically. I needed more – I had to travel.

I thought my aspiration to see the world was reasonable, but a lack of cash thwarted my plans. I knew about the serious explorers of course; they always seemed to have enough money. There were the hippy types, bumming around the world trying to find themselves after reading Kerouac. Not for me. I had to do something useful. Then there were the clever people with qualifications and skills to sell – they all travelled. But for me as a commercial trainee, basically one step up from a humble clerk, it all seemed quite unrealistic.

After all those years of study, I had eventually found a respectable nine to five office job. It was with a company that manufactured gaskets! Essential products but dreadfully dull! Working diligently over the years, I would arrive at my office each day with the steamy mist of the Slough Estates cooling towers and the smell of chocolate from the neighbouring Mars Bars factory assaulting my senses. The low-lying cloud and frequent gloom of the weather did not help my demeanour much either. One day it all became too much and I decided I'd had enough. I was earning a supposedly reasonable salary, but I was perpetually broke. There was no prospect of saving enough to live in a decent place, let alone travel.

My place was one room in a damp old house, right beside the Thames in Maidenhead. It meant sharing a kitchen and bathroom with a couple of guys, and there were three more pretty crazy guys, living in the flat upstairs. The social life was tremendous, but the living conditions were dreadful. One night a large piece of the ceiling fell and landed on the floor a foot or so away from my head. The mould-streaked glossy yellow walls of the kitchen dripped condensation when we boiled our veggies. Then, one Christmas, I came back from visiting family and found a dead mouse in the bottom of the empty garbage bin in the kitchen. Beside it was lying the head, four feet and the tail of what had been another mouse. What a ghastly place. It was near-squalor with few prospects of escaping this or the monotony of my job.

Some months earlier my employer had told me I would be first in line if I wanted to go to the new office being set up in Germany. They even paid for language classes. A flat-mate and I would get home of an evening laughing as we practised our 'Guten Tags' and 'Wie geht's' with affected German accents. We thought we were pretty good, until we discovered the grammar!

But now, with the downturn in the economy, all businesses agreed it was not a good time to expand. My employer ditched the plan and with my travel hopes dashed I was facing the same old office work, now and into the distant future.

To improve my chances of getting anywhere I applied for a course to study management. Surely that would stand me in good stead? At around the same time, I saw a small advertisement from a rather vague-sounding organisation called the British Council. Could this be a front for MI5 perhaps? It turned out to be something a lot less exciting, but still quite fascinating.

The British Council ran a programme called Voluntary Service Overseas (VSO), and yes, they were looking for volunteers. It sounded much more fun than marketing gaskets, and it was overseas. The catch was that they wanted trained teachers, nurses or professionals and I doubted my auto-engineering diploma would appeal. It was none of these things. But I applied anyway and enrolled to study management at the same time.

Of course, as luck would have it, I was accepted for both. Being reasonably level-headed, I put my adventures on hold, the British Council deferred my posting and I commuted up to the Polytechnic of Central London for a year. Now, with overseas travel within reach and despite an ongoing weakness for partying, I got serious with my studies and, for once, passed with reasonably good grades.

Why was I so keen to see the world? The truth is, I was born to travel; it was in the family. The craving had started long before all this, back in my childhood in the English countryside.

CHAPTER 3

TRAVELLER'S GENES

I grew up in rural Wiltshire, a hundred miles as the crow flies due west of London. Freshford, Bratton, Westwood, Limpley Stoke, Winsley – these were the villages of my childhood. An old stone cottage with a thatched roof here, shared rooms in a house with gas lighting for a while; cold and dark old houses. Village lanes with dry-stone walls, cows in the fields, walks in mysterious woods. I coughed and spluttered over smoking Old Man's Beard, the plant we kid's called 'woodbine'. This was my playground, a beautiful, unspoilt part of the West Country close to the lovely old city of Bath.

An idyllic childhood, one might assume. It wasn't really; my early years were quite unsettled. Not that my father was an itinerant or on the run from the law or anything exciting like that. On the contrary, he was a very conservative man, supplementing his income as the Deputy Architect for Wiltshire by renovating houses and selling them on, hopefully at a profit. Consequently, my mother, my older brother and I spent a lot of time moving from house to house. I went to ten different schools before I was ten years of age, and lived in as many different houses. It is true that each time we moved the house was slightly better than the one before, but any money Father made from all his hard work was ploughed back into the next project or spent down the pub, and, much to Mother's frustration, we were perpetually broke. Any friends I made were soon forgotten as I moved on to the next new school.

Eventually, in the late 1950s, having moved yet again, we arrived at what was to become our family home. Rather grandly, if unimaginatively, known as 'East Hill', it was just 156a, Trowbridge Road, Winsley, with the address being the result of one enormous old house being divided into two, with 156b being correspondingly titled 'West Hill'. Our half was still large: two storeys, four bedrooms, metre-wide stone walls. It was big and it was horribly cold! Having been built ninety years earlier, it carried with it the characteristics of that earlier age and had a fireplace in every room. We would only have the one fire going however and, as kids, we had to carry buckets of coal from the scullery at one end of the house to the living room at the other each day. The rest of the place was freezing and the old lead pipes froze and burst in winter. We had coal, we had paraffin stoves, we had electric heaters; we had every form of heating known to man and still we were cold!

The village itself was pleasant. Each Sunday a small cohort of the faithful frequented what I thought was the rather suitably named Saint Nicholas' Anglican Church. Mother dragged me along to a service here some weeks, but father and brother somehow managed to escape this duty.

The real year-round nerve centre of village life was the Seven Stars pub. And then, for each at their designated time, the cricket and soccer fields were appropriately lively venues. But apart from Burghope Manor and the council estate behind the church, the village was little other than a narrow lane, winding its way through a series of tortuous bends between high stone walls and ancient houses. The big green Number 48 double-decker bus (Bath to Trowbridge and return) would squeeze through this meandering route with incredible agility. Unfortunately for us two kids, looking for some excitement, it never had a head-on or even left as much as a graze of paint on the walls.

I always considered myself a bit of a loner, but I was also a bit enterprising. Certainly not like the early missionaries in deepest darkest Africa, but venturesome enough to get out and about. Moving house and school over the years contributed, I suppose. Perhaps I got some inspiration from my brother who, when he was home from boarding school, was always up to some crazy antics or other. Hot-wiring the family car for joy rides at night was our favourite; that was until we ran out of petrol miles from home and our very irate father had to rescue us! Or maybe I just wanted to get away from the family? As an eleven-year-old, I did not apply too much reason to what was going on around me. But after getting a decent bicycle for my birthday (straight handlebars, black paint with a fine red stripe, three-Speed Sturmey-Archer gears *and* a speedometer), I got the notion that I had to go somewhere, anywhere really.

I decided to ride up to London. I planned the trip in minute detail: how far I thought I could ride in one day, how many days I needed overall, where I would stay overnight etc. I joined the Youth Hostels Association (YHA) and made bookings myself by telephone (with a bit of help from Mother). Then, on the next long school holiday, with ten shillings in my pocket and a change of clothes in my panniers, I set off.

As I cycled down the road and got to the first junction, I was thinking 'Gosh, what am I doing? I can't go back after all that preparation'.

Cycling on, talking to myself, worrying about taking the wrong turn and consulting my little map, I was pedalling so fast I thought my little legs would fall off. The weather was excellent; the traffic was light, there were few cars on the road and it was safe. If there were any problems with child abduction or kids disappearing, you never heard about it in 1958.

After cycling along the old A4 on my first day's ride and by now with a very sore backside, I waddled into the YHA in Marlborough to sign in. The Warden looked over my shoulder to see who was with me and, being a little taken aback by my explanation that it was just me, started saying something about minors having to be accompanied. Some older guy behind me, a stranger who heard what was going on, piped up and said 'He's with me' and with that the Warden turned a blind eye. I had ridden nearly fifty kilometres that day and was pretty sore. I didn't want any fuss.

The second night I spent at Streatley, near Goring Gap, in 'a large Victorian house in a very picturesque village on the River Thames,' another fifty-four kilometres further on. Then, pedalling away like a loony and slowly nearing London, I started getting nervous. It was all so hard and grey and built up; dingy and soulless. It was not anything like the Wiltshire countryside.

But I had made it. I had got to London!

After only one night spent with a lot of strangers in the cold, smelly and noisy YHA dormitory in Oxford Street and feeling very lonely, I turned around and did it all over again. This time I was in a hurry; I wanted to get home!

How Mother had let me go I shall never know, but she trusted in my abilities. By the time I had got back I had cycled over three hundred kilometres, from a little West Country village up to the Big Smoke and back, at the tender age of eleven; well okay, eleven and a half, I suppose!

A few years later a disaster hit the family. Father suddenly died. He was only forty-eight. I was still a kid and had just started getting close to him. I well recall the last time he and I chatted; we were walking in the back garden. He was probably telling me some job he wanted me to do around the house. He was always one for doing things. Next thing, I was helping Mother carry his body from the bathroom to the bedroom. One slipper came off and I dropped his legs and ran out of the room crying. I found it hard to deal with the 'one minute he's there, the next minute he's gone' scenario. With my brother away at boarding school, it left a dreadful quiet emptiness in the house. I knew the situation was serious, but I had no idea what to do about it. I was not so much feeling sorry for him as I was for Mother and myself. I called my friend Pete Slater, and he and I went down to a pub in Bradford-on-Avon, where I cried over a pint of beer. I never really knew my father, but the effect of his passing added a little more to my already restless nature.

CHAPTER 4

SO, THE JOURNEY BEGINS...

Back to 1972, and after years of study in Bath and Worcestershire, distracted as they were by a lovely girlfriend, my need to travel had taken on international dimensions. I needed more than the English countryside and wild, boozy parties in Maidenhead. I had finished my study of management and, true to their word the British Council had come back with details of my posting and had told me to report for a briefing session 'forthwith'!

After that orientation night and now knowing the job was to captain a boat, I suddenly had cold feet. What had I got myself into? I had volunteered with all good intentions, but had

I overstated my public spirit a little? I just wanted to see the world really and now, having found a way of doing it, was I being dishonest?

Of course, I wanted to help others, isn't that why one volunteers? But then I wondered if pursuing my interest to travel conflicted with the 'doing good' bit and cancelled out my altruism. I thought about that for about ten seconds and said: 'What the hell!' Someone was going to get my services for free, and after so many years of trying to get to travel here was my big chance. I certainly wasn't going to give it up now.

And, so, before I knew it, on Tuesday 19th September 1972, after a riotous farewell party thrown by my flat-mates the night before (disco music, lights, dancing and plenty of booze for good measure), I was at Heathrow Airport with a cheap cardboard suitcase containing three pairs of underpants and socks, a couple of shirts and slacks and my toothbrush rattling around inside.

"Now make sure you brush your teeth regularly and get plenty of sleep. And don't drink too much dear!" said Mother. I was being farewelled by her and my favourite aunt. I hate farewells. What is there to say?

They themselves had both made a long journey just to see me off. Any travel for Mother, who had MS and was shuffling around with walking sticks, was an effort. Her sister Joan had travelled all the way up from Plymouth to Bath by train. Then she and Mother had caught another train up from Bath to Heathrow, coming via Paddington Station – just for an hour or so to say 'Farewell'.

Being a young guy in the company of other young guys, I didn't care too much for the mothering smothering. Although secretly grateful, I still hated farewells and I could not get away soon enough. There were big kisses all round and 'Love you dear, take care'. Was that a choke I heard in her voice? No, not really. Mother didn't cry at that sort of thing, well not in front of me at least, and this twenty-five-year-old gung-ho bloke didn't worry too much about his mother's feelings and concerns anyway.

Checking in with me were Martin Daintith and Dave Clarkson, and with the 'goodbyes' ringing faintly in our ears, we were on our way. From then on, we each shared our views on the world, where we had come from, where we were going and what we thought we were going to do.

Sipping whiskies until we were nicely mellowed, we chased the sun to New York. Flying at 35,000 feet and travelling at 600 miles per hour in a Super VC10[1], we felt like kings. It was our first flight ever, and it was a real buzz. We refuelled in NY and flew on to LA, then in quick succession to Honolulu, Nandi in Fiji and finally, for a while at least, on to Sydney. Having lost a day somewhere along the way, we arrived on Thursday 21st 1972. Even though we were sitting down most of the time, it was exhausting.

A representative of the British Council met us at Sydney Airport, gave us a taxi voucher and five Aussie dollars each, and the name of a hotel. That night, the Secretary of the British Council sent around a car to pick us up and treated we three to dinner at his beautiful residence overlooking Sydney Harbour. We sat outside, under a stone-columned loggia, a gentle breeze wafting through and cooling us down after a sweltering day. We were even more impressed by the pretty young waitress dressed in her far-too-short black mini skirt and white pinafore, but she stonily returned our secret, lecherous stares, looking disdainfully down her nose.

The Secretary, a Pom himself of course (and a slightly snooty one at that), had landed on his feet. He had a great job, mixing with a veritable Who's Who of Australian society and spreading good ol' British culture wherever he went. He chatted about what the British Council expected of us and how it operated, but I didn't take much of it in. We were suffering from a new experience called jet-lag and were naturally, just a wee bit hung-over as well.

Nevertheless, we learned the British Council had far wider responsibilities than simply placing us 'jolly vollies' into some project or other. He must have found entertaining us rather scruffy twenty-five-year-olds all a bit below his dignity, and, in return, we were a little bemused by his urbane and somewhat condescending manner. Even so, we had a lovely evening.

Next day we looked around town. We did Manly by hydrofoil, went up Australia Tower, went shopping for cameras and then, having developed a thirst, went drinking our way around countless pubs. We sampled as many of the unusually cold beers as we could handle and had a brilliant time.

Too soon, we were off again, flying on to Brisbane, this time in a Boeing 727. From there, we flew on to Port Moresby, the capital of Papua New Guinea, learning in the process that it was, somewhat affectionately, referred to by its airline acronym, the same moniker commonly given to us by the Aussies, 'POM'!

Dick Bird, the VSO Field Officer, met us on our arrival at Jacksons Airport, along with a humidity that hit us in the face like a hot, damp towel, something we could never have imagined. But before we could worry about that, our fresh-faced, chubby, matter-of-fact leader bundled us all into his car, crammed our luggage in the boot, and we were off.

We drove along hot, dusty roads, one minute in stark bright sunlight and the next in tree-blackened shadows, weaving in between slower, beat-up vehicles and dodging the occasional pothole and errant pedestrian. We passed rows of utilitarian houses, all similar in style: single-storey, grey 'fibro' walls and corrugated iron roofs, all quietly roasting away in the heat of the day. Instead of being built solidly on the ground, many were half a metre or so higher, sitting on concrete posts. As Dick explained, to allow the frequent and torrential downpours of rain to run underneath and not through the building!

Eventually, we arrived at Dick's own place, not a thatched roof hut in a native village but another 'fibro' house like those we had already seen, and in a very European-looking suburb with the charming name of Boroko.

Being a bachelor, Dick clearly didn't have much time for domesticity. His house was sparsely decorated and the crush of people easily overshadowed whatever meagre furnishings were there. I had thought we three were 'it', but a whole gang of other volunteers picked up from earlier flights packed the place. Dick introduced us to the crowd in general and to his friend Margaret, who, he explained, helped him out on these occasions.

Martin and I made a beeline for a couple of pretty-looking girls we spied across the room. But, after introducing ourselves, we found they were not VSOs at all, but lay missionaries, from an order known as Palms! I had assumed we would all be from the same organisation, but Margaret had brought these girls over just to help them settle in. Our interest waned further when we heard they were going to some place up-country and nowhere near our own postings!

After a few refreshments, Dick and Margaret packed us all into a mini-bus and, after explaining that we were to spend the afternoon on the beach 'to relax and acclimatise', drove us down and around the many steep, alpine-like corners towards Moresby CBD.

Eventually, travelling along beside a stretch of a treed and dappled shady land, we had our first glimpse of the sparkling blue waters of the Coral Sea. A hop, skip and jump out of the bus and we were on the golden sands of Ela Beach. A real tropical beach!

We were all so excited to be there, but none of us had thought to bring our swimming gear. Some sat around in the shade chatting, whilst I and others went off for a paddle and soon found the water too shallow to swim anyway.

We waded around happily, sea-grass tickling our toes, until suddenly a yell went up from one of the girls. Running swiftly back up on to the beach, she cried out that she had been stung. Not to be outdone, I also quickly hobbled out with a sharp pain in my big toe.

We had not been stung at all but in fact pricked by sea urchins. These little blighters, hiding among the sea-grass, had spikes bigger than any splinter I had ever seen, and they hurt! I was fortunate, I only got one spike; others got several.

Without any fuss, Dick got iodine from the mini-bus, dabbed our wounds and assured us it was nothing serious. There was a few brave-faced folk limping around for a while after, and much more sitting and much less paddling. Welcome to Paradise!

Our stay in POM was as brief as could be. On the Monday we went to our different projects around the country and immediately lost track of each other. Dick took me to the airport, gave me my ticket, put me on a plane and told me someone by the name of Stewart would meet me at the other end. From then on, I focused on getting to my posting.

I flew in a noisy, but sturdy, twin-engine, turbo-prop Fokker F27, from POM to Lae and then on to Rabaul on the smaller island of East New Britain. Soaring over and through cotton-boll clouds, I mused at how, in the past few days, I had gone from the temperate and sophisticated epitome of middle-class Britain to this supposedly primitive South Pacific island. I was now about as far as I could physically be from my earlier haunts and totally intrigued by my new environment, so brilliant in contrast to the grey skies back home.

Funnily enough, I found the place was not so alien. In fact, the differences were far less extreme than I had envisaged. Much of the language was English (well, Australian English), the food so far had been European and even the buildings were sort of Western and not the grass huts I had imagined there would be in a primitive country.

But then there were the inescapable physical differences. It was very hot and very, very humid and the native people, who I soon learned were respectfully referred to as 'locals', were very black. However, there again, there were also plenty of white people around with the Australian administration employees providing something of a reassuring buffer between 'them' and me. I also spotted what appeared to be some 'local' foreigners. It was hard to put my finger on it but there were some subtle cues, such as the nature of their clothes, a swagger in their walk and perhaps more obvious, with the Europeans at least, being slightly more tanned and much less pink than us real expats. I found later these were largely people of Chinese extraction, who, along with a smattering of people from other countries, had indeed been born and raised in Papua New Guinea.

So far, having been nicely sheltered by VSO, I had not met any native Papua New Guineans and was yet to experience any genuine cultural contrast. Knowing real differences were far more than skin-deep and would take a while to appreciate anyway, my concern now was more about the on-going nature of my journey. Before I had set out from Britain, I had not given much thought about how long it would take to get to my posting. I knew I had wanted to travel but now, after six days or so on the road and still not yet there, I was not too interested in the complexities of cultural difference. As we approached Rabaul and buckled up for landing, I felt I just wanted to get there.

CHAPTER 5

THE REALITY OF
THE SEA

Hot air blasted my face as I stepped down from the aeroplane and followed the gaggle of passengers across the tarmac. 'Whew! This'll take some getting used to,' I thought.

Swinging wearily in the heat-haze, the weather-worn 'Welcome to Rabaul' sign seemed to nod in agreement as I hurried into the air-conditioned arrivals hall. Immediately a rather dishevelled-looking fellow stepped out from the waiting crowd.

"Nick Brown?" Standing before me, in a scruffy T-shirt, a pair of dirty old blue shorts and rubber flip-flops was a real Robinson Crusoe. Although, from his accent he was without doubt British, he looked like he had been away for quite a while and adapted well to island life.

"Hi. You must be Stewart?" I said.

With a broad smile under his tousled blond hair, Stewart took my outstretched hand and, before I could ponder further, cheerily said, "Come on, grab your things, I've still got some shopping to do, and then I'll introduce you to the crew. We'll take a cab into town where we can pick up the car."

With perspiration running down my nose despite the air-conditioning and even with a confusion of thoughts in my mind (shopping, taking a taxi to a car?), I was happy to see that at least I would not be dressing like my colonial forebears. A collar and tie would be intolerable!

"Oh. Okay, but why didn't you drive over?"

"You'll understand when you see the car!"

After a little while, the cabbie dropped us off in a shady lane running alongside the Catholic mission house. Sitting adjacent to the fence and looking like it had been there for several years, was a dusty old blue and cream Holden station wagon. Stewart reassured me it worked well but needed jump-starting. So, as I stood behind, Stewart removed a rock from under a front wheel, hopped in and yelled, "Push now!"

With exotic tropical shrubbery catching my hair and now sweating even more profusely, I pushed the old wreck down the slight incline and out on to the road and jumped in. Stewart eased off the clutch, the engine spluttered into life, and we were away.

In a faint but cultured North Country accent contrasting strangely with his rather scraggy appearance, Stewart went on, "The old dear goes quite well really, but the battery needs replacing and the area around the airport is too flat to bump start in this heat [I'd never have guessed!] Besides, she's not registered, and there are too many cops around there. Having a car in Rabaul is a real godsend. We're jolly lucky. Our work would be a lot harder without it."

Stewart came across as a happy-go-lucky, can-do sort of guy, used to mucking in and sorting out whatever problem happened his way. There was a slight touch of sarcasm in his voice, coupled with a frequent, nervous little laugh, but not at all self-deprecating. He was full of enthusiasm and with a natural way of brushing off the negatives!

Eventually, having parked the car on a slope, he and I then spent the next couple of hours wandering around Rabaul. Stewart had to finish shopping for the Society and, equally as important, I needed to buy some clothes to replace my uncomfortably hot, Northern Hemisphere slacks and boots with some shorts, thongs and T-shirts!

So, while buying up half the town's supplies and getting a cheery 'Hello' from the storekeepers in the process, we chatted about each other's background and how we came to be there. Stewart hailed from Warrington, up north, and, somewhat reassuringly, had owned and sailed a sizable boat for a few years in Britain. By some small coincidence, he had also left a job in the car industry.

Later, shopping finished, we headed off to the harbour. As we drove past a profusion of tropical shrubbery growing out of various nooks and crannies, Stewart explained that Rabaul was known for being one of the most beautiful towns in the Pacific. It was true, the hibiscus, frangipani and bougainvillea neutralised the rather bland uniformity of the Western-style buildings. Huge, green-fronded coconut palms towered overhead, and under them the roads ran hither and thither in ragged and dusty contrast. Oddly enough, the lack of kerbing and unfinished edges of tarmac suited the place; anything else would have been out of character.

Further on, a little way in the distance, I could see a few low grass-covered, rounded, breast-shaped hills encircling the bay. Although blocking more distant views out to sea, they provided an attractive backdrop and more importantly, maintained the calmness of the waters.

Rabaul certainly looked like a tropical wonderland, but as skin colour gave little clue to cultural difference, I knew this landscape could also belie character. I would wait before passing judgement.

Eventually driving down to Simpson Harbour and out on to the quay, I finally saw the boat that had been on my mind since that night in London. It was a solid-looking craft. The dirty salt-white of the hull was off-set by pale, equally grimy, blue detailing around parts of her superstructure (vaguely hinting at some ambiguity between work and leisure). Stewart said she was Chinese-built, all wood construction (with a copper bottom to

MV *Kiriaka Aro* with her two-tier superstructure providing excellent visibility. Photo: Chris Powell

keep out borers), she had a capacity of up to thirty-five tons and was fifty-four feet at the waterline. Stewart reckoned she would do a respectable eight knots with a clean hull. She had been given the name *Kiriaka Aro*, which translated as 'Kiriaka Brothers'[2], and reflected the name of the villagers who owned her.

Somewhat unusually, to my uneducated eye at least, the *Kiriaka Aro* had two levels above deck. The first comprised a part-enclosed cabin and then, for about a quarter of her length forward from the stern, open-sided, airy, sleeping quarters. Above all this and set high and slightly forward of centre, was a small bridge, just big enough for three, or four at a squeeze, and allowing excellent visibility all around.

She looked functional and seaworthy, although perhaps a little top-heavy. But then I was looking at her with the eyes of an infrequent solo sailor on a calm English lake and under no illusions about what sailing the South Pacific Ocean demanded of a vessel.

On hearing our arrival, a solid-looking guy in dirty blue singlet and shorts appeared on deck. And, jumping ashore, he grabbed me by the hand and with an expansive grin, simply said 'G'day'. With a cap of tight curly hair, a high forehead, bloodshot eyes, fine white teeth and shiny, jet-black skin, he was a pretty impressive sort of fellow.

Stewart introduced me to Jacob, the First Mate.

"Hi, Jacob. Pleased to meet you," I said. I was thinking, 'My life's going to depend on this guy, I hope he knows what he's doing'.

Then, in the uncomfortable pregnant pause as Jacob and I stood grinning somewhat foolishly at each other, Stewart explained that our conversation would be limited as Jacob spoke mainly pidgin English[3].

Jacob was the first Bougainvillean I got to meet, and not a

little intimidating at that. His smile was friendly enough, but his body language was confusing. I figured it was part shyness on his part (of all things), but that he was also a little dismissive, perhaps sizing me up and wondering if I was up to the task. I shared his concern!

It was clear that learning pidgin was vital if I was going to take over, and now the reality of the task began to sink in, if you'll excuse the pun.

Stewart saved the moment by introducing me to the other crew who had started loading the results of our shopping, now being delivered to the docks. Each was as black and as curly-haired as Jacob, but their chuckles and friendly smiles were a little more welcoming to this wet behind the ear's white fella. I shook hands with each one in turn, simply saying 'Hi'. They all looked very black and very similar and I knew I would not only have trouble remembering their names but also putting a face to a name.

Later, lying on a dirty sheet over a rubber mattress and with the *Kiriaka* wallowing gently on the harbour waters, I pondered on my wish to see the world. I had not really considered the conditions of my travel and now realised I had been dreaming if I had thought the boat would be anything like passenger liner. I had swapped the comfort of my bed (albeit under a decaying ceiling) to sleep on a dirty bunk in a smelly cargo boat in the hot and humid tropics. It had been a tiring day, but I couldn't sleep. There was a strong whiff of fish, diesel and urine interspersed with something else I could not quite fathom. I eventually nodded off, sweating away gently and wondering 'How much further?'

Next day we were back into town for more shopping and then eventually went over to one of Stewart's friends for a most welcome shower. We arrived to find Alan and several other folk sitting around in a strangely darkened living room. It was late morning but the blinds were still down, to keep out the heat of course!

As we went the rounds introducing ourselves and as Alan explained that his friends were staying over after a party the night before, one very pretty girl hung on to my handshake a second longer than usual. She was gorgeous! Was I dreaming? It had been a long time between drinks.

After nattering away for a while, someone called out, 'Come on, time for a swim,' but while the others rushed off to change, Jenny and I hung back. For reasons that one could only guess were something to do with chemistry, we found ourselves talking like we had known each other all our lives. I had only just arrived and here I was with such a lovely girl already. I was not sure what I was thinking, but one thing was clear, it only involved Jenny and me!

As we continued to chat away, only vaguely aware of the others splashing and whooping around outside, we were suddenly surprised when a couple of guys ran into the house. They quickly grabbed me by my arms and legs, bundled me outside and threw me into the pool! As I scrambled about gagging, with water up my nose and down my throat, Stewart warned me that Jenny was Alan's girl and he got a bit upset with her flirting and was not averse to throwing the odd punch or two. With some sort of minor epiphany, I realised I had better watch out!

Eventually wearying from the crazy pool antics, we returned to the cool of the house and, with Jenny having prepared a meal, spent the rest of the day eating, drinking and sharing stories about life in the tropics.

Later that evening, with Jenny surreptitiously smiling a farewell in a pseudo-innocent sort of way which hinted at something that could have been but never was, Stewart and I took our leave and drove back down to the *Kiriaka*.

At midnight, on a high tide and with the forecast of a fair sea, we prepared to set sail for Kuraio. Jacob fired up the Gardener 6LX, Stewart helped with the rest of the crew and I stood and watched as we cast off and moved slowly away from the wharf. There didn't seem much to it really; sailing out of the harbour was easy.

It was a beautiful night with a black velvet sky perforated here and there with stars as bright as diamonds and wisps of clouds racing across the face of the moon. In the now balmy air, calm waters and with few other ships around, it was all 'bloody marvellous' really. But then, as we ran out of the harbour, Stewart described our route.

"We're making a few stops before Kuraio. We'll call into Buka and say 'Hi' to the priest there. I've a little job to do at Tsiroge, near Sohano, then we're dropping off stores at Sipai before we head on down to the Mission."

Somewhat ironically, after eight days on the road, I was getting a little tired of travelling. For some reason I had assumed we were sailing straight there, so I was a bit surprised. I asked, "So how long before we actually get to Kuraio?"

"Well, if the weather's fair and we make good progress, we'll hopefully be there in a couple more days."

I bit my tongue. What could I do? We would get there when we got there. But after the drinks earlier in the evening, the meeting and leaving of Jenny and length of the journey so far, I was starting to feel a bit jaded.

Stewart went on to explain that as the *Kiriaka Aro* was the only regular cargo vessel in the area, we, that is the West Coast Development Society, ran her from Kuraio down to Torokina, back up to Sipai, Sohano, Tsiroge and Buka, then across to Rabaul and back again every three or four weeks. Indeed, he said, it was the only way for us expatriates to get off the island and back to civilisation, apart from hacking our way out through the jungle. And he was not kidding![4]

The journey started smoothly enough, but the weather turned squally until it was quite unpleasant. With the possibility of a rogue wave drenching us, we moved down below. Sitting aft, with the breeze blowing through the open sides, was more comfortable, but with waves the size of which I had never seen before in my life, I had to admit I found it a trifle nerve-racking. Indeed, despite my love for sailing, I started feeling quite ill; the diesel exhaust wafting back and forth, combined with the urgent motion was having its effect.

There was something else that also roused my nausea, that horrible smell again. What was it? I made a note to ask Stewart later, but now, around two in the morning, I was too tired to bother. Instead I watched the rippled moon on the blackness of the waves and listened to the urgent slap of the sea against the hull, reassuringly offset by the solid pulse of the engine down below. Eventually, thinking of Jenny and me on a golden beach under the shade of a gently swaying palm tree, I fell into a fitful sleep.

Too soon, the rays and the heat of the sun woke me, and in that drowsy, half-sleep state I imagined I was now dressed in my smart captain's whites, running a container ship on the high seas, a nubile young lass waiting on me hand and foot, serving me bacon and eggs in the privacy of my own cabin…

But then, wide awake, Stewart popped his head around my

bunk and with a peremptory 'Morning!' thrust a packet of dry biscuits and a cup of black tea into my face. Great timing, but I could not expect even this kind of service to last – I would be getting my own in future! Any romantic notions of sailing the Coral Sea evaporated in the reality of rising dawn on this smelly Chinese trader. Now, in great contrast to my euphoria on leaving Rabaul, I was feeling the results of too much booze from the night before, the heat, the unfamiliar surroundings and that same damned smell. In terms of a typically British understatement, it all now seemed 'a bit of a shock'.

After the biscuit breakfast and being determined to track down the source of the smell, I rolled with the waves, staggered along the gangway and checked out the main cargo hold. The results of our shopping packed the place. There was a jumble of cases and packages, tinned fish, sacks of rice, cartons of soap, a bicycle! Plus, the all-pervasive aroma, but it was not coming from the cargo or the dunny.

I called out to Stewart, "What is that smell?"

"That? Oh, nothing much, it's the cocoa and copra, you'll get a better whiff of it when we have a load on board and make our next trip back up to Rabaul. What we've got now is the residue from our previous trips. You'll get used to it."

I realised I had no idea what either copra or cocoa was or what either smelled like in the raw. I had assumed cocoa beans would have a rich, chocolaty smell, perhaps like the Mars Bars of the factory next door? But the odour was more like human excrement, so I said as much to Stewart,

"No, no. Well, perhaps partly that, but it's mainly cocoa. You see, properly treated, cocoa beans don't smell much at all," he said. "The problem is, we do get a bit of mould in them now and then when they decompose, and that's what causes the foul smell."

"So, if that's the cocoa, what's copra then?"

Now a trifle exasperated and as if to say, 'You mean you really don't know what copra is?' Stewart said, "That's the dried kernels of coconuts. We harvest it on Bougainville, take it up to Rabaul and sell it to CPL, who then process it to be turned it into cooking oil."

'Well of course,' I said to myself, 'Everyone knows that, don't they!'

I found out later that, although copra does not smell particularly bad, it attracts thousands of purple-grey moths. These little critters enjoy a habit of quietly and imperceptibly settling anywhere and everywhere and then, when disturbed, swarming up like a blanket in your face.

By this stage, having observed that there was not much to do once underway, and now being out of sight of land altogether, I felt it time to raise the subject of running the boat.

"I've been meaning to ask you Stewart, VSO must have made a mistake putting 'Boat Captain' on my badge at the briefing session in London. Were they seriously expecting me to run this thing?"

"Nick, it's like this see. The second brief, the one they recruited you on, was for someone with an engineering background, someone who could look after mechanical equipment and manage the Society. We put that request in because they had tried to recruit a captain for the boat before but no one applied. So, we changed the brief, thinking that if we got someone with an engineering background, we could persuade that person to run the boat also. Simple as that really."

It appears that someone in the very different world of administration in London, miles from any South Pacific island, had, despite knowing about the difficulties, got a bit mixed up and put 'Boat Captain' on the badge anyway.

"Well, that's a pretty big assumption to make, Stewart. Seems a big ask. I'll have to see how it goes."

With a hint of disappointment in his voice, Stewart said, "Jacob is leaving at Christmas, so we have to get someone to manage the *Kiriaka* soon."

I made a quick visit to the bridge to check on our position, but with the vast expanse of sea and no land in sight to give me a bearing, there was nothing to answer my question. So, with a quick nod and smile to Jacob and his mate (and assuming they knew where we were and what they were doing), I went back below. I settled into my bunk and stared out at our wake for the next few hours. It was bright and sunny and although the temperature was climbing, the breeze from the sea moderated the humidity and the heat. It all looked very agreeable, but the sparkling blue of the ocean did not match my mood. I was getting fed up with the journey, and now worrying about the practicalities of running the *Kiriaka*. With people's lives at stake, the boat and all the cargo, it was beginning to seem a little scary. On top of this, there was just this tiny issue of communication. The Bougainvillean crew was chattering away in a mixture of *tok ples*, the local dialect, and pidgin English. I thought I recognised every other word of pidgin but then missed the overall meaning. I would have to learn the lingo pretty quick or I wouldn't be going anywhere.

After a few hours of sitting around, and with the sea now settled into merely running an active swell, I decided to look at the engine. My experience with diesels to date was in the test labs at college and from trucks standing on firm ground. I was comfortable with how they worked and what ills might befall them, but as I started down the narrow steps into the bowels of the boat and saw the hot, green, greasy object of my interest slowly rolling around in front of me I was a little less confident. Up until this time I had been quite enjoying the exhilaration of the sea air, but down in the engine room it was stifling and murderously hot. I ran the gauntlet of some stray electrical wires, kept my balance on the few remaining bilge boards to avoid the oily swill, noted the engine was running nice and steady, and dashed back up on deck. The heat and the swell started my stomach churning and, with that 'I'm going to be sick' moment and gulping fresh air, I hung out over the side until the breeze sorted me out.

Shortly I went back and joined Stewart resting in the cabin. While chatting about getting one's sea legs, he suddenly remembered something.

"By the way, don't go jumping around on your bunk Nick, because I put the dynamite[5] under it, so it was out of the way. But, don't worry, it's quite safe as long as it doesn't start sweating."

"Thanks Stewart, that's great! What am I supposed to do? Take it out every half an hour to see if it's still cool?"

"Don't worry," he said again, "It won't go off without a detonator, and I've got those under my bunk."

All very well to say that, I thought. I was already doing plenty of sweating and now knowing I was sleeping on dynamite I thought I would sweat even more!

Before I had time to get too carried away with my nausea and worries of a more explosive nature, Jacob called out, "*Mi lukim Buka!"*[6] I hurried back up on deck and saw we were now close to land, passing the northern part of one little island and entering a narrow passage between two others. Stewart said the stretch of water between the island of Buka and the northern tip of Bougainville was only 300 metres wide and, with an incredibly strong (4-6 knot) current, it made for tricky navigation. Indeed, I could see the swirl of a powerful undertow just below the water's surface. Common sense indicated the need for care and precision in control of the engine and helm. Up on the bridge again, I watched Jacob steering us towards land, running the wheel this way and that for a few seconds each time, raising and lowering engine speed as the need for care in progress demanded. Finally, we came up along-side one boat tethered to three others lined up in parallel against the jetty. With the *Kiriaka* giving the neighbouring vessel a solid thump as we rose and fell with the wash, one of our crew jumped on board and tied us up quickly before the current carried us away.

After giving Jacob a few instructions, Stewart and I clambered over the other boats to get ashore and the heat and humidity hit me yet again. Once off the water and walking up into town, I realised being wet and clammy in a perspiration-soaked shirt was the new norm.

Buka was just a few buildings, much smaller than Rabaul. There were a few trade stores, the Post Office, a bank and a bit of sealed road. Here and there was a jumble of rather sad detritus, forty-four-gallon oil drums haphazardly stacked up on what would be the re-fuelling bay, the mangled wreck of a car, an up turned canoe. But despite this muddle and its modest size, with the number of Chinese, expats and local Buka folk milling around, it had a lively air.

Not stopping to look around, Stewart and I wended our way through people going about their business, past groups of others just hanging around, passing the time of day and set off to trek the few kilometres up to a little place called Hahela. Stewart explained that this was one of the various missions that gave us volunteers somewhere to have a bit of a wash and brush up and something to eat as we made the journey between Rabaul and Kuraio.

Arriving at the Catholic mission house, we knocked briefly and walked right in, just as a diminutive figure came hurrying down the dark, cool corridor to meet us.

"Father Fey, meet Nick Brown, he's going to replace me at Kuraio," said Stewart. "Nick, meet Father Fey, he's the priest in charge of the Buka diocese."

"Hi Nick, Stewart, welcome to both of you, come along in." Father Fey, a pale and oval-faced fellow, ushered us through into the house and sat us down in the cool of his sparsely decorated lounge room.

As expected with one of the cloth he was a picture of serenity, but was he just a little too subdued? His brown, somewhat beady eyes studied me intently. Perhaps he was trying to read my reaction to the place? Whatever he saw, he could not have guessed my concerns were not about PNG, or the prospect of what lay ahead (for how should I know?) but more to do with my frustration of getting there. This was my eighth stop in as many days! But the moment soon passed and Father Fey said, "Come on, Stewart knows the routine, he's stayed many times with us, he'll show you your room and the bathroom. Have a wash and I'll see you both for supper."

Later, after a most welcome shower and then being waited on by a native cook-cum-housekeeper, we chatted over the first decent meal I'd had for a few days. Father Fey spoke.

"Nick, I'm sure you'll find Kuraio just fine. It's almost as big as the mission here, with a school and of course a church and the Priest. You'll get to meet him; he's a bit of a character actually."

Apart from some chat about the price of cocoa and copra that Stewart had just got in Rabaul, the conversation went on with Father Fey playing down any concerns he thought I might have with my new home. As I had no preconceived ideas about the place and was now being told it was not so bad, I started to wonder. But I put my imaginary worries to one side and had a good night's sleep on the already longed-for stable bed. Early next day, we were back down to the docks and off on the *Kiriaka Aro* once again.

Having been late arriving the day before, we had ended up as the last of the four boats tethered alongside each other at the wharf. And, now, having cast ourselves off from our neighbouring vessel and starting to head back up the channel, we saw the next two boats also leave. Looking astern, we saw to our consternation that these boats, still bound together and apparently without power, were being carried sideways down the passage by the rip! They eventually separated, but the current brought them together again and as they collided, there was a nasty splintering sound. Part of the roof over the rear deck of one boat collapsed, dangling off to one side like a bird's broken wing. The yelling and cursing of the crew carried across the water as they disappeared from our view. It was not life threatening, but it certainly emphasised the need for skill in nautical matters!

Colliding boats - Buka Passage

On sailing away from Buka, Stewart explained why we were going to make another brief stop before Sipai and the reason for the dynamite under my bunk – he had arranged to help clear some land at another station. So, we now headed off a few miles south of Buka Passage, to Tsiroge. This was the headquarters of the northern vicariate, and home to Bishop Leo Lemay[7], the head of the Catholic Church in Bougainville.

As we sailed on, we passed another island on our starboard side. Stewie said it was here, on the island of Sohano, where the Japanese had kept the missionaries they had captured, but had not killed during the Second World War. Until now I had not given any thought to the depth of the Catholic Church's involvement in PNG or the implications for me; I was not a missionary. And although naturally saddened, I was preoccupied with more immediate and exciting things.

After one of the crew rowed us ashore on to Tsiroge, we tied up at a rickety jetty. Then, with Stewart carrying an old canvas bag full of his precious explosives - and me following at a safe distance - we made our way up from the shore to a large expanse of grass. It must have taken an enormous amount of human effort to flatten the area. But there, right bang in the middle of it, was a huge clump of old tree roots which had presented an obstacle that even human muscle could not overcome. Not being familiar with the characteristics of dynamite and not wanting to get in the way, I left Stewart to his devices, walked back a couple of hundred metres to some trees closer to the sea and sat in the shade to watch the fireworks.

I saw him crouching down and then fiddling about for a little while before getting up and striding purposefully back towards me. Seconds later we watched as three massive tree stumps rose, ghost-like, in a puff of smoke and then, with a muffled whumpf and a shower of earth, fall dramatically back down to the ground.

"Great!" said Stewart, a little flushed with excitement. "The priest will be happy. Now they can get on with completing the playing field for the kids!"

He had that crazy, half-mad look in his eyes and dare I say he got a real blast (sorry!) out of the venture!

Sailing along the west coast of Bougainville for a few more hours, we made our way down towards the Catholic Mission at Sipai. For a long time we were running just a kilometre or so offshore, past some of the most impenetrable parts of the island. I watched the dark and gloomy coastline slip by and, recalling one of Rousseau's paintings, imagined a jaguar slinking away through the undergrowth, startled from an attempted kill. Every now and then small sandy coves interspersed the rocky shoreline, each dotted with palms growing at improbable angles, some practically horizontal to the ground. Above them was thick, mysterious and somewhat forbidding jungle, but, so far at least, no sign of wildlife. Then I thought, perhaps instead of wild animals, a tribe of native savages might come screaming down the cliffs, paddle furiously out in their dugouts, scramble on board and take us hostage, for dinner perhaps?

Emerging from my reverie, I now saw some real action. Just below the surface of the water, between the shore, and us were swarms of jellyfish. There were hundreds of these creatures floating floating horizontally alongside us, each trailing four or five metres of scary tendrils from their huge, milky, alien-like heads. These were Portuguese Man o' War jellyfish[8], the most venomous marine creature in the world with a sting that could kill a horse, and a real danger. There would be no dangling our legs over the side on this trip! We sailed on, seemingly forever, through blooms of these creatures, continuing past the still menacing shoreline and on past a backdrop rekindling my memories of tropical lands I had read of years before in 'A Pattern of Islands'.

Eventually, approaching Sipai, Stewart assured me this was to be our last stop before Kuraio. I had been living out of a suitcase for ten days and was looking forward to stopping and settling down at wherever it was I'd been sent to help.

Anchoring a little way from land, we hopped into the dinghy and as one of the crew paddled us to shore, we spied figures running down steps cut into the steep cliff face before us. With excellent timing, no doubt born from practice, an older guy and two young women arrived at the water's edge just in time to save the dinghy from tipping over as we ran on to the sand. Amongst all the confusion of getting out of the boat and the excitement and breathlessness of the welcoming party, Stewart introduced me to the priest in charge of the Mission, Father Bourgea[9], and his assistants, nurses Sary and Donna.

Eager pleasantries dispensed with and with each of us carrying an odd assortment of supplies, we climbed slowly back up the cliff, up towards the Mission above. Panting and pausing for breath on the way, Father Bourgea, a scrawny, tanned and bespectacled forty-something American, explained how the Marist order had established the place way back in the 1930s but that he had taken over just a couple of years ago. It was a largish place with a school, an aid post and a church, all quite hard work to maintain along with the duties of the ministry, so he was grateful for the two nurses help.

Finally, having made it to the top of the cliff and pausing again to catch our breath, I looked back between the coconut palms and tangle of tropical vegetation and saw the little bay where the *Kiriaka* now lay at anchor. Appropriately enough the view was quite heavenly.

"Come on, let's go in," Father Bourgea called out, as we approached the main building. "We've been wanting some company for a while now!"

On chatting with the girls, it became clear they were quite different folk from the ones I had met in Rabaul, or indeed my girlfriends back home. Apart from being dressed plainly, Donna and Sary possessed other characteristics, something I felt as being of caring and kindness. They were both gentle types; most unlike other girls I had met before – pretty and feminine, but also seemingly practical and sensible. Clearly, they'd had the initiative and strength of character to move from the comfort of their own homes to this isolated outpost, their training as nurses no doubt reinforced by a certain commitment to God. Despite being about the same age as Stewart and myself, Donna, with hair pulled back and tied in a matronly bun at the back of her neck, was definitely in charge!

With visitors being infrequent, they naturally showed great interest in finding out what was going on in the outside world, and, as I had just come from there, I had an attentive audience. We chatted away, and as the day wore on and we had eaten, I realised Stewart had disappeared. I glanced down at the bay where we had anchored the *Kiriaka Aro* and to my surprise saw she was no longer there.

"Father Bourgea, where's the *Kiriaka* and what's happened to Stewart?" I asked.

"Oh, it's okay. Stewart's gone on down to Kuraio. He said he'd be back for you next week."

"Oh my god! But I thought I'd be on my way to Kuraio by now." Now I was angry. "I've had just about enough travelling and living rough for a while. What am I going to do? Where will I stay?"

Father Bourgea looked a little taken aback at my outburst and said he thought I knew the plan. I suddenly felt dreadfully miserable, and for the next half hour or so, I wondered how much longer this bloody journey was going to take. Sydney, Moresby, Rabaul, Buka and now here. How many more places did I need to stay at before I got to my posting? I had wanted to travel, but this was ridiculous!

Then suddenly Stewart appeared in the doorway,

"Fooled you!" he cried.

"You bugger!" I said, ignoring social niceties and the possibility of a novice's blush. "Where have you been? You might have told me. To be quite honest, I'm getting a bit pissed off. When are we going?"

"I just took the boat around the bluff to the little cove at Kivikee where it's easier to drop off the heavier stuff for the mission," said Stewart.

The joke had indeed caught me out and being a bit travel-worn I couldn't find it amusing. It was a relief to see him back however and I eventually settled down. But, by now all I wanted to do was to get to Kuraio.

That evening, while Father Bourgea attended to his priestly duties, and for the want of some entertainment, the four of us played Monopoly. Perhaps as a small consolation to the big tease, I won, and without cheating either!

Next day, in farewelling the girls and Father Bourgea, we reminded them that they were all welcome to come and visit. We promised the next time we came back from Rabaul we would pick them up and take them down to Kuraio for a break.

At last, we were off on the final leg!

On sailing down from Rabaul to Buka, I had not only been dealing with the uncomfortable rolling swell of the seas but also the rollercoaster of my emotions. But now, travelling on from Sipai, we found calmer waters and with the more regular motion of a quieter sea, at least that part no longer bothered me. Indeed, the last stage of the journey was pleasant, and I decided that sleeping in the boat was quite relaxing. 'Must be getting my sea legs', I thought. Although my emotions were still up and down, it was a good time to just sit and chat, and Stewart told me the about the difficulties they had with transporting the crops.

"Getting cocoa and copra on to the *Kiriaka* at Kuraio has always been a real problem. There's no jetty or deep-water close to land, so we must anchor a couple of hundred metres offshore and then load and unload the stuff by dugout. Paddling through the surf is time-consuming because canoes can only carry a few sacks at a time, and there is a real danger of water damage, or even worse, total loss, if a dugout gets swamped. All of which reduces the money we get in Rabaul."

He went on to explain that the Society had considered building a jetty but the cost was prohibitive. So, some months earlier, they had a marine company build an aluminium surfboat in Rabaul to do the job. Stewart continued, "The boat included a heavy tarpaulin cover fitting snugly over the gunwales to keep the cargo dry. When the boat was finished, we tied it astern of the *Kiriaka Aro*, fitted the tarpaulin and set sail. We ran into a light swell in the late afternoon, so, just to be on the safe side, I shimmied down the tow rope to check to see if any water had got in, but found it to be quite dry. As an added precaution, we got a couple of the boat's crew to keep a lookout and warn us of any changes. But during the night the weather picked up and the sea became quite rough. Right under the watchful eyes of the crew, but unbeknownst to either Chris, who you will meet shortly, or myself, the surfboat gradually filled with water. The weight of the water snapped the rope, and the darn thing sank to the bottom of the ocean, never to be seen again!"

Sadly, despite all their best efforts, it was back to square one with the problem of loading cocoa and copra on to the *Kiriaka*.

By now I realised I was going to have to push the boundaries to get anything done. But now, hearing of this, I wondered what other challenges might lie ahead!

CHAPTER 6

KURAIO AT LAST

The *Kiriaka Aro* swept gently forward as Jacob slowed the engine. From just a couple of hundred metres offshore the place looked entirely different from the idyllic tropical island I'd had in mind. Visions of white sandy beaches and swaying palm trees evaporated. Instead there was a narrow strip of mottled grey sand, strewn with the messy detritus of driftwood, beyond this, a ragged grassy bank rose just a few metres above sea level.

Suddenly a shout went up and the rattle of the chain running through the windlass shook me out of my reverie. Jacob cut the engine, the anchor dug into the seabed and we heaved up on the swell to the eerie silence of primal isolation.

The spell passed as the crew went about their tasks. On the beach, ant-like figures scurried around several dugouts. Above them, along the bank, there was much excitement, as a gaggle of villagers gathered; now waving and shouting at our arrival. The ants turned into people, as they manhandled the canoes into the sea and paddled frantically away from shore to avoid being swamped by the surf. In no time at all they were alongside and then, with someone guiding my legs and strong arms steadying me from above, I was lowered awkwardly into a dugout which was rising and falling on the swell. Landing on my backside in the water sluicing around in the bottom, I found myself at eye-level with the waves. Without delay a couple of wild-looking Bougainvillean's paddling hastily and skilfully, and with me hanging on for dear life, brought us ashore and ran us on to the sand. Before I could worry about being dunked in the surf, someone bundled me out of the dugout, onto the beach, onto my feet and upright. Just!

After eleven days travelling halfway around the world via air, land and sea, from sophisticated London to this primitive place, I had arrived. I was tired and dirty and my pants were wet, but finally, here I was at last, standing on firm ground!

The figures on the beach now took form and I could see women in a variety of grass skirts and non-too-clean blouses and men in shorts and tatty T-shirts. Children's dress code ranged from the natural look, i.e. nothing at all, to shorts or tiny dresses. Some even reversed their style with tops but no dresses or pants, '*em tasol*'!

With my emotions swinging from relief to apprehension and back again, I recognised that this was the tropical island where I would be living and working for the next two years. My new home was here – somewhere in the middle of nowhere.

With Stewart, a horde of islanders and what now seemed like a hundred children, all hiding their smiles and giggles behind their hands, I walked the short distance up from the beach and at last saw Kuraio. Nestling in among lofty palms, swathed in mottled blue-green shadow, was a scattering of large, multi-coloured timber buildings; the Catholic Mission and home of the West Coast Development Society. There was a lush green expanse of grass that in another context might be unkempt lawn, but here it made islands of the buildings. Other smaller 'islands' stood out: an old tractor, a few other bits of rusting equipment, a pile of timber; basically the sort of junk you would expect to find in a scrap yard!

To the left of the path, as we walked up from the beach, a newish and unpainted two-storey weatherboard stood out by way of contrast. Stewart explained that this was the Padre's house. We carried on walking, with Stewart pointing out more buildings in the distance: the '*haus sik*', the nurse's house, a teacher's house, the primary school, sheds and workshops, the church. All the buildings, except the church, were of weatherboard; some houses painted pink, some a pale blue and again, as I had seen in Moresby, all raised well off the ground.

My spirits rose somewhat. I had expected two or three buildings at the most, possibly even some grass huts. But here, as Father Fey had said, nestling in the dappled shade of a hundred palm trees and surrounded by jungle, was a reasonably large enclave of Western-style buildings. It had something of a surreal aura about it and really didn't look too bad.

As we approached one house, painted a shade of almost grass green, Stewart explained that this was where we, as the managers of the Society, lived. And, as he did so, my Pied Piper moment came to an end. The excited crowd of children and locals who had followed us up from the beach melted back into their villages, somewhere 'out there', on the edge of the Mission.

The house at Kuraio L to R: The author, Chris Powell
and Stewart Gibson, 1972. Photo: Christine Sullivan.

Before going in, Stewart steered me towards a dark shed next to
the building. "And here's the kitchen Nick," he said.

I took a quick peek inside and my heart sank. It was as black
as night and I knew that, like my earlier dream of breakfast
on the *Kiriaka*, the chances of having a good feed were slight.
Conditions were not conducive to exercising any kind of culinary
skill, let alone maintaining any degree of hygiene. I backed
out, trying not to think about the effects there might be on my
stomach.

Moving on into the house itself, my first impression was that of
a spooky film-set for an abandoned dwelling, only re-discovered
after many years. Stewart explained that the locals had built the
place, with the guidance of the priest, in the 1960s, and so now it

was a bit run down. Cracks in the walls allowed sunlight to seep through here and there, highlighting an abundance of dust motes. The exposed timber frame revealed the building's construction. It was unlike anything I had ever seen in Britain, except perhaps on a farm. Instead of windows, there were simple openings in the wall, propped above each of which was a timber flap which, I later found, was shut at night. But even though the openings took best advantage of the onshore breeze, the corrugated-iron roof meant it was still as hot as hell inside.

As my eyes adjusted to the gloom, I saw well-worn cane furniture on dusty bare floorboards, a few books and papers scattered here and there; in one corner a fine collection of cobwebs. I should not have been surprised. Only a few weeks earlier I'd been living with two other guys where tidiness was not on the agenda and who could not agree on housekeeping, so why wouldn't the same scenario exist with Pommie guys sharing a house on this side of the world? And then I noticed another smell I could not quite place, this time a slight chemical odour.

Even though I had not done anything other than walk up from the beach, I was again dripping in perspiration. The cumulative effects of my journey, the exhausting heat, the humidity and my roller coaster emotions told me I had had enough. I simply had to stop, but before I could, Stewart called out, "Meet Chris. He's looking after the agricultural project."

A young man rose awkwardly from his chair, shook me by the hand and laughingly said, "Hi Nick. Welcome to Hell!" Dressed only in shorts and thongs, he had developed a great tan to go with his solid physique. Combined with hair as sun-bleached as Stewart's, I thought he would be a real killer with the girls.

With a broad smile, deep-set, dark brown eyes and an easy-going way, despite his reference to the underworld, he looked like he was quite enjoying himself. But then I noticed why he had got up so slowly; the lower part of his right leg and ankle was red and swollen.

"It's nothing much," said Chris, "Bit of a scratch that's turned into a tropical ulcer. But it's getting better."

Stewart explained, "I've been playing doctor and giving him a shot of penicillin, now and then. You should have seen it last week!"

I had already taken a liking to Stewart and now meeting Chris, it appeared we three were well matched. Clearly, despite the somewhat disheartening facilities, at least we would get on well together.

Stewart said, "Come on, dump your stuff over there and I'll show you around." With Chris hobbling and Stewart pointing out its various features, I was given a guided tour of the house: there was the central living/dining room area, several bedrooms, the toilet and shower, but of course, no kitchen. Chatting away, Chris told me he was from Fleet in Hampshire, south-west of London, and Stewart, I already knew, was from up north. With each of us having come from such a different part of the world and a very British way of life, I figured we must have an adventurous streak in us, or we would not be there. But then I wondered if there was something else. Was it that we were also slightly mad, or perhaps eccentrically altruistic? At this stage, I was not sure which it was, or indeed which, if any, of these characteristics fitted me.

"And this is Mark's room," Chris said. "He's away at the moment, back next week when we pick him up from Sohano."

"Oh! Now who's Mark then?" I said. More information was emerging slowly. I had not heard about Mark until now, or even much about Chris' agricultural project for that matter.

Stewart explained, "Mark Roberts is a lay preacher from Phoenix, Arizona. He took over from the priest who started the place way back. He's been at the mission for quite a while now and naturally he's involved more on the spiritual side of the project, working with the local priest."

I looked into his dark and dusty room. A ghostly mosquito net dangled over an unmade bed, gathered up to a crude iron hook in the ceiling, a few clothes scattered around here and there; overall, it looked awful. Where was I going to sleep?

After the tour we at last sat down and with mugs of coffee, my new colleagues started telling me about the origins of the West Coast Development Society (WCDS).

"This place was set up here in the 1930s," Stewart said, "But serious efforts at commercial development only started around 1961[10], after Bill Mentzer[11] arrived. Bill was a bit older than us, in his late thirties, when he climbed up from the beach. He trekked inland to where the Kereaka lived and essentially said, 'Throw in your lot with me, and I'll show you how to organise your lives, improve your health and bring you education and wealth.'

"Of course," Stewart joked, "having a gun in his hand made his offer hard to refuse!"

"Amazing stuff when you consider the locals were big into the cargo cult" said Chris.

"Goodness me! What's the cargo cult then?" I exclaimed.

Noticing my rising concern, Chris only half answered my question. "Apparently the Kereaka were a pretty wild and desperate lot. Seeing the wealth of others all around, the cargo frustrated them because they could not figure how they could get hold of it themselves. So, they did as Mentzer said and followed him, thinking they would all benefit."

"But what do you mean, cargo cult?" I insisted.

"Well, in the Second World War, the natives saw supplies for the American troops falling from the sky on parachutes. They thought that if they did the right thing, they could also get their hands on this 'cargo', hence the start of the cult."

"Yeah," Stewart interjected. Excited by telling the tale of Mentzer's exploits, and again avoiding a direct answer to my question, he said,

"And that's where Bill Mentzer came in. His idea was to convert the enthusiasm of the cargo cult to bring about some form of spiritual fulfilment, through economic development and of course to introduce Christianity".

"Indeed," Stewart continued, "Mentzer himself assumed the role of a cult-like figure[12], promising them they would gain wealth if they were to follow what he said."

"Hmm, a bit like a glorified 'rice-Christian' bribe," said I.

Stewart carried on, "So, over ten years or so, indeed just up until last year, Mentzer managed to encourage close to a couple of thousand Kereaka's to move down from the mountains and resettle in new villages on the coastal plateau around here. He got them to clear tracts of land, plant thousands of coconut trees and cocoa bushes and over the years, helped them increase production of both. You saw the coconut trees as you came up from the beach. Tomorrow you'll see the cocoa. Mentzer managed to get a Freedom from Hunger grant, and with that he bought a tractor and built a timber mill. That is the tractor you see with the grass growing around it as we came in. Bit old and shagged out now!

"Essentially the economic initiatives of these two priests, Mentzer here and his colleague Father Brosnan, the predecessor of Father Bourgea who you met up in Sipai[13], helped arrest the cargo cult. "But," he went on somewhat ominously, "it's not been fully eradicated. Bill Mentzer left last year and Mark replaced him. You'll get to meet him shortly. Mark's job is to continue Bill's work with the local priest, supported by us volunteers. That's about it really. Mentzer deserves a bloody medal for all the things he's done here".

This background was fascinating. I had not even thought about the history of the place, I had just come to help. But this story put an entirely new meaning to the job. And, although how the place started was fascinating enough, I suspected there was something more about this cargo cult thing. Something was being held back.

After hearing about the labours of Mentzer, I saw things differently. This was a serious, groundbreaking and culture-breaking venture. I could not start to guess at the changes in the Kereaka themselves. But while the natural environment around Kuraio remained quite beautiful, I could see the buildings and particularly the equipment was getting a bit tired; the place had seen better days.

"Oh, and by the way, you can stay with the Father for a while, just to get you settled," Stewart continued. "As you can see, things are a bit disorganised now. You'll come on over to the main house for meals and to relax." The look on my face was enough for him to quickly add, "Of course you will have Mark's room when he leaves, but as you can see, it needs a bit of a tidy up and besides he hasn't left yet. Anyway, come on; enough stories for now. Let's go over to the priest's place, and I'll introduce you to Father Peter."

It was getting late in the day, and by this stage, all I really wanted to do was to eat something, have a shower and go to bed. But back across the station we trudged, back to the new two-storey weatherboard to meet the priest.

Although only in his late thirties, Father Peter Tatimuss, a dumpy, round-faced, cheerful sort of guy, was going bald. Chris whispered that they indeed called him 'Baldy' or 'Paka' behind his back in *tok ples*. Of greater significance, coming, as he did from Buka, was that his complexion was much paler than other Bougainvillean's further south. Indeed, he was sometimes mistaken as a Papuan from the mainland. So far, I had not thought about the differences between one Papua New Guinean and the next. However, clearly, most Bougainvillean's were very black and the other folk I had seen in Moresby and Rabaul varied from dark to light brown. This difference in skin colour had not even crossed my mind, but it was significant to the Kereaka. They called the Papuan's 'red skins' and apparently didn't much care for them, particularly when they came over to Bougainville and took their jobs. I realised we whites were not the only racists in the world.

Father Peter was one of the first two Bougainvillean's ordained and had only been at Kuraio for a short while. But, as I was to find out later, for reasons other than racial prejudice, he had already got a bit of a reputation.

"Hi Father" I greeted him cheerfully, still ignorant of any of the issues about him being a bit of a radical. "Apparently you're putting me up for a while?"

"Come in, come in, m' boy. Please, you quite welcome in my house."

We four sat around the sparsely furnished room while his *haus meri* brought us lukewarm soft drinks.

"Okay Nick, you have room at top of stair. Bed was table one-time, but mattress will make comfy. Olsem bathroom 'e stap long corridor," Father Peter said.

We chatted away for a while, but I was too tired for small talk. So, while Stewart updated Father Peter and Chris with all the news, I made my apologies and went to bed. I had had enough!

I found my 'room' to be a sort of semi-enclosed alcove on the landing at the top of the stairs. A bit lacking in privacy, but at least there was a bed, of sorts, as well as a window. Peering into the darkness through wooden slats, I could just make out I was facing inland. Frustratingly I couldn't see too much because of an enormous rainwater tank, on a platform outside the window. I could just pick out a few shadowy figures of villagers going about their business a little way off into the distance, backlit by what I guessed were cooking fires. The scene reminded me of a strip cartoon in one of my childhood comics. A pith-helmeted white explorer, tied up by cannibals, was sitting in a cauldron, beads of perspiration on his plum-red face, being slowly boiled up for supper.

I showered, changed and climbed up on to my bed-table and was sound asleep within seconds.

An hour or so later I woke to an almighty shaking. The bed was shuddering around so much I thought I'd fall off. It took me a few seconds to figure where I was and why there was a strange noise of sloshing of water and where it was coming from. Was I having a nightmare? I jumped off the table and ran downstairs in panic and shouted, "What the hell's going on?"

It was as if I was in a dream. Chris and Stewart had gone and now, instead, there were a few locals calmly sitting around the dimly lit room, smoking and drinking with Father Peter.

"Nick. No worry my friend, only earth tremor, *guria* you know. Happens all the time."

"What! An earthquake? Wow! Thanks for the warning. Bit scary, being so close to the cliff and all that" I said, quite agitated.

"Ha ha. Olsem, yu no sit under tree. Man 'e sleep under palm tree one-time, coconut fall and bingo, him dead outright. Coconut heavy too mus. Couple of kilos you know, husk an' all."

"Well, thanks for the advice. I will remember to keep away from the trees. Are you sure we're okay and not going to slide into the sea?"

"You go sleep Nick. All okay."

I returned to my dreams, but instead of some dusky young maiden serving me breakfast, there were now coconuts raining out of trees. I was rolling down the hill in an empty water tank and floating out to sea.

Heaven or hell, I suddenly woke up to another significant issue. After seeing the others sitting in the gloomy light of storm lanterns, I realised there was something missing, something I had taken for granted all my life. What a shock – there was no electricity!

Next day, Stewart explained the situation. "The generator blew up a few weeks earlier and we can't repair it on site, so we're going to have to take the whole-darn thing up to Rabaul. It is such a big machine we'll have to take it to bits first, to get it on the boat. I know it's our number one priority, but it takes a bit of effort to organise. You'll get used to doing things by kerosene lamp. If you keep the wick trimmed, it can be quite adequate."

Now I understood what the faint chemical smell was I had noticed earlier.

Combining the lack of electricity with the constant heat and humidity seemed to make everything just that little bit harder. Even carrying a kero lamp around wherever I went after dusk, it seemed all I could see were just things right in front of my nose.

The stories about Father Peter and his reputation were revealed over the next few days. Apparently, he had a regular habit of socialising with the locals. Nothing surprising for a man in his position, but there is socialising and socialising, and his socialising included some habits unbecoming to a representative of the Holy See. Smoking and drinking were not so bad and chewing betel nut, a common habit, tolerated and, again, not such a big deal. But it was certainly frowned upon for a Roman Catholic priest to have women in his house at night. There were complaints about teachers wasting too much time at his place, and there were concerns the men and the nurses were even alone there together.

Eventually, the situation had deteriorated to such an extent that the big-men called a meeting between the schoolteachers and nurses, after which they forbade the women from going to the Father's house altogether. Thereafter, by way of retaliation, Father Peter forbade everyone from his house and was essentially sent to Coventry. It was his own fault, but I felt sorry for him; being such a sociable person, he must have ended up feeling pretty lonely.

As well as this and being mistaken for a Papuan 'red skin', and thus not a true Bougainvillean *wantok*[14], there was probably another reason for resentment on the part of the villagers. He, unintentionally, had assumed some of the status of a big-man, with the privileges of tribal leadership and all else that it involved, and the villagers and certainly the actual big-men would have questioned who had given him the right to this position. Nevertheless, although he did not quite fit the criteria of a priest as expected by Mark Roberts or Father Mentzer, Chris said both he and Stewart got on well with him. But then, to a certain extent, it was a matter of necessity.

Despite all this, you would not really know there was any palaver; Father Peter still carried out his religious duties and the faithful still flocked to the place of worship each Sunday. And, thus, on my first Sunday, we three volunteers dutifully went along to church, joining what seemed to be the whole of the Kereaka clan.

The church was a rambling and reasonably attractive old building, blessed with that indefinable sacred air reminding me very vaguely of St. Nicholas' in Winsley. There was a large archway forming the main entrance, under which was a nice homely touch, a community notice board; inside were rows of hard wooden pews standing on a beaten earth floor. And then, at the end of the aisle, a couple of steps led up to the altar in a sort of fibro-sheet walled sanctuary. Again, there were no windows, but below the extra wide eaves there were metre-high woven Pandanus walls to the nave, providing a relatively cool, light and airy space in which to pray.

Being more familiar with the small numbers of parishioners attending St. Nicholas', the size of the congregation that Sunday amazed me. The place was so packed, that many would-be worshippers were sitting on the grass outside. I am sure they were not all there to welcome me, but it did seem that way; after all, the arrival of another *white pela* on the Mission was a pretty rare event.

The service included lots of enthusiastic and emotive hymn singing and prayers spoken in pidgin. But not being much of a churchgoer or familiar with the language meant a lot of it went over my head. Nevertheless, with Father Peter now all dressed up in his red cassock and white surplice occasionally mentioning 'Nicholas', I assumed they were praying for me. And, now, having learnt a little more about the state of affairs, I felt I needed all the prayers I could get!

I heard my name again towards close of the service when Father Peter was giving out the social messages, and despite my limited understanding, it was obvious I had now been formally introduced to the locals and officially welcomed on to the Mission.

After church, I at last had a bit of time to myself to take stock, familiarise myself with my surroundings and start thinking about the tasks ahead. On the downside, it appeared we had a fair amount of rather worn equipment (which I would have to investigate later). There was the occasional earthquake, plenty of insects (including millions of voracious mosquitos and *very* noisy cicadas), a very hot and humid climate and no electricity. At the end of the day, there was a thin layer of sponge on an old table upon which to rest my bones and a mosquito net – which, I discovered, kept the little blighters in as well as out.

Apart from the lack of electricity, I soon found that the other critical facility missing in our house (but not Father Peter's) was piped water! Not washing in the evening was impossible. In a climate where merely sitting still involved perspiring, it was uncomfortable, let alone unhygienic. Chris and Stew informed me there were several options. Initially, this was not a problem for me as I was staying with Father Peter and he had the water tank and a shower. But later, when I moved into our house, it meant going back and forth to Father Peter's, along an ill-defined path and in the pitch-black of night.

It was not the dark or the oft-elusive trail that was such a problem as much as the possibility of stepping on something. Thus far in my life however, I had not really been in the habit of walking across fields at night. And so, the first time I did so, I jumped with fright when I experienced a squishy sensation and a gentle wheezing noise from underfoot. Looking down, I saw a large cane toad, with a hugely offended expression on its face, staring back up at me. Taking a few seconds to re-inflate, Mr Toad then hopped back into the dark as I carried on my way. There was a real abundance of these not-so-little creatures on the Mission, and I am sure they did not really enjoy being stepped on any more than we enjoyed stepping on them!

But apart from the threat we posed to toad and frog life, there was another reason we didn't make a habit of washing at Father Peter's. It turned out that he was justifiably a bit funny about using his water because, surprisingly, there had not been much rain for a while. So, even though it was clumsy and awkward, we sometimes made do by having a splash bath in our own house. This involved squatting in the base of the yet to be connected shower, scooping cold water from a big tub with an old plastic container and splashing it all over our bodies. It was a rude awakening for this spoiled *white pela* when I found cold water was still cold even in the tropics.

However, the most adventurous way to keep clean was care of the Tsinamutu River[15]. Being a ten-minute walk away from the Mission, going down to the river for a good clean up after some mucky chore was both exhilarating and frustrating. On the one hand, it was great fun as the river was quite fast flowing, but on the other, it was exasperating as the track was either dusty or muddy depending on the weather. We usually got back to the house either dripping with sweat and covered with a fine layer of dust or wet from the rain and with muddy ankles. Washing like this also meant using a whole bar of soap each time, as the current had the habit of snatching it out of your hands. More importantly, we needed to finish washing in the river before dusk. What with the rough nature of the path, the potential for a bite or a sting from local fauna, stepping on a squishy toad, or perhaps even providing a crocodile with his evening meal, it was much too hazardous after dark.

The fourth and most obvious way was right on our doorstep, the sea. However, although great fun for messing about in, I soon found salt water simply doesn't have the same restorative qualities as the fresh variety.

Apart from these few minor worries and fortunately fewer major ones, I recognised things were generally pretty good. Here I was, living on an exotic tropical island, with three meals a day, board and lodging plus a few dollars of pocket money each week. I thought the place was more a tropical paradise than the 'hell' Chris suggested. But then I had only just arrived and still had not actually done anything. So, after taking stock of my environment, I next focused on work. Different as it was from an office and factory in England, it still involved tasks and people with responsibilities.

Father Peter oversaw the Mission, along with a council of big-men[16]. The latter ostensibly oversaw the West Coast Development Society, but all were quite remote from daily activities and, as far as operations went, Stewart, Chris and I were 'it'. We were there to manage and give technical support for the welfare of the Kereaka people and do whatever needed doing to keep the place going.

We were not quite alone. Mentzer has trained a few Kereaka over the years, and Stewart and Chris continued with this. Amongst them was Jacob, the First Mate of the boat and the five or six crew members; we had a *kuk-boi*, a mechanic/driver, Thomas and his trainee Boracede, and a few others besides.

I was a bit surprised to hear Father Peter was not more directly involved in the operations. After all it was the Catholic Church, through Mentzer, that had set it up in the first instance. Apparently, there was a bit of history there and some part of that involved the cargo cult. It was not until later I found out what was really going on and meanwhile, I kept focused on what I was there for.

We three sat down and had a chat about what 'management and technical support' actually meant. Broadly, Chris was to tend the cattle and I was to run the boat, look after the mechanical equipment and manage the business. But to help clarify the specifics, we made a To Do list, which included the following:

- Collect the cocoa and copra and pay the farmers.
- Run the boat and visit the various Mission stations on the West Coast; collect their cocoa and copra, sell it in Rabaul, buy trade store goods and deliver them back to the Missions.
- Supervise our cocoa drying to make sure best quality; build more drying beds as needed.
- Service and repair the machinery and vehicles.
- Husband the cattle etc.

- Manage the cash and accounts.
- Help run the trade store.
- Train the locals.

As Mark was due to leave in a just few weeks and Stewart and Jacob were leaving after Christmas, all this would fall to just Chris and me. Adventurous as we were, both Chris and I realised Stewart would be a hard act to follow and this was a big responsibility for us two young Brits plonked down on a tropical island.

Chris explained further that his job with the cattle was to care for their health and help with breeding. The aim was to give fresh milk and meat. The problem was that by the time he had arrived from Britain the cattle were running wild and getting into the villagers' gardens and ruining them. Naturally the locals were not too happy about that, so his priority had been in corralling them by building fences to keep them out of trouble. He said they had sold the meat to the locals and helped improve their diet somewhat, but the lack of refrigeration had limited this to the immediate market as the meat soon went off. They could not supply too far afield, even to the next Missions, so it was hard to make it a commercial operation[17].

Even though this was a frustration and keeping the livestock out of the gardens was a challenge, Chris made it clear he loved the life and was steadily getting to know many of the locals on the Station in the process. But Chris confided later, it was Stewart who almost single-handedly ran the boat and the Station. Stewart bought machinery and managed the building of the roads out to the villages; he maintained and repaired the machinery; kept the power supplied (until recently that was); and helped train the locals to work the equipment and manage their affairs. He would indeed be a hard act to follow.

On a lighter, but important note, and after experiencing the indigestible results of the cooking facilities thus far, I suggested we focus on improvements in that area, as a priority!

CHAPTER 7

GETTING ON WITH IT

For me, eating properly was far more critical to being able to work in this sort of climate than washing. But cooking, particularly at the end of the day, was a chore, so it was great to hear the Mission had assigned us a *kuk-boi*, a lad by the name of Ignatius Calimo.

Actually, the title was only partly correct. He was definitely a boy, but there was a big question over whether he could actually cook. It is true that he provided us with meals each day, and even though we hardly expected cordon bleu standard, they were usually pretty bad.

It was perhaps a bit unfair to criticise him. He was young and relatively new to the job, and whatever culinary expertise he had gained thus far was tested by the quality of the raw materials and ingredients and, of course his working conditions! Opening tins, boiling taro[18] or kau kau (sweet potato) or whatever in the windowless black hole of that kitchen would be a challenge for anyone. So, it was hardly surprising that he generally ended up in a lousy mood and ruining whatever food he was preparing.

The meal-time routine was pretty standard. We three would sit expectantly at the dining table, listening to the cussing and crashing of pots coming from outside. Calimo would then emerge from the kitchen, walk the few metres separating the buildings, up the steps and swagger into the dining room, dishes balanced on his arm waiter style, and with a look that could turn milk sour, serve us what passed for our evening meal.

Apart from the awful working conditions, the other reason for his sullen way was that when the wet weather started again, Mother Nature took great pleasure in coordinating rain with our meal times. We would either sit waiting for it to stop, or, if we were in a hurry, Calimo would dash through the torrential rain to bring it in. The result was that our food was either cold and dry or hot and wet!

All this was incentive enough to convert a spare room in the house into a kitchen. Fortunately, the task had been on the To Do list for a while and thus, many of the materials were already to hand. So, one day we got busy. We moved the stove from the old hut, installed a couple of old kero freezers which had lain idly by, knocked up a couple of benches and covered the surfaces with laminate.

The results were rudimentary but adequate. There was no more waiting for dinner during the evening downpour, Calimo's mood and the quality of his culinary efforts picked up enormously and he was even known to smile now and then!

Having established better cooking facilities, we were now

more confident of avoiding food poisoning, despite still having weevils in the rice. We were better fed and better prepared for the routine of collecting and shipping cocoa and copra and all the other items on the list.

Unfortunately, as I had already observed, much of the mechanical equipment on site was getting a little weary. Annoyingly and in line with Sod's Law, much of it seemed to break down just when needed the most, case in point being the truck. This great big, drab-grey, rusty, 10 tonne, all-wheel-drive Japanese monster, of 1960s vintage, was critical to bringing in the cocoa and copra from outlying villages, but it was getting old. Apart from dodgy brakes and lack of synchromesh the clutch had given up the ghost just before I arrived, so one of my first jobs was to help replace it. Stewart and I spent several hours sweating profusely in the greasy dirt under the truck's nether regions. It was not a complicated job, but it was messy and I recalled with some irritation the clinically spotless facilities at Massey Ferguson back in Coventry. Fortunately, it all went back together nicely, and worked perfectly first time.

Finally, I got the opportunity to drive the beast. It was a large machine, with seats that had seen better days, and being only of modest stature, I found it a stretch to see over the steering wheel, let alone reach the pedals. However, as it turned out, this was the least of my worries. Driving over to pick up some cocoa from Cacasipi village, the truck went well enough but we could not go far because the rains had washed the road away! Hurrying back to the Station, Stewart fired up the JCB[19] and, with me driving the Isuzu we trooped over to the river. Stewart scraped up gravel from the riverbed, dumped it into the back of the truck and off we went, back over to the section of damaged road. I dumped the gravel out of the truck, Stewart stacked it up with the digger and I then drove backwards and forwards over it until it was solid and the road passable again. All very basic, but necessary and time-consuming nonetheless!

As time went on, we would hear by word of mouth when crops were ready for collection. We would take the Isuzu off to various pre-arranged spots beside the road, where growers had brought their produce. Stewart would jump down, 'scale' the sacks and get them loaded up on to the back of the truck. After paying the growers, we would be off to the next village until the truck was full and then head off back to the Station.

Life continued like this for a while, collecting crops, working at various maintenance jobs during the day and relaxing by reading or writing letters in the gloom of a kero lamp in the evenings. But leisure time was about to change, and for the better.

To a certain extent, reading by kero lamp had become acceptable, but doing other chores in such a dull glimmer was a bore and after a while we all got tired of being without electricity. It was impossible to fix the big generator at the Station, but fortunately there was an older, smaller jenny. Apparently, it still worked but it was not powerful enough for the whole Station and would only generate enough for us and perhaps Father Peter's place. Knowing other folk would not be too impressed seeing we had electricity while they had none, we first made sure word went out that this was a temporary arrangement and full power would be back on as soon as possible.

Stewart and Thomas isolated the wiring of our place from the rest of the Station, installed the old generator, threw the switch and (thank the Lord) there was light! After the dull illumination of kerosene storm lanterns, even a few forty-watt bulbs brightened up our evenings no end. The others would have to wait a while, because getting the broken generator on to the *Kiriaka Aro* was a big job and carrying crops was the priority; the generator would just have to take its turn.

But then, with the electricity back on again, I almost wished it wasn't. Chris had a fondness for the dreadfully morose Canadian folk singer Leonard Cohen and had one of his records. Unfortunately, he only had the one, and he played it incessantly! I didn't say anything but instead retaliated (in jest) by playing my Hendrix LP 'All Along the Watchtower'[20]. The Station would alternate between the reverberations of his brilliant howling guitar and the laid-back singing of Cohen. If the locals hadn't thought so already, this would have convinced them that we were all mad!

However, on a more positive note, with the electricity back on, and despite being in the middle of nowhere, I discovered we did have some form of contact with the outside world. At six-thirty each Tuesday evening, we were allocated a fifteen-minute block of two-way radio communication on the Catholic Church radio 'sked'. This was to allow us to report on our current situation, make requests and share any news. Although the Church decided on whether one's queries or messages warranted transmission further afield, it least was contact with someone else and provided a certain degree of comfort to us three foreigners in relative isolation. And, as another bonus of having electricity again, I could now listen to the news broadcast by Radio Bougainville and hear official pidgin English spoken, which helped no end in learning the lingo.

Mark finally appeared from his latest round of pastoral work in the villages, but then, with the briefest of 'Hellos', immediately set off up to Rabaul with Stewart on the *Kiriaka*, carrying the latest crop of cocoa and copra.

I stayed back with Chris who was still nursing his infected leg and set about getting a better idea of the status of the various bits of equipment on site. I needed to prioritise my work and asked Thomas to show me around and explain the state of each item. It did not take long. With Thomas' vocabulary limited mainly to '*Em i bagarap big taim*' or '*I dai pinis*', combined with my still poor understanding of pidgin, I was none the wiser about the detail of why something did not work. Nevertheless, a visual inspection was usually enough to see some pieces of equipment were so dead I could not justify spending any time digging around in the entrails.

On getting back up to the house after this rather superficial survey, Chris called out, "We've got an invitation from Barclays"[21].

"Oh! Who on earth are Barclays now?"

"You didn't know we have a few other expatriates in this neck of the woods? Well, Barclays are building a road down to us from Sipai and then all the way further on down to Torokina, south of here. Once it is finished, we'll be able to drive up to Sipai."[22]

"Well, that's great! How long before it's finished?

"Well, I dunno… but, anyway, Barclays said they've only a few kilometres to go and apparently, although still a bit dangerous in places, the road's just about passable by four-wheel drive. So, anyway, the point is, they're throwing a party at their camp to celebrate and they want us to come along."

We thought about this for a minute or two and then realised there could be a bit of an issue with us middle-class, do-gooder Pommie lads from a Christian Mission station, socialising with the roustabout road builders.

"At the very least, there would be both women and grog at the party," Chris said. "It might not look too good for us being up at their camp carousing, and apparently doing so in the name of the Lord. We'd better seek divine guidance before sending our reply."

Knowing Father Peter's lack of interest towards our activities and not wanting to stir the possum so to speak, we decided to ask Father Bourgea up at Sipai. Getting up there would give us a legitimate excuse to see if the road was passable. Great!

So next day, with Chris driving (and insisting his leg was not *that* bad) and me as pillion, we set off on the 120cc, two-stroke Suzuki trail bike we used for getting around the Station. All went well to start with and although bumpy and uncomfortable, we made good progress. About halfway there however, we found a bridge over the river near the village of Matterio was still under construction. It was simply a couple of steel girders, each only a few hundred millimetres wide. It would be impossible to ride a motorbike across unless you were some sort of circus artist!

Fortunately, the Barclays' *wok-bois* were there and being used to such tricky circumstances, carried the bike across for us in a trice; and so we carried on. Later, despite being told the road was nearly finished, we found some sections were still just a couple of muddy tracks. Chris got used to steering towards whichever looked the least slippery and bumpy, and hoping! We were skidding away so much we would end up with one wheel in one furrow and one in another, then slide slowly over and find ourselves walking along-side the bike! It was muddy and exhausting work and would probably have been quicker to have just walked.

Eventually, we made it up to Sipai and, getting over the

surprise of seeing us, Father Bourgea gave us his advice. He said representatives of a Christian based society mixing with road-builders would not look too good, with the women, booze and 'everything else that might be going on'. We were hardly surprised and so, happily accepting the decision had essentially been made for us, we ate a bit of lunch, chatted briefly with the girls and set off back to Kuraio.

By the time we got back down to the bridge at Matterio we found the Barclays crew had knocked off for the day! This was a worry. However, on closer inspection we saw their work had progressed a little and perhaps anticipating our return, they had laid a few 200mm planks along the steel girders on one side. So, with Chris awkwardly pulling from in front and me pushing from behind, we cajoled the bike back across the bridge. Unbelievably, halfway across, we had a *guria* which shook the entire structure for what seemed an eternity. With the girders each a couple of metres apart and nothing but thin air between, we stopped pushing, hung on for dear life and waited for the tremor to pass. Ending up a mangled mess of bike and limbs in the swollen torrent below had been a real possibility.

After things settled down, we continued our struggle through the muddy terrain and finally made it back to Kuraio. Having taken five hours for a journey of probably only thirty kilometres, the road was evidently still a fair way from completion. Nevertheless, Chris and I claimed the doubtful honour of being the first and second person in history to travel from Kuraio to Sipai and back by motorbike!

Somewhat perversely, with Chris having a legitimate, but weak, excuse in the shape of his still injured leg (now inflamed again from the bike ride), and me feeling genuinely ill from the last typhoid jab I'd just been given at the *haus sik*, we were able to send our apologies to Barclays because of 'ill health'. Declining their invitation on moral grounds would have been too pathetic for words.

And then, after being back home for a couple of days, and just to keep us on our toes, we experienced yet another terrifying *guria*. This time, we were in the house and it felt like the place would collapse around our ears!

Over those first few weeks, I started to appreciate that the best thing about Kuraio was not what had been the work of man but, appropriately for a Christian Mission station, the work of God. The earthquakes meant it wasn't exactly the Garden of Eden, but apart from that Kuraio was a wonderful place.

Nature's beauty spoiled us and, indeed it was hard to imagine a better scene than that provided at the conclusion of each day. With the house just thirty metres from the cliff edge we could sit looking out over Empress Augusta Bay and the vast expanse of the Solomon Sea. There, framed by the dark silhouette of sloping palms, the last rays of the sun singed the clouds and added blood-red accents to the greying sea. The greatest pleasure however was from the pounding surf that delivered a welcome counterpoint to the incessant racket of cicada, toads and frogs. It had the appearance of Paradise and the sounds of a madhouse.

So, had Chris been right when he suggested it was hell? I knew it was a throwaway remark, and even though there were a few drawbacks, we did have the most magnificent views and an abundance of flora and fauna.

I withheld judgment a while longer as I gradually took it all in. The island of Bougainville was generally lush, green and rugged, and perhaps through some trick of the light or some natural phenomenon, the vegetation even appeared to have a bluish tinge about it. Included within all this were many exotic and ordinary, edible and inedible plants, which looked entirely different from anything I had ever seen in England. The most obvious and prolific were those introduced for commercial purposes: coconut palms and cocoa bushes, the latter shading a few experimental coffee shrubs. Planted under Mentzer's guidance in the 1960s, there were palm trees as far as the eye could see and they were now showing their age, some were very tall and dying. Some, with only a few fronds sticking out of the tops of their branchless trunks set at a rakish angle, resembled an enormous North American Indian's headdress!

Walking around the outskirts of the Station I was puzzled to see what looked like old blankets thrown up into a few trees here and there. Chris patiently explained they were the bundles of leaves the locals tied around papayas and bananas to stop the bats eating the fruit – of course!

I was no expert on fauna, but obliged to become aware of it, sometimes for safety's sake. Living creatures comprised two broad groups. There were those that were a bit of a pest but relatively harmless, and those that were dangerous. Luckily there seemed to be less of the latter than the former!

The most prevalent pests were the toads to which I had already been introduced. Some clever soul introduced these delightful creatures, known locally as *rokrok's*, into the country, in the 1930s to control hawk moth larvae that attack the sweet potato. They now numbered in their thousands and apart from getting under our feet, they teased us with their operatic airs. Being the antithesis of what many prefer of children, they were mainly heard but not seen. They would start in a wave of cacophonous croaking and simply go on and on forever. Just when they were at their worst and you thought you would go mad, they would stop. There was just time to breathe a sigh of relief at the silence before they would start up all over again! We swore the noise was a significant factor in sending many an expatriate 'troppo'. Frog and toad noise, along with that of the cicadas, was so pervasive and was such a part of the way of life that one just had to put up with it!

In addition to the frogs and toads there were some enormous spiders and other creepy crawlies to look out for, including a species of giant centipede. This charming creature tended to live in rotten wood and apparently its sting was so painful that even tough soldiers in the war demanded morphine to quell the agony.

There were also many birds, bats and rats and, apparently, a few rare butterflies and then there was the ubiquitous gecko. These pale, pink, pop-eyed creatures would suddenly appear from nowhere, stick themselves to a wall at an impossible angle and lie there, motionless, before darting off to catch a bug. Approaching quietly and getting close enough without frightening them off, you could see their internal organs pulsing through their translucent skin. They were our friends, because they kept the mosquitos down and were far nicer than the eye-stinging repellent coils we would light and put on the floor around our chairs of an evening. We had started taking anti-malarial prophylactics before we had left England, but they didn't stop the mozzies biting or the later torment of itching and scratching.

Perhaps the most irritating creatures were the sweat flies. These annoying little critters had the habit of getting in your face and in your eyes, and no sooner had you batted one away than their mates were back with alacrity. They were responsible for the infamous Australian wave, where the hand, swept across in front of the face to swat one away was mistaken by foreigners as some form of peculiar Antipodean greeting!

There were also some dark brown, hairy, semi-wild pigs, husbanded by the locals and rooting around the outskirts of the mission and of course, the eighty to ninety head of cattle Chris was managing. But there was one, large and dangerous native creature. Downstream from us as we swam and washed in the Tsinamutu, there were crocodiles. We assumed they were already well fed on fish, frogs and crustaceans and were not really a threat. However, they were occasionally seen swimming across the bay and best kept at a distance.

There were a few other creatures although not in the same league and certainly less dangerous. Bright red and green parrots flitted dramatically around in between feeding among the coconuts, and then, even more benign, a species of duck on the river. Chris managed to shoot some of these and they made a nice change from the tedious tinned meat. And then there was the flying fox, a big black bat-like creature the locals rather appropriately called *blakbokis*[23]. We would often see them swooping and swerving around the sky at dusk. Being quite prevalent and voracious feeders on their husbanded crops, particularly the paw-paw and banana, the local's shot and ate them whenever they could. Somehow, they did not appeal to our (more sophisticated?) palates.

Tales from Durrell and Attenborough of exotic animals from around the world, had spoiled me and I had rather expected a greater variety of wildlife – monkeys perhaps, peering out from the jungle surrounding our camp. But I guess it was just as well that, apart from the crocs, there was really nothing that was too dangerous. All we had was fascinating enough and besides, there were plenty of other issues to contend with without having to protect ourselves from any more mischievous creatures in the night. And I was soon to learn a little more about these other issues.

Mark and I had somehow missed meeting and talking to each other for a while. He had been away, off-site somewhere or other, visiting a village doing his pastoral work and had then shot off up to Rabaul with Stewart. But now, back on site, we had chance to get better acquainted. We relaxed, took a break from the afternoon heat and sat chatting in the living room.

It was hardly relaxing. Mark, thin, pale and lanky with a mess of dark hair, was an intense and fidgety sort of fellow; always adjusting his spectacles, pushing them back off the tip of his nose or taking them off and wiping them. However, as much as he could, he settled down, and in his Southern States drawl, related his (supposedly far-fetched) stories. The others said he had been out here too long and exaggerated. However, they seemed realistic enough for some concern.

"Y' know Nick, one of the big-men came to see me the other day when I was up at the Mission on Tsiroge," Mark began. "He told me there was a strong possibility of some danger. Bit frustrating because he would not say what sort of danger he was on about! But, knowing the history of the place, I understood it to be in the context of the cargo cult. Y' know; it's lessened in recent years, but it could easily return."

Mark went on to explain that, as the people were originally animists, they thought that if they carried out their traditional ritual's 'cargo would continue to fall from the sky'. Problem was despite them carrying on thus, no goods arrived. And because they knew it was the missionaries who tried to stamp out the cult, they blamed them for making the cult ineffective.

Mark continued, "In May '61, because cargo failed to arrive when expected, the priest here at Kuraio, Mentzer's predecessor, had to flee in fear of his life."

Amazed as I was to hear all this, I was more concerned about what it meant for us.

"Wow!" said I. "So, what happened then?"

"Well, Mentzer managed to calm things down y'know[24] and for many years, he encouraged the people to work. They are all still at it, farming cocoa and copra, as you can see. But the speed of progress towards material wealth is frustrating them. It is all too slow. So now the story going around is that the big-men believe the Tambaran, their deity, is angry because of the many bad things happening here. In addition to the no-show of cargo, they are talking about the poor weather (it had been unseasonably dry), also about Father Peter's behaviour and the mine at Panguna. And now there's been all the trouble in getting someone to captain the *Kiriaka Aro*! Man, they're even complaining about Barclays building the road to Sipai!" He pushed his glasses back up off the end of his nose, yet again. "All of this, along with their attitude to white man's lifestyle, y'know, our material stuff, etc, I worry deity worship may have taken over again."

"So, what does all this mean for us?"

"Well, what it means is the potential for the people to go back to their old, dark ways, the ways before the white man. For example, I've had it on good authority there was a child sacrifice back in April."

"Wow! Really? That is shocking," I said.

I eventually left Mark to complete the writing of his pastoral report and wended my way back across the frog and toad obstacle course to Father Peter's. I wondered if, having lived here so long, Mark was imagining all this and making it up.

Sometime later, as if to support what was going on and to add even more to my concerns, Stewart told me about *spik poison*. This, he said, was the form of black magic in which Bougainvillean's believed[25] and was the means by which someone had recently been killed. It was very serious and the danger to us whiteys was highlighted by the fact that Mark had already been attacked twice since he had arrived! On one occasion, some *longlongman* had taken a swipe at him with an axe whilst he was in bed. He missed, but since then, he had been sleeping with a knife next to him for protection. The worry was that the individual who attacked him was not crazy but someone trying to scare Mark, to hasten his and us other whites' departure so the cult could start up again.

But then, both Stewart and Chris again said that Mark exaggerated his stories. And when, later, I mentioned to Chris what Mark told me, he said he wasn't sure how real the re-emergence of cargo cultism was. He had always felt very safe. Strangely enough, despite the stories of voodoo, child sacrifice and issues with the cargo cultists, and the fact that Mark told me I should go back to England and not worry about the Mission, it sounded all so far-fetched that it really did not bother me that much either[26].

Later, at last, Mark made up his mind and said he would soon be leaving. After nearly four years on the island, he knew he had been there long enough. Stewart and Chris explained they had been encouraging him to return home for some time, as they had felt he had indeed been showing early signs of going troppo[27].

Mark's departure was still some time away, but in preparation for taking over, I learned more about the usual routine for the *Kiriaka*. While she was based at Kuraio and was mainly for the benefit of the Kereaka people, she also sailed further afield, both up and down the coast. Other Missions had the use of these freight and transport services, when they asked and when weather and scheduling permitted. Generally, most journeys ended up in Rabaul, the main centre of trade between Bougainville and the rest of the world.

So, as part of this routine, in early November, Stewart and Chris took the boat south, down to Torokina. This was about equidistant between the north and south of the island, and the purpose of the visit was to see how the people were and find out if they wanted anything. The pair reckoned to be away for a couple of days, and as Mark was also away visiting villages and telling them he was going to leave, I stayed behind to hold the fort. This was a good opportunity to spend more time with the *wok-bois*, improve on my language skills and to check on the other on-going projects. Both the sawmill (*somill*) and grass cutter needed fixing, and most important of all, we needed to complete the fermentary for the cocoa beans. Our agents, ANGCO and CPL in Rabaul, told us, concerns over my olfactory senses aside, we could expect a better return on our crops if we ensured proper processing of the beans.

When Stewart first arrived, processing facilities included two bed-dryers and a single Rotary dryer. And now, as he had already started building a third bed-dryer, it would be a relatively simply job to get it finished[28].

I met the two *wok-bois* out at the dryer's one morning as arranged and started telling them what we needed to do – dig post-holes, make up the concrete, put the DYs in the ground and cement them in; it was not so hard to understand. But there were blank stares all round. The lack of plans didn't help and my lack of ability to communicate was clearly a problem. However, I knew it was not that the *wok-bois* did not understand me; their lack of enthusiasm was more a matter of not wanting to exert themselves in the heat.

Nevertheless, with the existing beds close by as a guide, with me doing some parts myself, and explaining by example, we eventually got some of it done.

Despite these day-to-day frustrations and through this sort of interaction, my pidgin English gradually improved. And after a couple of months of chatting to folk and listening to Radio Bougainville and hearing lots of '*long*' and '*pela*' and '*yumi's*', I found I was getting the hang of it and could now get by.

A few days later, with the Kiriaka having returned from Torokina, Chris and Stewart said they wanted to see a bit more of the island and decided to hike up the 3,000-metre-high volcano, Mount Balbi. Apparently, none of the locals or their forebears had ever known it to erupt and they were assured that it was dormant.

Safety aside, as it was located somewhere off to the north of Kuraio and right in the centre of the island, it was going to be a fair hike through virgin jungle. Biobeara, a member of the boat crew, said he would guide them on their expedition (despite him probably being afraid of the spirits of the dead being there.)

With nothing much going on at the Station they said I should come along as well, but by now I had realised I was not quite as venturesome as these two. With no proper camping gear, I was not keen on sleeping rougher than I already was and was quite happy to stay back and look after the place.

With Stewart, Chris and Biobeara off on their hike first thing next morning, I then realised it was true, there was not much to do. But, instead of sitting around, I decided make a more thorough check of the various bits of equipment I had earlier written off, just to see if I could save any of it. I went and got Thomas to come around with me and see if we could get to the bottom of their ailments.

This time, I managed to understand a little better what was wrong with the tractor. Thomas told me someone drained the engine oil out over at the refuse tip on one side of the Station and then driven the tractor back to the workshop on this side and filled her up with clean oil. 'Not by me', he hastened to add. This had naturally ruined the bearings, and, as Thomas said, '*Em e baggarap big time*'. I knew that to fix it meant splitting the tractor in half and then some; taking the crankshaft up to Rabaul to have the journals ground and then rebuilding the engine with new bearings. It was an even bigger job than the generator, and as I didn't have the manual or much of the equipment needed (and getting it from Britain was simply too hard), I decided to investigate something a little more manageable.

With timber always in demand and now needed to complete the dryer beds, I next went to look at the *somill*. It was not far from the Station, perhaps a kilometre or so. Thomas and I walked over to have a look. As we approached, my first impression was that of a rotting and run-down grass shed abandoned many years ago. Peering into the gloom, I saw something that looked like it had been associated with cutting timber; lying there in a state of exhaustion was a dark clutter of sharp and dangerous looking bits of metal. Thomas announced that this was a Dolmar rig.

Now, despite my extensive interest in things mechanical, I had never heard the name Dolmar before. However, I did recognise the source of its power. It was like lifting the boot of a Beetle, for there, stuck on the end of the sizeable chainsaw, was a Volkswagen petrol engine. So, after surveying this sorry collection of greasy old machinery and while Thomas made himself busy sharpening the chain-saw teeth, I checked out the motor.

There was fuel in the tank, the plugs were connected, there was oil in the sump and I couldn't find anything particularly wrong. But to make me feel like I had done something useful I cleaned and adjusted the points. Thomas and I then took it in turns to crank the motor. We persevered for about twenty swings of the handle, but couldn't get the stubborn beast to even kick back. We exhausted ourselves with so much effort we had to call it quits. The trouble was that with no electricity on the Station the battery had been left flat for so long it had not the slightest spark in it and was well and truly dead. Another item for the shopping list for our next visit to Rabaul!

A day later, with Stewart and Chris still off-site trekking up the volcano, I heard the characteristic clatter of rotor blades of a helicopter. I ran over to the source of the noise just in time to see an ugly machine descending from the sky. It hovered for a while, twenty metres or so off the ground, presumably to scatter the cattle grazing in the paddock, then finally landed in a swirl of leaves and dust. Hordes of inquisitive villagers and the usual giggling children arrived out of nowhere and joined me as we all stood around expectantly. Anyone visiting by such means in our neck of the woods had to be a big man, although no one seemed to know who it was.

Eventually, with the rotor blades drooping and ineffective, the pilot stepped down, helping out his VIP passenger. Edging his way through the throng, the pilot came over to me and said, "Meet Paul Lapun, the Minister for Mines from central government in Moresby".

"Good afternoon Minister. Welcome to Kuraio," I said.

As I was the only white face in the crowd, the pilot had assumed I should be the point of contact. But Lapun had other ideas and looking over my head somewhat dismissively as we shook hands, tried to spy someone more relevant. Despite all my worries over the *Kiriaka Aro* and the project in general I hardly expected a government Minister, let alone the Minister for Mines, to come to see me about them. He was looking for a local representative, perhaps someone he knew? Lapun soon recognised those he'd really come to meet and, muttering something about Shell and 'telling the locals', he quickly walked past me and greeted the group of big-men. Meanwhile, breaking the 'What am I supposed to do now?' spell, the pilot produced a small box from his leather attaché case, indicated a patch of shade and, as the Minister talked, we sat and played a game of chess – as you do when you have a bit of time to kill in the jungle! The pilot explained that the Minister was here to tell the big-men and the gathered throng that Royal Dutch Shell was about to start prospecting for oil and gas off the west coast. To help the ships get their bearings, they wanted to set up a radio repeater station exactly where Stewart and Chris probably were now, on Mount Balbi. Lapun was there to explain what it all meant and seek their permission so he could move forward with approval for Shell.

His speech done and with lots of smiles and handshaking all around, the Minister got back on board the chopper. The pilot wound up the revs, and after a short pause seemingly stuck to the ground and trembling in fear of itself, it rose up through its own clattering noise. Tipping its nose in salute, it roared off over the treetops, taking the VIP to his next meeting further inland. I wondered briefly if it was only the Shell repeater station he had come to see about, or perhaps more significantly, something to do with the mine at Panguna?

A few days later Chris and Stewart reappeared, looking even more like a couple of Robinson Crusoe's, and this time complete with Man Friday, Biobeara, in tow. They gabbled on enthusiastically about their expedition. They had slept under the shelter of leaves, found a huge limestone cave, fed on pigeon and *blakbokis* and bathed in icy cold mountain waters (good for them, I thought). Chris explained how the villagers told them the water of the stream was so acid it would sharpen an axe left in it overnight! They said that even though steam and sulphurous gases emerging from the fumaroles near the crater warmed the immediate environment, the air was freezing; only about four degrees Celsius. They insisted they'd had a great time, but still I didn't envy their roughing it.

While they had been away, I had had plenty of time to ponder my situation. I found Station life was following some sort of pattern. Apart from the ever-present heat and humidity it was not particularly hard work. Something more significant, usually something important to repair, occasionally interspersed the few regular tasks. But we would often start getting into one project and then, frustratingly, would have to stop for one reason or another, usually through lack of parts or equipment. The remains of unfinished or unfixable jobs were all around us. Aside from this frustration, I was getting into the swing of things and was even starting to enjoy myself a bit. But I was still concerned over whether I was able to run the boat. However, despite Mark's warnings, I decided to hang on in anticipation that we would find someone else to do the job.

Meanwhile, one of the regular tasks we had to do was to help run the trade store. While the locals mostly ran it themselves, now and then and with no formal roster, we took it in turns to help out. This was both amusing and, as with most of the other jobs, very hot work. The store was basically a corrugated iron shed with a door on one end, a large window flap and counter along one long side and shelves behind. When the store was open, we raised the flap to allow customers to see the merchandise on the shelves inside. It was something of a mix between a 1950s British village store and a roadside hot food truck.

With Serisu the *stor-boi* showing me the way on my first morning, I undid the huge padlock and went to push open the ill-fitting door. The whole building echoed with that distinctive grating noise of corrugated iron scraping against itself, but the door would only open part way. Pushing harder and peering in I saw why. A mess of stuff covered the floor: tinned goods, bars of soap, T-shirts and even kid's toys. Many items had obviously fallen off the shelves and simply been left there. I didn't know if this was the result of the latest *guria* or simply untidiness, but to me it looked like they had been there for some time.

Serisu, quite unfazed by the situation, pushed past me and walked in over the detritus. Following him in, I could not bring myself to leave it like that, so I shoved what I could behind the shelving and asked him to sort it out. I said to put the good, undamaged items, back on the shelves and put any badly damaged stock out at the back of the store and give it away.

Big mistake. I had only just started opening the serving flap, when, seeing Serisu throwing stuff out, locals appeared from nowhere. Perhaps thinking the cargo had arrived at last, they grabbed whatever they could and ran off at lightning-speed before anyone else could beat them to it! I'd almost caused a riot!

I quickly swapped roles and while Serisu was serving, I finished tidying up and then checked on what there was in stock. There was a good variety of merchandise, but no records, what was on the shelves was what we had. Another job, for later: set up some system for stock control and re-ordering. In the meantime, being a Sunday and the busiest time of the week, things literally started hotting up after church and I got busy helping behind the counter.

The heat was exhausting, but it was nothing compared with the patience required to serve the average shopper. My first customer pointed at the tinned *pis* (fish) on the shelf behind me. I put a can on the counter and she immediately pointed at the same item again! I repeated the exercise until she had the required number of tins (only three in this case). She then went through the same process for biscuits, asking for one packet at a time. It was a slow process! And, with the goods on the shelves being at least a metre away from the customer's finger, the accuracy of this form of communication had its limitations. But, there again, so was the language. While my understanding of pidgin English was now adequate, when customers added a bit of Kereaka *tok ples*, just for good measure, I was confused!

And then, as if this was not hard enough, even understanding pidgin English was not that simple. They called women's blouses '*meri's dress*', but this was also the name they used for the skirt! Lighter flints went by the name '*sitone*', (as in stone), '*stik tabak*' for twist tobacco (smoked in a huge, long, cigarette made of a sheet of old newspaper); torch bulbs, globes (the standard Aussie name), and so on it went. It took a while and, though I hate to admit it, it tested my patience. I found myself talking a little more brusquely to locals than was fair.

Food for our own meals also came from this store. Calimo would simply go and take what was available, tinned meat, tinned fish, tinned vegies, everything and anything that one could find in a tin. But even though he had the new kitchen to prepare all this, some food was simply beyond improvement. And, one evening after yet another dinner out of a tin, we concluded that we were sick and tired of our diet.

Stewart said, "Chris. We need real meat! What do you reckon about killing one of your cattle? They're going feral anyway. Okay with you?"

"Well, sure," said Chris, "the husbanding task's almost impossible so that sounds reasonable." Then, turning to me, he said, "By the time I got here they were running all over the place, the gardens, the old airstrip...."

"Great!" said I, nodding to give my own two bobs' worth of approval. "I'm fed up, if you'll excuse the pun, with what we have to eat every day. Let's do it."

Then, having taken a nanosecond to register that Chris mentioned that there was an airstrip at Kuraio, I said,

"Oh. What do you mean, airstrip? I thought the only way to get to Kuraio was by sea in the *Kiriaka*? Of course, there'll be the road eventually."

"Well, they built a grass strip here some time ago, but it wasn't maintained and the cattle have taken it over as their favourite pasture," said Chris. "They've helped it along the path to degradation with their cowpats and hoof marks and ruined the surface. It's quite unsafe for any aircraft now, except helicopters of course."

I pondered on this and realised it was yet another example of the challenge of maintaining the place in reasonable working order. However, back on the topic of food, it was clear our supply of protein was somewhat limited to either tinned meat or tinned fish. The meat was a disgusting sort of product like the well-known Spam ('Special Processed American Meat') and the fish was mackerel. As I had discovered the latter was known locally, and rather appropriately, as *pis*. Imported all the way from Taiwan this had the most dreadfully overpowering taste and smell of anything that had ever been put in a can and we ate it only in desperation. That was it. After a few meals of these two, it really became deadly boring.

There was a bit more variety when it came to carbohydrates. Complementing the locally grown taro and kau kau we also had rice, (usually well speckled with weevils for decoration) and some tinned vegetables. Amongst these was a mushy mess drowned in a thick, black, disgusting sauce, tasting something like wood but described on the label to be mushrooms. It surprised me that the locals would buy any of this, particularly the fish. After all, surely, they should be out there catching them from the sea or the river maybe? But then I realised that Mentzer had brought these folk down to the coast from the hinterland and the Kereaka had no tradition of fishing. Somewhat contrarily, considering they were now so close to the sea, they had been encouraged into farming the land.

Anyway, with plenty of motivation to get some real meat, all we had to do now, if you will forgive another pun, was to execute a plan. But how does one kill an animal that might run faster than a horse, weighs around a tonne and is practically wild? The answer of course is to shoot it! It should be easy. We just had to identify one specific beast and then, bang! Simple! But there was a bit more to it than that. Trying to shoot it on foot was pointless as the cattle ran away at the slightest hint of danger, and firing in the wrong direction could readily put human lives at risk. No. We needed to get a steer into a place where it was safe to shoot, and to do that we required something that was quick. There was only one option. The only thing, apart from the trail bike, that could travel at anything like the speed of a running steer was the truck.

So, early next day, with Stewart brandishing the old .303 BSA ex-WWII rifle and muttering something about the sights not being too good, we boarded the Isuzu. With Stewart wedged securely against the cab up in the back of the truck, rifle at the ready, Chris acting as my guide and with me driving, we set off to hunt beef.

Unsurprisingly, as soon as the herd saw us coming, they took off, running wildly, scattering all over the airstrip and surrounding paddock. As Stewart said we should take a bull, we spent a good deal of time charging around in the truck, trying to separate one from the rest[29]. Eventually, I managed to corner one in a small copse in the corner of the paddock, well away from any errant human beings. Stewart took aim and fired – but nothing happened! With the sights on the old gun proving as dodgy as he suspected he eventually had to fire at the poor beast many times before it finally expired. Not a pretty sight! We agreed next time it would be better to build a corral, entice an animal in and then put it humanely out of this world with a solid hammer blow to the forehead.

If the shooting of the *bullemecow* was ghastly, it was nothing compared to the next phase of getting meat closer to the plate. In preparation for what was to come, Chris went and got the JCB, dug a large hole in the ground between two palm trees and strung a wire rope between them, a couple of metres off the ground. Then, tying a rope around its rear legs, we dragged the carcass behind the Isuzu over to our makeshift abattoir, threw one end of the rope over the wire between the trees, re-attached it to the back of the truck and drove off, hoisting the corpse up in the air, dangling over the hole in the ground.

With a good idea of what was going to happen next, I went back to the house to sharpen some knives to prepare for my part of the job, leaving the others to do their worst with theirs.

Sometime later, coming back to the kitchen, Stewart and Chris deposited two enormous and still warm quarters of *bullemecow* in front of me and proceeded to tell me the gory details. They had slit open the body, dumped the intestines into the hole, removed the hide and cut the carcase up into quarters. Now, even after having given so much of it away to the locals, including the other two quarters, we found there was still far more than our needs.

In starting on the job, I recalled having seen a diagram of the traditional joints of beef behind the counter of Mum's butcher's shop in Bradford-on-Avon. Unfortunately, I had not taken enough notice to recall the detail and now struggled to see the connection with that and the lump of gore in front of me. So, I just got down to it and spent all afternoon chopping, cutting and carving the quarters into smaller pieces, butchering away as best I could.

Strangely enough, despite it being a gruesome exercise, I felt okay with cutting up meat disassociated from the living creature. It was physically hard work, but apart from that and the slimy blood, the worst part was the damned flies. They were horrendous. Swarms of the little buggers suddenly appeared out of nowhere. They had obviously been waiting around for this once in a lifetime opportunity and were now gate-crashing the slaughtering party with a vengeance.

After a grisly day's work, we ended up with a huge supply of vaguely recognisable joints, enough to keep us in meat for months. We stacked them up in the old kero freezers and took ourselves off down to the Tsinamutu to literally and metaphorically wash away the sins of our deeds.

CHAPTER 8

APPREHENSION

One hot and sunny November morning, we left Kuraio on another trip up to Buka and Rabaul. For some reason, the boat was jam full of people, this time. Villagers, knew the Society owned the Kiriaka, and assuming they could use it when they felt like it, they simply materialised when they heard it was going to leave. I didn't know if anyone counted or tried to limit the numbers, but overcrowded she was. I got the impression people would have continued to board and fill her up until she sank. Sense prevailed, however, and once all of those who wanted to travel were on board, we upped anchor and set sail, low in the water.

Arriving in Buka, Stewart and I hitched a lift up to Hahela to chat with Father Fey about the situation at Kuraio. We talked all evening about the various issues: about the state of the equipment, the amount of work and number of jobs for Chris and me after Stewart and Jacob left and, more specifically about running the boat. I made it clear I was not comfortable about taking on the responsibility and Father Fey did not seem particularly surprised, or forthcoming about what, if any, additional support the Church might give over the matter. He said this and the various other problems had been around for many years before I had arrived and that Mentzer had only got qualified support for his project. He said I had a couple of choices: I could carry on and do the best I could, or simply leave. Faced with these obvious alternatives I said I would give it another few months, and hopefully, a replacement captain would be found and allow me to focus on the jobs on land.

Next morning, I went down to Wong You's, the Chinese trade store, for supplies of lolly water (soft drink), eggs and bacon and a few other things, arranged for them to be sent down to the *Kiriaka* and then went on up to the Post Office to pick up the mail. While I was there, I telephoned Dick in Moresby and told him of my conversation with Father Fey and what was going on with the Society and the *Kiriaka*. He gave me a bit of encouragement, confirmed the alternatives and said it was up to me and to take it a day at a time.

Going back down to the boat, and after helping supervise the loading of the stores, we sailed over to Tsiroge to pick up and drop off their things before heading on up to Rabaul.

It had been another busy day, but by this stage and particularly after the pep talks from Father Fey and Dick, I began to see the brighter side of things. I felt more up to tackling the problems at hand. On the surface of it, the boat, littered as it was with chickens, crates of beer and lolly water (and still lots of people) was enjoyable – in good seas. Nevertheless, I was still concerned about the slightly critical issues of reading charts, navigating reefs, using a compass and my ability to communicate clearly with the crew. I was still not confident or foolish enough to take charge, but now, I decided I would investigate further - if necessary.

A few days later, after being worried again by the rough seas on our return from Rabaul, we stopped off at Sipai. We waited just long enough to drop off their stores and, as promised, to pick up the girls and Father Bourgea to take them down to Kuraio. This would be a nice break from their relative isolation and a welcome change of scenery and, of course, there was now the party to farewell Mark.

The sea got a bit choppy again en-route, but all we arrived in good spirits. And after the locals had paddled us ashore, we trekked up to the house, rustled up some food and went down to the Tsinamutu for a picnic. Stewart and Chris had discovered a beautiful spot further upstream from where we would usually wash and where the trees cast a welcome, cooling shadow. The water was shallow and so clear you could see the bed of mottled brown and green weed-covered pebbles, highlighted now and then when the sunlight managed to sparkle through. It was a lovely place; too shallow for swimming but great for cooling one's heels.

We dumped the picnic things, set ourselves up comfortably in the shade and then, with a sense of déjà vu, revisited our respective childhoods, splashing around with gay abandon. Eventually, all grown up again, we sat under the trees chatting, ate our picnic, drank a few beers (even Father Bourgea) and then, avoiding the temptation to sleep by the river, wandered back to the house.

All told, what with the journey down from Rabaul, Buka and Sipai, the heat and the beer, we figured we deserved a rest for the remains of the day and didn't try to fight it. Father Bourgea looked like he was enjoying his day off from pastoral duties and was soon snoozing in a comfortable chair; the girls went for tea with their friends the nurses, in the *haus sik*, and I settled down with a copy of Robert Louis Stevenson's *Kidnapped*. I read that David Balfour, the main character had been enticed into boarding a boat and now seemed destined to be sold into slavery! With my imagination getting a bit carried away, I could not help but see the story adding a certain *je ne sais quoi* to my own situation.

Come evening and back to reality, there were now a few more signs of life. After gathering around their fires most of the afternoon, villagers were now cooking rice and chicken in banana and taro leaves in their in-ground ovens and getting ready for the big feast. And, now, around six, just as it was getting dark, they started preparing for the sing-sing in Mark's honour. Chris, Mark, the girls and I hung around in the house, watching the various comings and goings and keeping out of the villager's way. Then, having slipped out into the gloom some time earlier, Father Bourgea and Stewart reappeared, stealthily carrying a box they must have brought up from the boat.

With curiosity roused, we went outside into the now pitch-dark and watched as the conspirators scurried around, clumsily bumping into each other and fiddling around with something or other. We could not make out what was going on but then, in boyish excitement, Stewart shouted, "Watch out!" and jumped back as a rocket spiralled up into the night sky. A loud 'Wah!' erupted from the small crowd of surprised local onlookers as the missile traced a fiery trajectory and then suddenly illuminated the sky with a thousand crackling stars. Stewart's box of fireworks, bought surreptitiously from a Chinese trade store in Rabaul, provided a brilliant start to the proceedings and a complete surprise for Mark and the rest of us, and especially the locals. With the ice broken, so to speak, we all joined in and had a great time letting off the remaining rockets, crackers and Roman candles. Then, as if inspired by the pyrotechnics, the now solid crowd of locals followed on with a wild, uninhibited show of dancing and singing, a warm up to the sing-sing proper.

A little later, silhouetted by their fires, we saw a mass of natives swaying around in a circle, energetically stamping their feet to the bizarre sounds of their bamboo pipes and *kovokovo*[30]. I watched and listened mesmerised; all this was music to their ears, but alien to mine. I had to check myself. Was there perhaps a shade of malevolence in their dance? No, I was imagining things. This was a Catholic mission station after all. Maybe the disappointment with Mark's impending departure had spawned this almost palpable atmosphere, or maybe it was just something exaggerated by the incessant heat.

Whatever the implications, by eleven thirty things were, figuratively and literally, really warming up. The Kereaka had boundless energy and one couldn't mistake the fervour in their singing and chanting, but, nevertheless, by this time I'd had enough and went to bed.

I could still hear them around three in the morning, so I got up again to see what was going on. They were still in full swing, but looking and sounding very much like the same scenario and not understanding any part of the tradition, I soon went back to bed.

The sing-sing went on until daylight, even dancing right around outside the house. I again wondered if there was some hidden message. Was this a warning to all of us that despite all the efforts of the Christian teachings, they were not letting go of their traditional ways?

Next day, putting to one side any real or dreamt-of implications of the previous night, we focused on at last fare welling Mark. We all of us, Father Bourgea, Father Peter, the girls, Chris, Stewart, myself and of course Mark, traipsed down to the beach, followed by Blaize, the headmaster and a whole host of schoolchildren. The sight of the *Kiriaka Aro* anchored a little offshore, riding gently up and down on a sparkling sea, contrasted confusingly with the mood of the children now lining up above the beach. It was a beautiful but poignant scene. As each of us took it in turns to shake hands with Mark and bid him goodbye, the children, under Blaize's direction, began an emotive rendition of *So Long, Farewell* from *The Sound of Music*. It was particularly moving, given they sang in pidgin and in pretty good harmony too; tear jerking in fact, in complete contrast to the dancing of the night before.

Mark, the girls and Father Bourgea sailed away with Jacob in the *Kiriaka* and, not to mess around, I immediately got down to work. I spent the rest of the day cleaning out his room, fetching my things up from Father Peter's and finally moved in. It was good to have my own private space at last.

After a restive night in my new surroundings, I woke to conditions that were hotter and even more humid than I had ever imagined possible. We were perspiring simply sitting around eating breakfast! I had been slowly adjusting to physical work in the heat, but the combination of the busy-ness of the last couple of days with the heat and Mark's farewell party the previous night, meant I was exhausted!

But, then, although reluctant to get going, we figured it was about as good as it was going to get for the day, so we started off to do some work outside. After spending half an hour messing about half-heartedly at some job or other, it started raining. Our prayers were answered, thank the Lord! Soon it was not just rain but a solid downpour of water, more intense than anything I had ever seen in my life, so much so you felt you could drown simply standing in it. We breathed a sigh of relief, for here was our excuse to laze around inside and get over our weariness. With the rain crashing down on the tin roof, the most effort we could afford was to go around checking and fixing a few leaks here and there. We hurriedly hid away Chris' record player (and his Leonard Cohen LP) and went about making sure nothing of importance would get wet.

On a more productive note, this was an opportunity to do some long neglected administrative work. I had been expecting to look over the finances of the Society and sort out the accounts and wondered at how complex a task it would be. But after Stewart gave me a box of papers containing a chequebook, a whole lot of bills and a mess of bank statements, I realised we hadn't even got to that stage. There really were no accounts per se. This was it!

It was not difficult to fix the basics. Over the next couple of hours, I had sorted out the papers, separated bills that needed paying from those that were already paid and written out forty cheques for several thousands of dollars. I eventually set up a simple system so we would at least know what we owned and what we owed. We hadn't got the proper books to keep formal accounts, so I made a note to get them (plus something for the store stock records and a new battery for the Dolmar) next time we were in Rabaul.

Meanwhile, the torrential rain kept on coming. It lasted for days on end after Mark left, which was a big relief. It had been a surprisingly long time since we had had a decent shower and we really needed the water. Now, the wets' resumption meant our newly plumbed-in tanks would fill and we would not have to traipse over to Father Peter's or down to the river to wash or go to the spring and back every few days.

A few weeks later, Stewart and I again set sail for Sipai, Buka and Rabaul, but instead of leaving at dawn, for a change we set off around six in the evening. We had spent the last few hours of the fading light supervising the loading of cocoa and copra, and this time we found room for the faulty generator. We had earlier separated the rotor and stator and, dangling each part one at a time off the front of the JCB, had run them down to the beach. We then gently placed one piece (essentially a huge lump of metal) into a dugout and, with heart in mouth, had it paddled carefully away to the *Kiriaka* riding offshore.

I went out on the first trip to supervise. What with the two oarsmen, the stator itself, weighing a few hundred kilograms, and me, there was only a few centimetres of freeboard. However, the guys were extra careful and with deft paddling, we arrived safely alongside. A couple of crew on board leant over and in a profusion of cussing, blinding and hysterical laughter, manhandled the thing up on deck. We then did it all over again with the rotor. Fortunately, there was a quiet sea; if we had been swamped, we would have had to kiss the whole thing goodbye.

Once under way, Stewart and I sat and discussed managing the boat. Word had been put out for a captain for over a year, but no one had come forward to take on the responsibility. Stewart now elaborated and told me that by law, to run a boat the size of the *Kiriaka Aro*, it required an Engineer's Certificate and a Master's Ticket. And, to get these, one must sit for, and pass, two exams.

I should not have been surprised. Over my short time in Kuraio and having seen what running the boat entailed, I figured it was not something one could (or should) do at the drop of a hat. I'd felt a good deal of conflict between people's expectation of me versus the reality of my ability and, let's face it, concern for people's lives. We talked about all this for a while and, then later, lying in my bunk with a fair sea and running along nicely at about seven knots, I mulled over the issues yet again. The whole affair frustrated me really, but although I had been worried since my arrival, I was becoming a little more comfortable with the situation.

Eventually I made up my mind. I decided to give it a go and told Stewart I would take the exams, captain the boat and stay on at Kuraio.

Then, just as some form of practical reality check, next morning, having picked up Sipai's cocoa, we arrived in Buka to discover the Jabsco bilge pump had stopped working. I took it to pieces and fitted a new impeller. But with my glasses steaming up in the heat of the engine room, I couldn't be sure I had done a proper job. By now it was too late to try it out, and besides we were hungry. We went up the priest's house for supper, then back to meet a friend of Stewart's, and we sat talking till late and then went back to sleep on the boat.

The next day we tried the Jabsco, but it still was not working so we dismantled it yet again. Neither Stewart nor I could find the fault, so we eventually gave up and ended up pumping out the middle bilge by hand for a couple of sweaty hours.

Trusting to luck we would have a calm sea, we left for Rabaul carrying our precious cargo of cocoa beans and the faulty generator. The day passed and, as a beautiful clear night fell and a nearly full moon appeared, Stewart said, "Come on Nick, let's prepare for your exam. I'll show you the basics of how you can get your bearings by doing a running fix".

"Well okay," I said doubtfully, "I'll give it a go."

Stewart went and got the compass from the bridge, and as we stood on deck, he explained how to use it[31]. Steadying myself with my back up against the bridge and holding the compass so I could see the needle, I peered into the distance, trying to take a bearing. With a reasonable swell running and in the dark, it proved elusive.

"I have to admit Stewart, I find it a bit tricky," I said. "I get the general idea, but learning how to do the calculations using dividers, parallel rule and chart is all a bit much to expect in one session and especially if we were in rough weather."

"I know, I know, but this is really important if you are travelling at night. At least you now know the general idea and with some more practice, that'll be enough." Stewart's can-do nature was again coming to the fore. I thought he was kidding to imagine one lesson would be enough for me to bluff my way through the exam. But by way of some sort of encouragement, arriving into Rabaul around nine in the morning, I found I had slept reasonably well and was now feeling more positive. It helped that the swell had subsided and we had enjoyed a beautifully calm sea. The calm did not last!

As soon as we docked, Stewart came down with a bout of malaria. Witnessing this for the first time was a bit unnerving, but with his teeth chattering like castanets, Stewart said, "I'll be okay in a couple of days. J… J… Just give me some of those Chloroquine."

"How come you've got malaria; I thought the Chloroquine fixed all that?"

"I stopped taking them a few weeks ago. D…D…Don't like pills!"

I hadn't thought much about malaria since I had arrived, but having sussed Stewart out as the gung-ho type that he was, I was not surprised.

"That's great! What the hell am I supposed to do now? Do you need to go to hospital?"

"N… No. Y…You take over, I'll just rest up."

He was shaking badly and I wasn't sure what to do with him, call an ambulance or just let him suffer and get on with dealing with the cargo. It was first thing in the morning, I hadn't had a decent meal for thirty-six hours, I was dirty, I had a headache and now this. I left him to shiver away and went to see about off-loading the cargo.

The trick was to make sure that a few sacks of cocoa and copra didn't suddenly disappear somewhere or other, so I watched with eagle eyes until they had all been discharged safely into the hands of the agents. And then watched again as, on cue, a couple of guys from the electrical engineers arrived with a fork-lift, hoiked our generator on to the back of a truck and drove it off to their workshop.

Eventually, with the paperwork completed, I left the boat in the capable hands of Jacob (and the incapable ones of Stewart) and went and picked up the Holden. I needed a break from all this palaver, so drove over to see a friend from England whose posting was at a school on Vuvu Mission. Blow it, he wasn't there. It was a wasted trip, and just to make my day a front tyre blew out going down the long slow hill back into town. The jack was a real pain; the nuts had probably never been off since the day they had made the car and it took me an eternity to change the wheel. As a result, half the day was gone before I could get back to the boat.

"How are you going, Stewart?" I called out. He was still shivering and shaking like hell and appeared no better than before.

"I'm f… f… fine," he lied.

"Yes, right. Even Blind Freddy could see you are not. I reckon you should go up to the hospital."

"No. No. I'm fine. There is nothing they could do. All I need is a good rest."

"Okay," I said reluctantly, "but I'm not spending another night on the boat – I've had enough of living rough for a while and I need some food, a shower and a decent bed. I'll go back up to the Mission to stay the night. Sure you'll be okay?"

I greedily ate a large meal at the Mission and chatted with the Father about Kuraio and now Stewart's fever, but then, despite my on-going concerns, I again slept well. And then, thank God, getting back to the boat in the morning, Stewart was up and about and looking much better. He was well enough for us to spend the morning shopping around town together for a few things I had missed earlier.

Later, we met up with some other friends of Stewart's, Tim, a salvage diver[32], Alan Feahy and his wife Margaret, and Alan

Jamieson (whose girl I had dreamt had taken a fancy to me, but who was not with him today). Following them in the old Holden, we drove a few miles out of town along the North Coast Road to have lunch at the Kulau Lodge. This lovely place with superb views across Talili Bay also, it turned out, provided excellent food. After a few beers we sat down to eat. We were half way through the meal when Tim dropped a brown, stick-like thing on my plate.

"What the hell's that?" I exclaimed.

"Oh, it's just a finger. A woman's actually," he said.

"Nice" says I, "Did you have a fight with your girlfriend or something?"

"No, no. It is probably from someone in the Dani tribe, across the border in West Papua. The story goes that when someone with a lot of influence and power dies, the tribe will cut off part of a finger from every woman who was close to the deceased. It's a sort of offering of a sacrifice to keep the spiritual strength of that person at bay."

With an unmistakable nail on the tip, it was certainly a finger, and being pretty shrivelled up, it had clearly been removed from its owner quite a while earlier. The others had seen all this before; it was Tim's party trick, supposed to make one feel queasy, something he did just for the fun of it, particularly after a few drinks.

I had to laugh. "Thanks Tim, remind me to return the compliment one day," I said. "I'll whip over to the morgue and see if I can get a withered leg or some other part of the anatomy to add to your collection of body parts!" It all seemed funnier after too many beers.

Later that afternoon, Stewart, again feeling the effects of his malaria, or perhaps the reaction to the grog on his extra-large dose of Chloroquine, went back to rest on the boat. I carried on and went over to the Yacht Club, swam in the pool, ate dinner and watched a movie. Just another hard day in the tropics!

Next day, Stewart was well enough for us to go and see about me getting my Tickets, so off we went and fronted up to the Harbour Master's office.

"Hello gentlemen. What can I do for you?" growled the unfriendly old Tolai Harbour Master.

"Good morning sir. I help run the *Kiriaka Aro* on behalf of the West Coast Development Society on Bougainville. Jacob, our First Mate, is leaving in December and I'd like to sit the exams for my Tickets to run the boat." I suddenly felt rather foolish.

The Harbour Master looked at us two young and shaggy whites and immediately switched on his official manner. Somewhat suspiciously, he said, "Well, OK. Can I see your apprenticeship papers?"

I looked quizzically at Stewart.

The Harbour Master continued, in a tired, patronising tone, "To sit the exam for your Tickets you've got to have studied for and passed examinations in a relevant apprenticeship. You have done your apprenticeship, I suppose?"

"Oh yes," I lied, playing for time to consider the request. "But I haven't got my papers with me right now. They're back in the UK."

"Well, okay, sonny. I will have to see them, so you send for your papers, come back when you've got 'em and we can talk again."

And with that, the Harbour Master dismissed us. Walking away, tails between our legs, we realised that neither of us had thought to find out what preparation was necessary to take one's

Tickets. Even though I had studied automobile engineering, I had never been close to doing any apprenticeship, let alone studying anything connected with sailing a cargo boat, or sailing anything else for that matter.

As for captaining the *Kiriaka Aro*, this was the end of the story really. I could not legally (or even practically, as I discovered trying to do a running fix with the compass) run the boat. Also, now the Harbour Master knew I did not have a Ticket I would be in big trouble if I ever tried sailing into or out of Rabaul in charge of the *Kiriaka*.

After realising the implications of the task first hand, and the dangers to others and to me of making a mistake, I was now legitimately excused from doing something I found I really did not want to risk doing anyway. Even though I knew I had let the side down, I felt somewhat exonerated by this turn of events. But nevertheless, we still had not resolved the problem of who was going to run the boat and we now needed some serious guidance.

We rang Dick in POM, explained what had happened and asked if VSO could find another volunteer with either the right qualifications or who was technically able to get them. Dick already knew London did not have anyone scheduled to come out in the next batch of volunteers due in January. And even though he knew it already, I again explained to Dick what this meant when Stewart and Jacob left at Christmas. It would be difficult enough for Chris and me to manage the place, but worse than this, it would be an impossible situation because the WCDS could not operate without the boat. For me, the prospect of being stuck on a tropical island with no way off, and a bunch of increasingly frustrated locals did not really appeal.

Dick promised to come over to talk as soon as he could, but not to hold my breath as he was flat-out with other volunteers.

He would try to get over just after Christmas. In the meantime, Stewart agreed to postpone his departure until at least Dick had come over and discussed the situation with Father Peter and the big-men.

Whatever was going to happen eventually, Stewart and I needed to get back to the Kuraio, so we sailed out of Rabaul again, this time, just after midnight. The seas were not too bad and even though I was grubby from working and sweating throughout the day this was now the norm and I was almost used to it. However, I vowed that if we could find someone to run the boat and I stayed on, the first thing I would do, would be to install a shower, so at least we could have a wash now and then.

After stopping off briefly to unload cargo at Tsiroge, Buka and Sipai we eventually arrived back at Kuraio on a dark and foreboding sea, the question of running the boat unresolved.

A little while later, after getting back to collecting and drying the cocoa, a treat awaited us in yet another sing-sing. Although happy enough in celebrating the occasion of a departing foreigner, Blaize had organised this one, as he did regularly, to celebrate the last day of school term. A group of dancers came over from a neighbouring school at Amun village, a little way to the north of Kuraio, and joined the Standard Six girls from our own school.

There was plenty of *kaikai* (food), and of course lots of dancing and singing portraying traditional folklore. The girls looked great in their grass skirts and not much else except wristlets, anklets of rattles and extraordinarily complicated headdresses. It was wonderful to watch and I felt privileged in witnessing such an event, one in complete contrast to the rather sinister dancing of the men a couple of weeks earlier.

As usual however, the dancing went on forever and showed no sign of breaking up. I watched for as long as I could, but the girls were still dancing even after I had gone to bed around eleven.

I got up again for a quick squiz at three and saw that the men had taken over. They had formed a huge circle and were stamping around, playing their drums, pipes and *kovokovo* and chanting away like crazy; it seemed even more dramatic and frenzied than the sing-sing for Mark.

Again, I wondered if, should I get too close, I might end up in the cooking pot; it seemed possible. The group was in a bit of a trance and looked like they had reverted to their primitive (and perhaps cannibalistic?) ways. Apart from my imagination running away with itself, the energy of the whole thing amazed me. They went on until six in the morning!

Shortly afterwards, with Christmas approaching, we were all looking forward to celebrations of our own, a bit of R&R and a change from Station chores. So, on the 23rd December the three of us packed our things and took the *Kiriaka Aro* up to Sipai. Apparently, the nurses, Sary and Donna were being joined by Christine Sullivan, a pharmacy student from the University of Sydney. As a member of the Catholic Youth Services organization she had been raising money for the Mission and had accepted an invitation to come and see the place. There were also some American nuns from Kieta on the east coast due to come over for a short visit later. It promised to be quite a party!

On Christmas Eve, the six of us rowed out to a little coral island offshore for a picnic lunch. With the water too inviting to resist we spent a few mad hours snorkelling, piggyback fighting and generally splashing around until exhausted. Even knowing we would get sunburned, it was a wonderfull respite from the constant heat and worth every minute of it.

That evening, after a lovely meal cooked by the *haus meri* (under Donna's guidance), and after attending a thankfully short midnight Mass, we all went over to a local concert, a little way out from the Mission.

We joined the villagers sitting around in an old Pandanus walled hut. Kero lamps spread their warm glow and darkening shadows up among the rafters and with what looked like straw on the floor, the setting was quite akin to that of a Country and Western barn dance. Things were already in full swing before we arrived, with the band of Bougainvillean's, one on guitar, one with a *kundu* (drum) and another on a sort of banjo, playing away for all its worth. Their part-Western, part-native instruments and grass skirts over Western short pants, bandannas and skivvies, were evidence to the changing nature of their culture. Counterbalancing all this however, the dirge-like, and to me entirely incomprehensible, continuum of singing was pure Kereaka. Earlier in the evening, despite the strong local flavour, I had easily recognised the Catholic Mass's relevance to the occasion, but this concert was something else! Singing at Christmas, for me, was all carols and freezing temperatures. But this style of this music, the heat and the bush setting, made for a very different sort of atmosphere. It was such a wonderfully inappropriate way to celebrate Christmas and such good fun, we didn't get to bed till well after two.

Next day, by way of contrast, Christmas progressed in the more traditional Western way, with too much food and drink! But before that and after yet another service, Santa Claus, resplendent in a red cape (looking suspiciously like an upside-down cassock) and sporting a big white beard (Chris had made up out of old pillow stuffing) suddenly appeared outside the front of the church! With appropriate joviality, great gusto and lots of perspiration, Santa, (alias Father Bourgea) dispensed simple gifts to the many faithful villagers milling around. Much to the everyone's delight there were sweets for the kids as well as some silly items such as a tin of boot polish (who ever polished their boots in this sort of place?), a bottle of grille lotion (far more useful) and a few other crazy things.

Later and after all that and with the usual excessive intake of food and drink at lunch, some snoozed and some went swimming. Having already burned myself to the colour of a lobster the day before, I kept out of the sun and again read a book.

Come Boxing Day, a light aircraft buzzed the Station. The pilot dipped its wings to check it was safe to land on the rarely used strip and flew so low we saw him wave as he zoomed past. Then, after a short while, and in an excited gabble of laughter, three more girls appeared at the house. Sisters Theresa, Jean and Louise Anne, all nuns in training, had literally turned up out of the blue. After yet another meal it was clear we needed some exercise to work off the excess. Despite the heat someone suggested we had enough bodies for a couple of teams to play basketball! Of course, being so energetic after a meal was a bit of trial and after plenty of laughter, but too much perspiration and some very suspect score keeping, we gave it away and went down to cool off in the water again.

After this most enjoyable Christmas, we three left Father Bourgea with his girls and set sail for Rabaul the following day, conveniently arriving just in time to celebrate the start of the New Year. Amongst the expatriates at least, Rabaul was one big party, but of a different kind. Unfortunately, with friends Alan

J, Tim and Alan F and Margaret all offshore for the break, our options for company and entertainment were a little limited. Not wanting to gate-crash any of the various private events (even though it was acceptable practice within the expat community), the only place to go on New Year's Eve, was the Returned Services League (RSL). The venue of this proud organisation (set up to support men and women who had served or were still serving in the Australian Defence Force) was huge and the number of people attending the celebrations certainly did the place justice. But being naturally a bit sombre, we found it was a bit of a bore compared with our preferred style of event.

In retrospect, I was not sure if my impression of the evening was a clouded by the amount of gin I drank, or perhaps I drank so much gin because the event was so boring. Whatever the reason, I couldn't recall a great deal of what happened after singing *Auld Lang Syne* except staggering back to the boat.

Fortunately, by way of contrast, New Year's Day celebrations were far more fun. Thanks mainly to the Chinese community, they were indeed boisterous and noisy. Even though their own official New Year (the Year of the Ox) did not start until February, the Chinese happily adopted the time of the Westerners' New Year as a good excuse to party, and, among other goings-on, they treated the town to the colourful display of a Chinese Dragon dance[33]. Out on the street we watched a small team of young men manipulate the fearsome looking paper, cloth and wood dragon. One guy held the ornate and appropriately oriental-looking head and operated the winking eyelids; others danced around and underneath the tail. Together with much enthusiastic beating of drums and crashing of cymbals, they spent an enormous amount of energy emulating the sinuous and undulating moves of this river spirit.

We watched the dragon as it pranced enthusiastically in and out of the crowds of locals, Australian expats and Chinese alike and made its way up to the doorway of a Chinese trade store. It stopped there for a few minutes, twisting and prancing in and around the many metres of red streamers hanging from the eaves. Suddenly, all hell broke loose. What I had thought to be decorative streamers, suddenly transformed into enormous firecrackers, exploding and flashing in a deafening cacophony. Puffs of grey smoke and red and yellow fire scattered shredded red paper cases confetti-like on the road around the shop. The popping and crackling went on forever, encouraging the dragon to even wilder gyrations. These were serious firecrackers; far more dramatic than any of the Guy Fawkes Night bangers I had been brought up on.

The sheer level of noise and the length of the dragon (the longer the better) could not have failed to frighten away all the stray devils hanging around and was sure to make for an auspicious start to the new year and good fortune for the store owners.

Next day, surprisingly none the worse for wear from all the partying, Chris, Stewart and I went scuba diving. Stewart had already undergone some form of training and had dived a few times before. With tongue in cheek, Chris said he had also had some training, as he had already dived. Once! All I knew was the bends and a painful death awaited anyone who ascended too quickly from a dive to any great depth! I hadn't undergone any training, but I certainly wanted to see what it was all about, so figured I would play it by ear and just make sure I came up slowly.

We drove out along the Nonga Road to the old wartime submarine base, a little way past the hospital, until the road ran out at Tavui. Here, thanks to Mother Nature, the coastline is somewhat unusual. For twenty metres or so out from dry land the water is merely waist-high, but then the reef wall suddenly gives way plummeting vertically over fifty metres or so down to the floor of the ocean. The Japanese had used the deeper water of this geological peculiarity in the last war to bring their submarines close in to land to load torpedoes and provisions, knowing they could submerge quickly if there was an air raid.

We hauled our gear out of the back of the Holden, strapped on the tanks, goggles and flippers and then, looking like aliens from some B-grade sci-fi movie, penguin-waddled through the water to the edge of the reef. Stuffing the mouthpiece of a regulator in my mouth and with brief instructions and encouragement from Stewart, I fell face first into the water and tentatively pushed myself out over the edge.

I had been worried about sinking but, frustratingly, the reverse was true. With not enough weights to go around and with nothing to compensate for my natural buoyancy, I couldn't get down more than a metre or so before bobbing back up like a cork. So, with concerns over sinking put to one side, I focused on what I could see. The water was clear as a bell initially and I could see many metres down before visibility diminished gradually to a dark green and eventually a solid black abyss. But, in front of me, schools of various brightly coloured fish, some with horizontal blue and yellow stripes, others orange and blue, some just bright orange were rushing around against a canvas of coral growths. On the reef wall there were blood-red anemones with voluptuous tentacles weaving seductively in the flow, some sort of shellfish attached to the rock and many other little creatures too numerous to identify.

Seen in their natural habitat, these creatures were really quite beautiful and a far cry from the poor dead things one finds in the market. And, although they darted rapidly away if I got too close, they otherwise swam calmly around in front of my eyes, as if they saw monsters like me every day of their little fishy lives. It was a whole new world, and all so different from anything one would see on land, from that moment on I resolved to dive properly, with weights, as soon as I could. I was hooked!

The following day, while Stew and Chris went off visiting their friends, I finally met up with Martin, seemingly a lifetime since we had flown out from Britain together. He and I spent time shopping and wandering around town and, swapping stories of our projects. As I was keen to compare his accommodation with my lot at Kuraio, we drove the thirty kilometres or so of jarring dirt road out to his place on the way to Kerevat, further inland on the Gazelle Peninsula.

What a contrast! His was as perfect a house as one could ever wish for: two bedrooms, a dining room, kitchen, bathroom, etc., basic, but all there – plus electricity and running water. He even had an overhead fan!

The best bit was the veranda out the back. We sat there with a few cold drinks and in an increasingly mellowed state, watched the sky through the trees and the last multi-coloured burst of rays in the clouds as the sun melted into the horizon. After too many beers and with the road being a little dangerous in the dark, I favoured the comfort of his place over the bunk in the *Kiriaka* and stayed for the night.

Picking up more shopping for the Society and mail from the Post Office back in Rabaul next morning, I found a message from Dick. He was coming down to Buka in a couple of days' and asked if we could pick him up. Then, on getting back down to the boat, I discovered Stewart had suffered yet another bout of malaria. I couldn't believe it. I remonstrated with him, asking if he had some sort of death wish, but no, he said, he simply did not like taking pills and so had stopped taking his Chloroquine. Again!

Having lost my patience with Stewart and not being sure how sick he really was, I drove him up to the hospital and dumped him there on the understanding he would fly on down to Buka when he had recovered. We would meet-up there, collect Dick and go on down to Kuraio together. Even though Jacob was still in charge of the boat, I worried that the Harbour Master would recognise me, and remembering my lack of qualifications stop me from sailing, particularly if there was no Stewart on board. So, with Chris having now returned from staying with his friends, he and I left Rabaul without signing out. The Christmas and New Year celebrations had been good fun, but we needed to get back to work.

Fortunately, with calm weather and a shiny blue sea, we enjoyed a perfect crossing and got down to Buka in less than twenty-four hours; a pleasant change from the usual thirty-eight-hour torment. But, just to spoil our fun, as soon as we arrived, it started bucketing down with rain. Chris and I got soaked walking up to the airstrip to meet Dick, whose flight from Rabaul, coincidentally and conveniently, had just arrived. Great timing. I could not help notice that he had chosen to fly to Buka and not sail down from Rabaul with us, but I let it go.

Back on to the boat, Chris and I, along with a surprisingly clean and neatly dressed Dick, sailed over to Tsiroge. Then, as luck would have it, as soon as we arrived, a message came over the sked to say Stewart was much better and he had flown down to Buka! So back over to Buka we sailed, picked him up and finally, Stewart, Dick, Chris and I, all together at last, sailed on down to Sipai.

With the weather now looking a bit threatening, after dropping us off at Sipai, Jacob took the *Kiriaka* back up the coast a short way to the more sheltered spot at Kivikee. Then, later that evening and quite unexpectedly, Thomas, our Mr Fix-it, turned up at the Mission. With the road still not yet good enough for the Isuzu, he had driven all the way up from Kuraio on the tractor and trailer and had brought with him a man who was gasping for breath and in great distress. As far as we could make out, the guy was complaining of a fish-bone stuck in his throat! To ease his discomfort Donna gave him a shot of morphine, which seemed to help, but he was still in a terrible state. With there being nothing more we could do for him at Sipai, the girls decided he should go up to hospital in Sohano, with its better facilities. The trouble was the *Kiriaka Aro* was at Kivikee, and there was no means to communicate with Jacob. So, with no other choice, soon after dusk, we put the poor fellow in Father Bourgea's truck and Stewart, Chris, Christine and I drove up to Kivikee. Dick stayed back with Father Bourgea to chew the fat.

As luck would have it, a few kilometres down the road the engine on the Isuzu died and we ground to a halt. Being familiar with our none-too-clean diesel fuel, I suspected a fuel blockage. Chris jumped out to run back to Sipai for the tractor, the only alternative transport, and to get some tools. But then, soon after he had disappeared into the night, blow me down, we got the truck going again. Leaving Chris to look after himself, Christine, Stewart and I carried on and drove our patient on up to Kivikee.

We got the unfortunate fellow aboard the *Kiriaka* and Christine, Stewart and Jacob took him up to Sohano.

On my way back to Sipai I met Chris, driving towards me on the tractor and waving a spanner wildly in the air. Quite a little mix-up, but with Chris on the tractor and me in the Isuzu, we drove on back to Sipai again, finally getting to bed early in the morning. With communications as limited as they were, we had to wait quite a while before we heard what had happened to the poor guy with the fish-bone.

Next day, with Thomas again driving the tractor and Dick, Chris and me hanging on for grim death on the trailer, we endured an incredible three-hour, bone-jarring journey back down to Kuraio; it is not something I would recommend! When we got off on arrival, I felt as if I had been gone over by a sadistic chiropractor and swore I could feel every joint, bone and muscle in my body!

Over the next few days, with Stewart now back on the *Kiriaka*, Dick organised a series of *kivungs* (meetings) to discuss the future of Kuraio and VSO support. He talked first with Father Peter, then met with the big-men and finally called a meeting of both parties. Dick had already heard our side of the story so did not invite any of us volunteers to attend. But afterwards, Dick told us Father Peter denied ever saying that he wanted nothing to do with the Society. We knew to the contrary. He had made it clear to us he did not want any part of it and had even gone so far as to say he wanted it off the Mission. Although knowing the Society had operated for many years, Dick also heard some of the big-men were complaining things were not changing quickly enough and did not feel it was helping the community adequately. They wanted more significant benefits, and they wanted them now.

I was really in no position to judge, but Chris and Stewart disagreed and felt the WCDS was very valuable to the Kereaka. Many of the locals they talked with seemed content with their lives and had expressed great appreciation for the help they received from all of us, Father Mentzer, Mark Roberts and us VSOs[34].

Mark told me earlier, and I had no reason to doubt him, any feelings of animosity were probably more related to the on-going belief in cargo-cult and towards the copper mine up at Panguna than the work of the WCDS.

The contradictions were unmistakable. Some people felt short-changed and expected greater rewards from the mine and to a lesser extent the Society, and others were more than satisfied with the way things were going. I reminded myself that I was not there to sort out these more sizeable problems[35]. Nor could I guess about their significance to Bougainville generally or to our specific project in the longer term. I had worries of my own. I knew I could still be of value in running the business and helping maintain the equipment, but being unable to help with the boat was a frustration. If we could not get a captain, if the priest was only lukewarm about the Society and if the cargo-cult was making a comeback and problems grew over the mine, things looked a little precarious, to say the least. I was more concerned about 'What next for Nick Brown?'

Eventually, after talking all this over with Dick, he and I agreed I could leave Kuraio. I was letting the side down, but I was relieved that I would not have to live at Kuraio with this uncertainty for another year or so.

Having fixed the date for my departure, Dick said that once he was back in Moresby, he would look around for another project for me, preferably one better suited to my skills and interests. What the future of the Society was, or what was to become of the *Kiriaka Aro* and Stewart and Chris, I did not ask and was not told. My involvement was ending, and soon.

I was pleased to be off the hook, so to speak, but now I had to wait until I got back to POM to find out what the future held for me. The Harbour Master had saved me from my worrying affair with the boat, and I knew the British Council would pay for my flight back to the UK if things did not work out. But I certainly did not want to leave PNG altogether; I had only just got here and felt sure I could be of use somewhere, hopefully with more enjoyable adventures ahead.

So, in mid-January 1973, after I had packed my bags, a crew member paddled Stewart, Chris and I out through the surf to the *Kiriaka*, we hopped on board and sailed up to Buka. Whilst there, we asked about the fish-bone man and heard the sad news that he had passed away shortly after we had brought him in. It was nothing to do with a fish-bone at all; the poor guy was suffering from throat cancer.

Then, still loathing farewells, I said goodbye, too hastily, to Chris and Stewart. It had been a difficult time and we were all disappointed I could not help. It was just not meant to be.

On the Friday morning I spent a frustrating time going down to the airstrip for a seven-thirty flight that did not happen, then going back up to Hahela for a bite to eat and going back to the airstrip again until I finally got on a plane to Rabaul later in the morning. By this time, I had missed the connection to POM, and with no onward flights until the Sunday I checked into the Community Hostel and called up my friend Martin again.

Hearing why I was in Rabaul this time surprised him and he soon came over.

After explaining what had happened and why I was now in transit back to POM, we sat and chatted about my alternatives. However, instead of sitting in the hostel and worrying all day and realising this would probably be my last visit to the town, we decided on a bit of exploration. Martin knew of some fascinating relics left over from the Second World War. The Japanese had excavated an enormous number of tunnels under Rabaul, using some to hide the boats they brought in to ferry supplies in preparation for their larger invasion in 1942. So, we went out to check out what we could see.

Along the road curving around Karavia Bay we found a few tunnels easily enough and peering in, we saw the first of a few old Daihatsu barges, lined up one after the other and slowly rusting away in the salty humidity. The dank interior and the boats themselves conveyed images down through the years of the dreadfulness of that time, conjuring up an eerie sense of Japanese army ghosts still drifting around.

Continuing with the WWII theme, we went and checked out the buckled and weathered remains of a crashed Japanese aircraft. The bodies were long gone, but considering how the plane had got here and of the trauma of those who died in the process, made for a sobering sight. Thinking more on bodies, we realised we had missed something. Rather macabrely, we backtracked to the small, spooky Chinese Cemetery. Here were the remains of nearly 700 people from China and India. The Japanese had brought these poor souls over from Singapore to work as their slaves in their determination to dominate the region, but of course we did not see any bodies there either. Simply neat rows of earthen mounds, at the base of which was a sentinel memorial column inscribed in oriental characters.

After expending all that physical and emotional energy, we went back to Martin's place to relax before going over to the Community Hostel for supper. Later, after meeting up with yet more friends, the six of us ended up going out to a bar for a drink.

We were just getting into one of those pointless inebriated discussions with a Papuan pilot, (one of the very few), when someone further down the bar started throwing punches. Just as quickly, riot police in their dark blue steel helmets appeared out of nowhere, laid into one guy with their truncheons, dragged him outside, chucked him in the back of their paddy wagon and drove off. All in a day's work, so to speak! We carried on drinking for a little while longer, but funnily enough, the mood was spoiled. And, feeling a little more sober than before, we bought a couple of bottles of Cinzano and went back to the hostel for a nightcap.

PART TWO

CHAPTER 9

INCREDIBLE FORTUNE

I'm looking through the window at the undercarriage of a Fokker F27. The engines rev and the plane shakes and trembles as the pilot holds it on the brakes. Finally releasing them, we are off yet again. The G forces push me back into my seat as I watch the undercarriage coming up and being stowed. We climb away from the shimmering heat of Rabaul and then, levelling off, fly over the harbour and through low thin cloud, briefly filtering out myriad trees scattered around the volcanos. Sadly, this is the last time I will see Rabaul and New Britain.

Now we are above gardens and jungle, all so green and so clear from a few hundred feet up. To my right, I can see the coast and the submarine base where I dived earlier, and the angular low hills, with sharp shadows leading down into the water. It is not a sunny day, but I can see a pool of water (a small lake?)

reflecting the blue and white skyscape. It's shaped like fingers giving the 'V' sign. *Ha! 'V' sign to you too Rabaul, I'm outa here, heading back to the big city!*

The last couple of days had been fun and a diversion from the worries of the past and, I suppose, a natural consequence of my relief at newfound freedom. But now I was concerned about my future and knew I would have to buck up and get on with things when I arrived back in POM.

Sure enough, on landing at Jacksons I was immediately faced with a couple of hiccups, just to keep me on my toes. Much of my gear had not arrived with me on my flight, I could not get in contact with Dick, and when I eventually did get out of Arrivals, I saw the backside of the last taxi disappearing down the road.

I tried calling Dick again, but still no luck; I guessed his phone was out of order. I gave up on my gear, assuming it would turn up eventually, and I was about to get a lift with some friendly expat when Dick turned up after all, full of apologies. It wasn't that his phone was out of order; there was a genuine reason for his delay. He had just come back from the funeral of a volunteer killed in a car accident. She had been based up in Mount Hagen and was apparently walking along the side of the Highlands Highway when a drunken driver hit her. Dick had been consoling her parents, who had flown out from Britain and were understandably very distressed.

I recalled how people were now so blasé about road deaths in Britain. Unless it involved someone they knew or there was something spectacular about the crash, it only rated a brief mention in the press. Logically, this should not have been any different. I didn't know the girl, but somehow, the fact that it had happened in a country so far from home and to a person of my age who had come out to help and then be killed by a local made a big difference to my emotional response. I supposed it could easily have been me: lost at sea or perhaps taken by a croc! The story sobered me up and put my own trivial dilemma back into perspective.

But now, driving into town with Dick, I realised I was back to the sort of civilisation I had craved. Here were offices, buses, cars, streetlights and lots of people, locals and expats alike. Although it was still definitely of third world standard and not very pretty, it was a relief to see a decent-sized town again. Exotic flora masked the less salubrious back alleys and provided a pleasant contrast to the dull, worn and drowsy shop fronts, baking in the heat. Somewhat perversely, much of this embellishment was from splashes of the brilliant purple and orange bracts of Bougainvillea. There were shops and traffic, people and pedestrians, all just doing ordinary things. Even though it had only been a few months, it was great to be back in the real world; a far cry from butchering cows and sailing on the *Kiriaka*.

On arriving back at his place, Dick explained that he was currently entertaining a couple of newly arrived volunteers. So, after brief introductions and a quick bite to eat, he took us all up to Burns Peak, a craggy hill overlooking the town. Dick declared to all of us that this was a favourite place for watching the comings and goings of ships bringing in the infamous 'cargo'. Then, to the quizzical stares of the newbies, he and I, somewhat conspiratorially, changed the subject and gave a quick and light-hearted explanation of the basics of cargo cult.

We enjoyed the magnificent views and even more, the relief from the heat brought by the fresh ocean breeze. We could see a few villages up on the coast to the west and then more, south, beyond the harbour, past what Dick explained was Paga Hill. After that there were low-lying headlands, the open sea and an enormous expanse of sparkling ocean. To our left, we could see for miles eastward down the coast until heat haze eventually shimmied away the detail. It was a remarkable panorama of contrasts between the messy presence of man and the pristine qualities of nature.

Quite by coincidence we bumped into someone Dick knew and who he thought might help with a job. He introduced me to Pat, who told me briefly about a wholesale trade store up in the Southern Highlands in need of a manager. Pat said it was a kind of school, and although they sold a variety of goods their main purpose was to train locals in how to run their own stores as a business. I was not too sure about going back up into the bush so soon after Kuraio, and with memories of the *stor bilong* Kereaka I thought I would wait awhile before pursuing the idea. I knew I needed to keep my options open, so I said It sounded really interesting and hoped like hell he didn't see through my insincerity.

Having sent the other two volunteers off to their respective postings, Dick allocated me the spare bedroom and I settled in for a bit of a wait. We both knew getting another placement could take months, but then, God willing, it might happen overnight. Then again, although Dick did not elaborate, VSO might want me out of there altogether!

One thing became clear – I was lucky to have Dick giving me his time. I was in his hands and not knowing anyone around town, finding work on my own would be tricky. But there was plenty of time to think. On the one hand, I was pleased to be back in a place with the essential services, but on the other, I was sad I had missed out on the real adventure that Bougainville offered. I had just been getting into the swing of things there and felt this was what volunteering was all about. I wondered if I had hurried away too quickly and if the future held anything more or less exciting than had I stayed on.

Rather than letting me sit around twiddling my fingers and waiting for answers to my concerns, Dick soon had me running around doing odd jobs. I took his car down to the garage to book it in for a service later in the week and whilst there I bumped into Margaret, the woman who had taken us all down to Ela Beach on our first day in PNG. After she had checked in her car, I ran her home on the way over to my next task and naturally, I found it necessary to explain why I was back in Moresby. She didn't seem surprised, saying it was not unusual for a mismatch to occur in postings now and again, but she assured me things usually worked out well in the end.

I carried on over to the Ansett Airlines offices to pick up tickets for other volunteers and then drove back out to Jacksons to find out about my gear. Apparently, the morning plane from Rabaul still hadn't left because of 'technical problems'. I would have to check back yet again later.

That afternoon a Mr Pugh from an organisation by the name of Pasuwe telephoned Dick. He was asking for me to come over for a chat about the store manager job Pat mentioned on Burn's Peak.

I went down to meet Mr Pugh in his dingy office in the CBD, and listened to the details. Some of it sounded quite good and I felt more than capable of doing the job. There was free accommodation and an attractive salary, but there were also some snags. Mr Pugh made it clear that Pasuwe was an evangelical

Christian organisation, which meant there would be no smoking or drinking! This was quite different from the relatively laid-back Catholics and an immediate turn-off for someone like myself who considered himself a Christian sceptic bordering on atheist.

His words, combined with the depressing ambience of the crummy little brown-walled office swayed my previously open mind. Giving up smoking was not such a bad idea, I supposed, but stopping drinking? That would be next to impossible! More importantly, however, the job was in Tari, in the Southern Highlands. And, now, after my experience in Kuraio and on my return to the city, I knew that living in a small town up in the bush somewhere, maybe without electricity again, was not really for me. I was adventurous but only in a spoiled, cosseted sort of way and was not really into roughing it for any extended length of time. Both Mr Pugh and I tacitly understood and so, even with no other jobs on the horizon, I bade a polite farewell and let the offer lapse.

I spent more time running around in Dick's car over the next few days; down to Steamships[36] for some stores, back to the airport again and finally got my hands on the rest of my gear. Somewhat perversely, even though there were some crazy and unpredictable drivers around, it was a welcome contrast to driving a truck in the isolation of Bougainville.

After a few more pick-ups and deliveries there was a bit of variety. Margaret asked Dick if I would do her a favour in helping to entertain her kids who were up from Australia on school holidays. They were bored, and as she was busy with work, could I mind them for a while? Of course, yes, no problems. Dick excused me from his somewhat confected duties and I went around to her place, collected her children, Judy (eight) and Ralph (six), and took them to the Crocodile Farm, a little way out of town. Even though I'd had nothing much to do with kids of this age and was not particularly fond of them, I found changing hats from being Dick's gofer to child-minder was quite enjoyable. Apart from the novelty of it, I was pleased with the respect they showed me. I guessed mother must have said 'Behave!'

On arriving at the farm, we watched a swarm of the dark grey ugly critters being fed. It was great to see the genuine excitement on the kids' faces as the crocs put on a dramatic display. With their huge toothy mouths gaping and then suddenly snapping shut, they fought each other fiercely when chunks of raw meat were thrown in to the cage. Then, after wildly splashing around in their shallow concrete pond, they returned to an almost death-like stasis, lying entangled over each other just as if their preternatural mate simply did not exist! The expression on the kid's faces amused me when I bragged a little about how we had had crocs swimming across the bay when I had been in Kuraio! Exciting for young and old! Thankfully, with the crocs well fed, they showed little interest in us white meat, so I brought both the kids and myself back home safely and all in one piece!

I had only been back in POM a week when Dick managed to arrange another interview, this time for a job in a government department. He introduced me to the Assistant Director of the Department of Business Development and the Principal Project Officer, Small Industries. These two bureaucrats talked about a role they had planned for someone to encourage the country's handicrafts and artefacts sector. Even though I was very much a private sector person, at least this part of the government interfaced directly with businesses, so it sounded interesting.

Also, the job involved marketing, which was the very discipline I had chosen to be the focus of my business career.

As we sat and talked, I realised I knew nothing about handicrafts or artefacts except both were totally different from engines and boats, but at least they sounded much more interesting than gaskets. What the heck – it was a job; it was a new position; there would be an office, the security of government support and a bit of a budget, and it was at the very cutting edge of development work. Above all, to some degree, it was up to my imagination as to how it would run. The job was more than just interesting, it sounded tremendous!

Quite apologetically, Eric Hovey, the guy in charge of small industry development, explained that I would only be employed on local (i.e. as a Papua New Guinean) Public Service terms and conditions. I would have to live in a hostel and probably catch a PMV (passenger motor vehicle[37]) to work each day. Did I think I could handle that, and would I be interested?

Putting any prejudices about Public Servants, hostels and PMVs to one side I jumped at the opportunity and said: "You betcha!" Despite the pay being less than the offer from Pasuwe, the job came with practically free accommodation and meals at the government hostel, where, rather worryingly (and recalling what Father Fey intimated about Kuraio) they assured me, 'Conditions are not so bad'. Just as importantly, there were no restrictions on drinking or smoking. It all sounded quite brilliant!

The opportunity excited me, but I did not know if they liked the look of me enough to give me the job. So, waiting on the outcome, I continued running around town as Dick's assistant.

I just started driving away from the Post Office on one of these errands, when I felt the steering on Dick's Ford Escort suddenly go funny. The car simply stopped going forward, the engine stalled and I skidded to a juddering halt, half on and half off the road. Worried that I had hit something, I jumped out half expecting to see a body under the car but instead, to my surprise, saw that the front wheels of the car were 'boss-eyed', one pointing to the left and the other to the right. I looked a little closer and saw a piece of metal hanging down near the inside of one front wheel. It was the drop arm, a rather vital component connecting the steering wheel to the front wheels. Contrary to its name, it is not supposed to drop off at any time, and certainly not while one is in motion! If this had happened at fifty kilometres an hour, I would have had a very nasty crash. The car might even have overturned and I could easily have killed someone.

I quickly recalled how the accepted behaviour after such an accident would be to get away as rapidly as possible. If the vehicle was still drivable, then drive, otherwise run like hell! The alternative was the strong possibility of ending up dead from a severe beating as payback by any wantoks or local passers-by. Indeed, there had been an event of this nature quite recently. Two Bougainvillean doctors working up in the Highlands accidentally struck and killed a child with their car[38] and had then been set upon by an angry mob and beaten to death. On hearing this I wondered at the fate of the driver who had killed the VSO girl up in the Highlands!

I caught a cab back to Dick's place and told him about the car. Naturally upset, he immediately rang the garage and gave them a severe telling-off. The garage collected the car and brought it back to Dick later in the day with profound apologies from the manager. Someone had obviously forgotten to tighten a vital nut.

Not to be deterred, I was back in the driver's seat and off on my errands once again as soon as I could.

As well as running around for Dick, there was time enough on my hands to check out my new environment. Driving down into town of an evening, through the reassuring noise and hustle of urban life, I saw scatterings of frangipani, their ivory waxen flowers adding a wonderful creamy fragrance to the evening air. Then contrasting masses of bright red hibiscus, making up for their lack of smell with spectacular trumpet-shaped flowers. The profusion of all this colour and aroma added a welcome counterpoint to the otherwise dowdy and dusty streetscape.

The flora was great, what there was of it, but I was a bit disappointed by the paucity of wildlife, rather surprising for the tropics. Apart from the occasional yapping of pi-dogs, it was the chirping of common or garden sparrows that greeted us at dawn and it was they that had to compete with the calls of what I guessed were the few native birds, which dared venture into town. With so many of their brethren killed and eaten over the years, it was hardly surprising their numbers were so depleted. There was the dominant cry of one native bird, a bit like a wolf whistle really, a single note that got higher and higher in pitch as it repeated, and then suddenly stopped and took a break before starting all over again. Even so, it was not half as annoying as the croaking frogs in Bougainville!

One evening during this interlude, I went back up to Burns Peak and just sat, mulling over my circumstances. The beautiful views were in great contrast to my still anxious mood. There was something special about a Moresby sunset; with the sun melting into the sea, the skies changing from blue into a palette of goldy-orange grey and then lavender and finally into black. Watching the flowers and shrubs disappear into their own shadows and feel the cooler night air provided a comforting diversion from my worries and a welcome boost to my spirits.

At dawn next morning there was a frantic knocking on the front door. Dick fell out of bed, raced down the corridor, opened the door and immediately cried out, "You can't come in here!"

Now wide awake, I ran to the living room to see what was going on, nearly colliding with a young Papuan lad coming the other way. Ignoring Dick's order, he just dashed past, plonked himself down on the sofa and sat there, all bare feet, dusty legs and knees and with a crazed look in his eyes. He was gabbling away so excitedly it was hard to fathom what he was trying to say. Finally, Dick calmed him down, and we learned both the police and his 'Mama' were after him. He had run away and given them the slip, and please could he hide out with us for a while? What a cheek! He went on to tell us that he was a Standard Five student, his name was Moira, and he just wanted to stay for a short while and lie low until his pursuers gave up the chase!

We didn't ask what he was running away from – we were more concerned about his incredible nerve in barging into the house at five in the morning. I didn't mention it, but I was surprised at Dick foolishly letting him in; however, it was too late now. We gave him a glass of water and let him stay for an hour, by which time the hounds must have lost the scent. Dick eventually managed to persuade him to leave, and we were relieved that at least it had not been a violent robbery.

A week or so after my return from the jungle the days started to drag, but there was another change. Dick said, "Nick, I've another batch of twenty or so volunteers coming through and it's going to take a lot of my time to organise them, so I've arranged for you to stay over in Hohola for a couple of days. There is this CUSO (Canadian University Students Overseas) volunteer, a stenographer/secretary who, like you, has experienced a bit of a hiccup with her posting. She's waiting for another job and happy enough for you to stay with her."

"Okay" says I, "No problem." My lack of a posting was stressful for both Dick and myself, and we began to wonder if Business Development was ever going to come back with an offer. Dick was probably wondering how he was going to solve the problem of me, and of course, I was worried about how my presence in PNG was going to pan out. Perhaps as importantly, Dick did not want me telling any of my Bougainville stories to the new arrivals and putting them off before they had even started. Apart from all this, I thought that sharing a house with a girl was not such a bad idea! So, on one thundery, overcast but unusually cool day, Dick took me around to Hohola and introduced me to Sally.

Maybe it was the weather, maybe she was upset at having to share her house, or maybe it was simply chemistry, but I immediately got bad vibes from my new (and frustratingly pretty) friend. I soon discovered it was not about me. Diminutive Sally did not seem to like anything much at all about PNG, and she whinged about everything. A few gripes seemed valid, but as far as I could tell, everything in her life was terrible! Although, she did seem justified in complaining about one thing – the neighbourhood of Hohola. The rows and rows of identical no-frills *dongas*[39], resembling one of those old British Butlin's holiday camps, was bad enough, but later in the day, after school was out, the sound of a hundred screaming Papuan kids and their yelling parents assailed our senses. This rather unpleasant environment, combined with a plague of mosquitos, contributed significantly to my pretty CUSO's bad ass attitude.

But then, eventually, she told me of the real reason for her dismay. Back in Canada, she had been led to believe that she would be working as a steno-secretary to a senior executive in the Public Service. But on getting here, she had found all they really wanted was an administrative assistant, a role needing a much lower level of skills, basically involving filing. She was so disappointed that she was just not able to adjust, (a bit like with the boat, but in reverse, I mused). She did have a point, but her constant whinging and criticism alerted me to avoid becoming like her.

Then, just one day later, amid all the gloom and negativity, a bright ray of sunshine arrived. Dick came around to say the Department of Business Development had offered me the job and asked when I could start! I was ecstatic and, perhaps more than anything, relieved. I moved out of the moody shared house as soon as I possibly could.

After signing on at Department, I settled myself into Ranuguri Hostel in Konedobu and soon had plenty of new acquaintances, mainly expatriates but a few locals as well. Of course, nothing is perfect, and I quickly understood why they had assured me the conditions of the hostel were 'not all so bad'. Sure I found it to be okay, but it was still a hostel; a large, impersonal building with a canteen, a common area for socialising and then rows and rows of identical bedrooms, each looking out over a car park. Razor wire surrounded all of this to keep out the *raskols*!

My room was small and basic: painted a vile pale green, (pastels being all the rage of about a decade earlier) it contained a bed, a wardrobe and a sort of side table. There were communal showers down the corridor. The room was not so bad, but the real problem was it was as hot as hell. There were no fans and even with the louvre windows fully open, there was little breeze; and, with the fly-wire having seen better days, there were also plenty of mosquitoes for company!

But on the upside, there was all the food I could eat. We could go down to a large canteen in the morning for a substantial breakfast and at night, there would a three-course dinner; they even did a pre-packed lunch to take to the office. There was also a laundry service! My *haus boi* (friendly enough, but nothing like Calimo) would clean my room and do all my washing and my ironing, and was happy enough in taking the trivial sum of $3 a week for his effort! There were no domestic issues to worry about.

It was an enormous improvement over the past few months and I knew I should be grateful and felt it would do for the time being at least. But, then contrarily, and almost immediately, I began to wonder if I could possibly live for the next couple of years in this open-prison-like environment.

On a more positive note, as it was a hostel for government employees, most people were quite educated, cheerful and conscientious. Naturally, there was a mix of folk; those keen to do the right thing by PNG but also quite a few who had come just to make money. I soon found, somewhat surprisingly, that the favourite topic of the mercenaries and others alike was the large (possibly exaggerated?) sums of money people said they were earning. Everybody talked about money! I even started to talk about it myself, but I kept my modest local pay a secret; I didn't feel I needed to explain such a personal issue.

After money, the next most favourite topic was 'going-finish' (*go pinis* in pidgin English). This was disheartening. Nearly everyone said they could not wait to *go pinis*. This was an anathema to me as a volunteer, particularly as I had just arrived, and I realised I really did have a degree of altruism about me. However, now, mixing with expatriate Public Servants, I found the constant focus on values and material things – good times, cars - were challenging my virtues, as modest as they were. It was the same stuff I'd had in Britain but which I could never afford in the quantity or the quality to really enjoy. Here, other than girls, material goods were almost the total focus of us mainly single white men, my new neighbours and colleagues. Some of these guys were even importing fancy brand-new cars, and as the best I had ever owned in Britain was a very second-hand Morris Minor, I was quite envious. Cars were perhaps the extreme example of material wealth, but with my background in the motor industry they were of natural interest. When one (quite nasty) guy took delivery of a brand new bright red Holden Monaro V8 he had brought up from Australia, I followed the gang out to the car park to ogle it.

After being in Moresby for a few weeks, and having already made a few expatriate friends, I discovered it was not so easy to gain much rapport with Papua New Guineans. It was not because of my poorly developed language skills. In fact, my pidgin was already better than that of many expatriates who made no attempt to learn it and all chatted away in English. Ironically, many of the more educated Papuans felt it below their dignity to speak in patois as they had their own language, Hiri Motu, and, of course, they also spoke English. So, it was not the language, it was more a definite 'us and them' mentality. There was more than a smidgen of racial antipathy. Many expatriates did not want to encourage friendships with 'orly'[40] with the unspoken question "What on earth would you want to mix with them for?" Conversely, having been patronised for so many years, some of the more educated Papua New Guineans held a similar degree of aversion towards friendship with expats.

Despite all this I soon made a few local friends. One guy, Loa Helalo, whose family came from the village of Tuberseria, a couple of hours drive up the main highway, had a decent sense of humour and was good company.

However, even with my new friends and an exciting new job, I soon discovered there were indeed some downsides to living in the hostel. The worst of these were the noises. In addition to the croaking of frogs and the incessant cicadas (which I now sort of accepted), there were quite a few others. The worst was from the packs of dogs that spent the night fighting in the street outside and expanded on their distress with the occasional bloodcurdling howl. Then, thanks to a few locals who had drunk too much, there was the sharp noise of stones landing on the tin roof in the dead of night. These woke even the soundest of sleepers. But, the saddest of all were the human screams. This was mainly the noise of kids from the neighbouring shantytown, along with a few obviously female voices. I hated to think what it was they were crying and screaming about, but it did not sound like anyone was having much fun.

All these various issues, when combined with the ever-pervasive heat and humidity, impacted on my natural equanimity in such a way I discovered an emotion I had never been aware of before – irritation!

Later, as another part of my re-integration into city life, I became even more aware of how much the locals also craved the material things they saw expatriates enjoying, and how frustrated they were because they could not get them. This was probably no different to the apparent frustration of some folk on Bougainville, but in practice it had more of an urban flavour.

As an everyday example, locals either walked to work or the market or, if they could afford the modest fare, travelled by public transport. This meant riding in one of the many beat-up and uncomfortable old PMVs that roared noisily around town. Invariably leaving a thick cloud of black exhaust fumes, these vehicles were little better than the trucks on which they were based and contrasted noticeably with the flashy air-conditioned cars many expats drove. Riding in the back of a PMV was nothing like riding on a proper bus and seemed quite demeaning. However, I guessed that for the locals at least, as an alternative to walking, it was not too bad. This situation was not so different from the on-going disparity of the haves and have-nots in so-called developed societies; it was just on a more basic level.

Alongside all this, and again as part of my initiation, I soon discovered that while everyone I met, native and expat alike, was very sociable, they all drank a hell of a lot. I thought I drank a fair bit, but while the usual excuse to sink another stubbie was the heat, more often than not the real reason was more to do with the frustrations of one's job and life generally. Outbursts of violent brawls amongst the locals, usually on payday and often near the pubs, were usually the result of too much grog. Expats kept their drunken behaviour a little more low-key, but it was still there. We knew there had been a call to curb the sale of alcohol, at least on a payday, but instead, the government allowed the opening of even more bars!

I soon got into the swing of things myself, because as well as feeling the heat and naturally getting thirsty, it was part and parcel of socialising. It was not long before I knew I'd have to go easy with the grog if I wanted to survive over the long term.

In early February 1973 I began my new job, as 'Handcrafts Marketing Officer' within the Department of Business Development. And, from now on, in amongst all the negative stuff going on around me, my life took an enormous turn for the better.

My new boss, Eric Hovey, showed me into a tiny little office in a rabbit warren of outdated facilities down in the CBD. There was an old regulation admin green baize-topped desk, one chair behind with one in front, and a phone. It was compact to say the least! And, with barely room to move and both of us standing awkwardly at the doorway, Eric said, "I hope you'll be comfortable enough Nick. Mother Nature's in charge of the air-conditioning. The breeze from the harbour is good at times, but non-existent at others. You'll get used to it."

There was no need to apologise. Simply having my own office was a miracle!

"That's great Eric. A telephone, a desk and a bit of peace and quiet are all I'll need," I replied.

With people continually dodging each other around the corridors the complex was indeed crowded, and hot, and not particularly quiet! But even though the facilities were old and, I supposed, a little uncomfortable, everyone seemed to have their own office. Some were larger than others of course, but the layout allowed one to get on with one's job. As far as I was concerned, it was all bloody marvellous, but the authorities thought otherwise.

Eric explained, "The Australian Government is going to increase the number of Public Servants over the next year or so, and we're building new offices out at Waigani to house them all. You can get up there and have a look if you like. It is about a half-hour drive away from the CBD. It's going to become the new admin centre and we and other departments will be relocating there later in the year."

Forget that for a while, I thought. I was more than happy to have my own office of whatever size, and I settled in comfortably.

Hovey soon called me into his office to tell me about my job, where I fitted in within the hierarchy, who else was involved and who was calling the shots. As he talked, I got a better chance to look at the guy who had saved me. He was a tall, tubby and genial sort of fellow with a full, flushed, oval face and a permanent five o'clock shadow. With his slicked-back greying hair and bushy eyebrows, I guessed he would be in his mid to late 50s. But whatever his age, with his shorts hoisted too high up his stomach and knee-length socks, he was a bad dresser!

Although genial enough, he seemed a bit stressed and I guessed he was relieved to have someone with whom to share his concerns.

Eric explained the hierarchy. "At the top of our particular tree, we have a Papua New Guinean by the name of Donatus Molar. He's the Minister for Business Development and a Member of the House of Assembly." (I immediately thought, 'teeth', 'dentist'; but later found out his name came from the Catholic Church, in memory of one of their saints.)

"Reporting to him is another local, Paulius Matane, the Secretary of the Department, he's like a Chief Executive Officer in a regular business. And then, there is the expatriate in charge,

Ian Wiseman, the Assistant Executive Officer. Plus, there are quite a few other expatriates involved, including the Assistant Director of the Department you met at the interview and then there is me. I'm in charge of small industry development."

All this time I said little and simply listened. From what my new friends at the hostel had told me I knew these expats were all on huge salaries and were also probably counting the days before they would hand over and leave.

Hovey went on, "Further afield we have offices in each of the Provinces and Business Development Officers with local staff located in each. Their whole raison d'être, and ours at Head Office of course, is the commercial welfare of the population. But these guys are at the coalface, and they'll be your contacts out in the field."

By now I knew there were over twenty provinces in PNG and many locals who made handicrafts and artefacts, so now I felt a little more comfortable knowing there were plenty of other people out there to help in our endeavours. Then, even though Hovey did not bother to elaborate, I knew that way down the bottom of the ladder, at HQ in Port Moresby, there was now me, the Handcrafts Marketing Officer, ex-ship's captain (not) and volunteer *extraordinaire*. I was more than happy to be a mere minion in the overall scheme of things.

Eric explained that his section was training a few locals in the production of handicrafts, woven goods actually and, by necessity, the government was now directly involved in business. However, the focus really was on training weavers and they did not want to increase their commercial involvement. Private enterprise was already trading traditional crafts and artefacts, and Hovey felt that with the right form of assistance, we could encourage many more Papua New Guineans to participate in the economy by using their own traditional craft skills and running businesses in crafts. The question was how to achieve this end, and what was the best way to help expand the sector. So, working under Hovey, that was primarily my job. I would have a relatively free hand to identify and work through the details, determine what would be the best way forward and eventually, help establish the plan. It was new to all of us, and an exciting challenge.

Although I was still a VSO volunteer, paradoxically, I was to get paid! Hovey warned me not to get too excited, because the local Public Service rates[41] were quite modest compared with regular expat salaries. It didn't worry me – I was relieved to have a job and very happy to be staying on in the country.

Hovey went on to explain that I was also eligible for a few perquisites. One of these was the use of an admin car, complete with a driver!

"Just telephone this number a bit in advance, and you'll get a car," he said. "But, again don't get too carried away, it's only to be used for local work journeys and not to get to and from the office and the hostel each day." Talk about style!

The real icing on the cake, however, was that the job required frequent travel around Papua New Guinea. And, because there were very few roads and none connecting the capital to any of the other major parts of the country, this meant flying regularly. In my previous life travel meant train or car, and flying within Britain was very much the preserve of VIPs. Here in PNG, even though it was common for those in business and government and the few tourists, it still had a certain degree of prestige. Also, never mentioned, there was also just a hint of apprehension. The country's tough flying conditions, extensive use of light aircraft and the occasional incident were well known, but the chances of a scary death rarely discussed.

The overall aim of the administration was for the local indigenise to take over from us expats and for them to then provide all government services. Hovey said, in preparation for 'localisation'[42] the task for each expat was to train a local understudy, then work him or herself out of a job and, as I had heard interminably from those in the hostel, to *go pinis* as soon as possible.

This was the idea, but, as Hovey explained, it was tricky to put it into practice because there were not enough locals with appropriate skills. A few Papua New Guineans had already received training in Australia (and there were a few qualified professionals such as pilots and doctors) but students had only been graduating from the local university since a year or two earlier (1970). And, although the plan was to have enough graduates to fill professional and specialist public and private enterprise jobs by 1975, right now there were just not enough to give everyone an understudy. He joked that also, contrary to the official aim, some expatriates deliberately worked in such a way as to delay the process of localisation because they wanted to amass their nest egg of a government pension!

During our discussions and off the record so to speak, I heard how some locals got their positions. Even though someone might not have much training or experience, locals in a job with a degree of authority would sometimes pull strings to get their *wantok* appointed; basically, it was nepotism. But then I recalled that I had got my very first job at the age of 15 (as, I am sure, did many others) based on the old British system of 'who you know'.

Underlying all this, everyone was aware the country was being prepared for independence, and despite the shortage of skills and contrary to some negative attitudes, most expats exhibited a genuine and positive approach in working towards that end. I had to pinch myself. It was an exciting time to be so directly involved in the development of a country, even with input of a relatively minor nature.

Hovey went on to tell me a lot about the historical, legal and social processes of what had been going on, but at this stage it was far too much detail for me to take it all in. As far as I understood it, in a nutshell, the territory's name was changed to Papua New Guinea, they had held elections for the formation of the first local Ministry and Michael Somare was elected as Chief Minister of a coalition government.

From what I had heard, the consensus was that people had a good deal of faith in Somare. He was articulate, possessed considerable charm and a certain presence that was appealing. So far, he had managed to overcome (or at least keep to one side) the parochialism inherent in the diversity of clans and tribes within the country. And, although the impression was that he would have his work cut out in keeping the country together, we knew there was the encouragement and full support of Australia's Prime Minister, Gough Whitlam[43]. The place was definitely on the move!

At this time and until independence (at a date yet to be announced), PNG still came under the jurisdiction of Australia. I discovered that above Molar and Somare, for a while at least, there was the Australian Administrator[44], Les Johnson[45]. Indeed, soon after my arrival, and fortunately for me, Johnson organised a garden party on the lawns of Government House to welcome the new British Consul. Even though I was one of relatively few

British expatriates in the country, I was somewhat surprised to receive an invitation. I had never moved in such circles before, nor did I aspire to now. But, as Johnson did the rounds glad-handing all and sundry, I suddenly found him talking to me! He did not introduce himself or even ask me who I was, and for a second I was not sure it was indeed to him that I was talking. There were plenty of other important-looking types wandering around, so he could have been the British Consul for all I knew, although his accent was a bit of a giveaway.

Not being at all familiar with the protocol of such events, I was a little taken aback by his arrogance. He could have at least asked how I had got to PNG and what role I played in the Public Service. Perhaps I should have felt honoured he even deigned to talk to me at all.

After he spent five minutes talking to me about this and that he moved on. That was it! Again, I was quite irritated. I had missed the opportunity to speak my mind about something or other of importance; a captain for a boat over in Bougainville might have helped!

I did not expect to be on talking terms with such VIPs, and certainly not on a regular basis. This was especially true in the Public Service, where it was clear that all communications further up the hierarchy were to be via my direct boss (and naturally, filtered by him). Also, even though in working for the Administration I was getting news first hand and was close to the goings on, it was seldom that anyone asked for my opinion when discussions got involved politically. I kept out of all that and focused on my own tricky enough technical tasks. They presented plenty of challenges – and opportunities for yet more travel!

CHAPTER 10

TRAVEL FOR BUSINESS

After doing the rounds of the offices and businesses in town and talking crafts and artefacts with a seemingly endless number of people, I was a little more clued up about the situation. It became pretty obvious I should first focus my attention on the weaving project. I doubted the sanity of those who had initiated a project in weaving woollen items in a tropical country, but there it was, it was already there and something of a known quantity. It was early days and way too soon to criticise the machinations of the Public Service.

I considered the various things that might need attention; pricing and promotion were usually of concern and then looking for market outlets, etc. It should not really be so hard to get some initiatives sorted out. Later, once I had got that organised, I would start on the other, more challenging, traditional crafts.

To take the first step, I needed to get more details of the items that were being made and what there was to market and to do that I needed to visit the weaving company. As luck would have it, this was miles away, up in the hills somewhere.

My dream had been to simply travel to see the world, and now it had an added dimension; I was to travel for business!

Out on the street bright and early one morning, I was waiting for the admin car I had booked to take me to the airport. I waited and waited and waited in vain. This was not an auspicious start. Hanging around any longer meant I would miss my flight, and that would not look too good on my first official appointment.

I rushed back inside, called a cab and finally got to the airport in the nick of time. So, now here I was, flying yet again in a Fokker Friendship. This time it was just a short trip up to Goroka, the capital of the Eastern Highlands Province, about an hour and 400 kilometres north from Moresby. We were flying quite low, and in the fine weather I could clearly see the dramatic crags of the Owen Stanley mountain range. This jagged terrain presented a nigh on impossible barrier to building a road linking the capital with other parts of the country, and it was the very reason I was flying and not driving up to Goroka.

I then recalled that when I first arrived in Moresby it was dry. The place was arid and brown, and resembled somewhere north of the equator. Dick then explained that it was these mountains that created a rain shadow, which gave POM its two distinct seasons. There was 'the wet' running from November to April and 'the dry' from May to October. Now, looking down, I saw nothing but dense, green, soaking wet tropical forest. Indeed, over the months I had been back in Moresby, I experienced the same incredibly humid, hot and breathless conditions of the drowning downpours I'd had in Bougainville.

I assumed that apart from the aberration of the Moresby 'dry', this was the way the rest of the country was going to be: hot, wet and sticky. So, when I got off the plane at Goroka I was surprised to find yet another distinctly different climate. There was an exhilarating freshness in the air.

Now was not the time to dwell on the climatic peculiarities of PNG however. A shortish, weather-beaten and very business-like Aussie appeared out of the waiting crowd, shook me firmly by the hand and said, "Welcome to Goroka, Nick. Have a good flight?"

This was Ed Hankin, the Business Development Field Officer for the Eastern Highlands Province.

"Hi Ed. Well, yes, I am glad to be here. I only just got my flight because the admin car never turned up and I had to catch a taxi."

"You were lucky to get up here at all mate. Old Gough [Whitlam] and his entourage have just visited and they've caused a hell of a mess with schedules."

As we drove over to the office, Ed continued, "Someone from his staff must have collared your car. You needn't have worried mate, there's nothing unusual about missing appointments, pick-ups or even flights. You'll soon learn it's an accepted hazard of working in the place."

I felt more at ease. Punctuality was the expected minimum back home, and earned a bad mark if not adhered to.

We chatted away about the usual topics. Ed told me he had decided there was more excitement to be had up here than counting sheep on his dad's farm in Victoria. Paradoxically I noted a faint air of resignation in his manner, which, I assumed was caused by the frustration of his job, but I didn't comment.

Then, after a brief introduction to his local staff and a quick cup of coffee, we jumped into a Land Cruiser[46] and drove a little way out of town to the Highland Weavers factory, close to the village of Makia. Negotiating the slippery gravel corners with the skill of a rally driver, Ed elaborated on the attitude he and the other Business Development field officers took to head office.

"Forget about HQ, this is where the action is – or lack of it!" he said. "Most of those guys down in POM are protected from everyday life out here in the provinces. They really have no idea what we do, or how hard it is to get anything done. So, I'm glad you have come up to see for yourself. I hope you have brought a practical attitude with you to make things happen. You'll need it!"

Ed explained that Highland Weavers was the key Government project, which had been set up as an example and incentive to get other, bigger crafts projects rolling. He confirmed that it should indeed be the focus of my attention and would provide an excellent initiation into *bisnis* Papua New Guinea style. This was now my opportunity to look at the operations, talk about plans for marketing and a chance for me to prove myself.

After bumping along the dirt corrugations of the Highlands Highway, we drove down an even rougher side road and parked in front of an old corrugated iron shed. As we hopped out of the Land Cruiser I looked around for the factory and then quizzically at Ed.

"Come on, this way," he said, pointing to the shed, "Let's go in and I'll introduce you to the guys."

This was it, the Government's much-vaunted Highland Weavers project everyone had talked about. It didn't look much and although it was not particularly dilapidated, it was still just an old tin shed; a tin roof over corrugated iron walls. And when I got inside, in contrast to the freshness outside, of course it was as hot as hell!

Apart from the stifling heat, the next thing that hit me was the clutter of looms and spindles, cones of yarn, rolags of carded wool; there was stuff everywhere. The second thing was the scale of operations. There were just five looms in a row, and only two weavers using them. Thirdly, as well as a few finished items hanging on racks, there was a large morass of woven goods piled up in a sort of holding bay over to one side.

Sifting through them quickly, it was clear many of the items were of such poor quality no one would ever buy them. Ed told me not to be surprised, and stressed this was a training facility rather than simply a factory. The place was such a mess, however, it reminded me a bit of the trade store at Kuraio; I didn't comment.

I soon realised there was more to this job than I had first anticipated, and certainly more than any marketing would fix. We would need to make an inventory, perhaps to rationalise what they were making, organise a range of garments and styles and only then look at promotion. It was easy enough to imagine, but probably much harder to do.

After coming to this fairly obvious conclusion and chatting on a little about the history of the workshop, I realised Ed seemed to have it mind for me to manage the place. He said the current manager was due to *go pinis* in a couple of months and was keen to get someone who would continue to run it. Knowing what improvements needed to be made was easy enough, but I was worried that trying to fix them would not allow me time enough for my bigger project. Developing a scheme for marketing handicrafts was a national project and Highland

Weavers, although important, was only one small part of it. Besides, even though Goroka seemed to be a more attractive town than Moresby, it was still up in the bush. Having recently re-acquainted myself with city life, I was in no great hurry to leave.

Ed told me he would put the idea of me taking over to Head Office and no doubt Hovey would decide in a month or so. Clearly there was a bit of wheeling and dealing to do to ensure I stayed in POM with my bigger job.

I took a few notes, looked at more of the stock and chatted to the two weavers who were actually working. After purposely avoiding commenting on what I thought needed doing, I decided I had seen enough for the day.

That evening I found myself in the restaurant of the Bird of Paradise Hotel. It had been an amazing few weeks. One minute I was stuck on a godforsaken Mission Station (if you will excuse the expression), eating tinned *pis* and rice and now I was in this fancy hotel eating Lobster Mornay. Having recovered from the initial shock of the prices on the menu, and relieved that the government was paying, I sat there thanking my lucky stars, swigging on my beer and downing more tasty morsels.

I went out for a breath of fresh air before retiring and now with the temperature even lower than when I had arrived, the idea of weaving woollen garments in a tropical country did not seem so silly after all. With Goroka some 1,500 metres or so, up in the mountains, it was freezing! I was more than happy to have a warm woolly blanket when I went to bed that night.

Another small surprise awaited me the following day. As Hovey had not told me anything to the contrary, I had assumed I was the only new expatriate recruited to help in the crafts sector. But now, Ed explained, he was going over to the airport to collect someone he had hired to provide technical support. He had mentioned technical problems the day before but it had not registered and he now explained,

"The weaving project was our initiative and we'd hired the manager in the first place, so it's quite reasonable we should also hire any other skills we think fit".

How could I disagree? But then I thought that if this provincial office had just hired someone and not told my boss at Head Office, there was a bit of a communication issue and perhaps a bit of territorial jealousy involved as well.

Whichever was the case, later in the day, having come back from the airport, Ed introduced me to Margaret Fletcher[47], who had just flown up from Adelaide in South Australia. She was a flouncy, blustery lady in her late fifties and quite appropriately very clothes-conscious; in fact, she looked a bit like a walking wardrobe with scarves, wraps and skirts whirling everywhere. I immediately labelled her an arty type and it turned out I was right.

Margaret knew her stuff about weaving, which was a relief, because the quality of the woven goods was a technical issue that I had no idea how to fix. But, gradually however, it became apparent there was something else – we held quite different views on what should be made. Margaret, (who was yet to see any of the woven goods) said she wanted to encourage the weavers to produce one-off high fashion 'works of art'. And with me having seen the quality of the weavers' work, I felt she must be joking. *My* immediate thought was that we should introduce a small range of simple garments that would be easy for the weavers to make and easy to promote and sell through craft shops. We needed to come to some sort of compromise.

As well as concerns over quality there was the high cost of wool, the low level of output of the weavers and, surprisingly, the high level of wages. In a nutshell, we faced trying to sell expensive, poor quality products.

Next day, Ed, Margaret and I went out to Highland Weavers to further explore what needed doing, and this time we got to meet the manager. Mike Weston, a very pale-skinned CUSO volunteer with an unruly mop of blond, almost white hair and a bit of a lisp. He had been away visiting retail stores around the province and now we got the proper guided tour and an overview of the patterns and techniques employed by the weavers. From his tone it was clear he was relieved to be finally getting the help he had asked for.

After the tour, he, Margaret, Ed and I got down to discussing the business. Mike agreed that the idea of selling at a premium price was all well and good, but the quality, style and design the weavers were capable of so far just did not match. There would have to be a fair bit more training to improve things. Eventually, we all agreed that prices, for existing products at least, were unrealistically high in relation to similar items in the market. So, we set up a new pricing structure allowing the same rate of pay for the weavers and enough to just cover costs for the business, but now including a margin for resellers. With the weavers seemingly some time away from being able to produce the sort of upmarket quality for which people would be prepared to pay, Margaret was happy to focus on improving everyday items while also spending a little time working towards her high-fashion dreams – for the longer term. We were all happy.

Next day, with Margaret staying back to focus on Highland Weavers, I flew over to another, even smaller weaving centre, in Kundiawa. There was a quite a delay at Goroka Airport, this time because of the arrival of a large group of fearsome-looking Kukukuku tribesmen[48]. They had been flown in from the Marawaka Valley specially to put on a welcoming sing-sing for Whitlam. They were very different from the Kereaka on Bougainville and were more like the mental picture I'd had of primitive tribesmen. Each wore a grass skirt over their nether regions, embellished by a kind of enormous sporran made of reeds (for additional protection against what, I never found out) and held in place by a bark belt. With cloaks of beaten bark over their shoulders and headbands of birds' feathers on top, they were something to behold. It was all quite bizarre, particularly seen against the backdrop of a shiny, sophisticated light aircraft and the Western-style clothing of the pilot. After a bit of a gawk I slunk around the back to make sure I got my seat just before the rest of the mob clambered on board.

Kukukuku about to catch their flight

Thus far my flights had been in medium-sized Fokker F27s, but now, sitting next to the pilot in this eight-seater Cessna, I began to experience a completely different type of air travel. I imagined the noise and vibration of turbo-charged engines screaming away either side of us, to be the kind of buzz one might get sitting in a Formula One racing car. The surge of power, the rush and blur of the scenery were straight out of Silverstone or Monza. But, with the pilot pressing buttons, flipping switches and then pulling back on the joystick, the disappearing runway proved it was more than racing on land and I was soon back to reality.

We had taken off despite dark, threatening clouds and a spatter of rain and I now faced the full visual impact of the brooding sky. I had been warned about flying conditions in PNG, but it was too late to chicken out. As we rose higher and banked away from the huge pillars of almost black clouds over to our right, I stopped myself from leaning into the bend as if on a motorcycle. But still we approached cloud, and then, getting too close to the fierce darkness, suddenly suffered a sharp drop in altitude. With the little craft now buffeted around by invisible turbulence, I mentally crossed myself and thought about the precariousness of life.

Thankfully it was only a short flight and we soon started on a more controlled descent. Circling over the township and between the mountains and magnificent scenery, the pilot lined up with the grass strip on a gently sloping ridge. For a moment I could see the Wahgi River several hundred metres below, what, in colder climes, could easily be mistaken as the take-off point of a ski-jump. Before I could worry about overshooting the runway, we did a quick one-eighty-degree turn, headed back up the other way and landed safely before the foothills of the mountains at the other end.

George Xavier, the Business Development Officer for the area, met me at the tin hut airport terminal and, after a brief chat, it being too late in the day for any work, checked me in to yet another fancy hotel, the Chimbu Lodge. There was no rush for the rest of the day so I enjoyed a stroll around Kundiawa, had another lovely meal and, thanks to the beautifully cool climate, another good night's rest.

George picked me up next day and we drove down to the Kundiawa Weavers factory in yet another tin shed! This was also a Business Development project, but there were no government staff on site; instead, we met up with a local expat businessman, Jim McEwan, who kept an eye on the weavers, just as a favour.

We three chatted about what further help was necessary and what we could provide. As with the project at Makia there were plenty of problems. But, with one of them being that of actually selling anything. So, by way of encouragement rather than any commercial sensibility, I took a dozen woollen ponchos and a few blankets on consignment. At least when these sold in POM they would provide cash to buy more wool and keep the weavers going for a while longer. With no direct government money being used, it really was a hand-to-mouth operation. I told them Margaret would visit as soon as possible to provide some technical assistance.

For my benefit, Jim and George explained that the government was finding it a struggle just to establish a simple weaving business here and at Highland Weavers. Indeed, the lack of skills characterised the problem being faced throughout PNG. A huge effort was required to train and develop enough Papua New Guineans to manage key industries in administration, education, health and commerce – just about everything, really! This was particularly so because any training needed to not only instil specific skills but address the general attitude to work. There was a vast chasm between growing up in a village, socialising and relying on subsistence farming compared with managing a business, a budget and perhaps a few employees. And even though the date for independence had yet to be fixed, working towards it was a distraction that again didn't much help. Admin staff in the provinces were really stretched in their endeavours!

After becoming engrossed in chatting about the various peculiarities of *bisnis* in PNG, George suddenly realised how late it was, rushed me back to the airport and put me on the last flight out of town, this time an even smaller plane, a single-engine Cessna 206. The pilot was sitting on the runway, impatiently revving his engine and waiting for me, his last passenger. Jumping in, I was surprised to see it was full of another group of locals. I didn't know which clan they belonged to; they were simply 'highlanders', different from the Kukukuku and smelling strongly of wood smoke and a bit shiny with pig grease. I squeezed in, wriggled around to close the door and finally, we zoomed off down the runway.

Seeing the ski-jump at the end of the runway and still firmly on the ground, I wondered if we were now a tad too heavy. But of course we took off anyway and in a long, slow, gentle climb to the right and with a bit of yawing around in crosswinds, we flew over the valley and into a slightly less sinister array of serried white clouds. With a tailwind, we were back in Goroka in just fifteen minutes.

Now, with my better understanding of the job at hand, and relaxing after the flights, I remembered there were two further tasks to complete before I returned to POM. My boss had set one of these tasks, and one I had set myself. Eric asked me to get him some vegetables! I was a bit taken aback by this but it was apparently fairly common practice. The veggies from the Highlands were better quality and cheaper than those in Moresby. With the ones in Moresby having been shipped up from Australia and now in varying states of decay, this was probably true. But, having seen the variety of fresh tropical fruit and the staples of kau kau and taro available in Koki Market, I could not help but think he was being a bit inflexible. But then he was the boss, and he must have his potatoes!

My own task was more to do with learning about the job. Having seen a few of the more commonly available traditional artefacts in the stores around POM, I wanted to buy one or two for myself while here and closer to the source so to speak. Eric had already phoned through his order for the vegetables to the supplier and all I had to do was pick them up, so that was the easy part. But finding some good quality artefacts was quite a lot harder. I eventually managed to track down a couple of decent-looking traditional masks and a distinctive silhouette-like carving, essentially a stylised head over a series of hooks called a *kamanggabi*[49]. I had seen a lot of similar but quite inferior items in the shops in Moresby and now, also knowing the nature of the quality of the woven goods at Highland Weavers, I realised quality was going to be an important factor in the task at hand.

I flew back to POM next day but then, having been so concerned about my own treasures I had traipsed half way back across the tarmac to the terminal before I realised I had left Eric's veggies back on the plane. Probably breaking some safety rule, I hurried back and picked them up just before the pilot thought he had scored them for his own dinner. Hovey would never have forgiven me!

I needed a break after such a hectic week, so early the following day I joined a few of my new friends for a swim out in the bay. We drove over to Kila Kila and boarded an odd-looking craft waiting for us at the jetty. It was not really a boat but more of a rectangular, flat-bottomed floating platform. But, with an awning for shade and a motor, it was more than adequate for our needs – in a calm sea.

The skipper cast off, took us out a couple of kilometres away from the mainland and eventually anchored just off the small, uninhabited island of Manubada. We had set off around eight-thirty and having got to the island fairly quickly, we spent the rest of the morning snorkelling over the shallows and generally messing around. Unfortunately, the marine life was a bit disappointing. The presence of so many rowdy human beings did not exactly encourage the fish to play along. Anyway, it was still good fun, and after a bit of lunch, by one or so in the afternoon, we'd all had enough and it was time to head back.

The guy in charge went to start the engine, but instead of the sputter of the motor we heard muttered cussing and blinding, followed by a deathly silence. We realised to our dismay he couldn't get the engine started! The battery was flat. No engine, no oars. We were stranded a couple of kilometres offshore. It was way too far to swim back to the mainland, particularly as we were already tired from messing around in the water all morning. Voices rose and fell as we anxiously talked through our options; then someone spotted a couple of local fishermen in their dugouts in the distance. They were still a long way from us and well out of earshot, but with only a few hours more of daylight they were our only hope.

A couple of guys felt comfortable enough to swim over to the fishermen and get them to take them ashore for help, so off they set. We watched and waited in trepidation, and eventually saw them contact the fishermen before they all disappeared from view. All we could do now was to sit and wait.

We got more and more anxious as the hours went by with no apparent action. None of us had brought much clothing, and as day turned to night, we got cold in the near-nakedness of our swimming togs. Finally, at ten-thirty at night, and with great relief, we saw the lights of a boat approach. It was the Water Police and after a good dressing down for not having any life jackets they hooked us up to their patrol boat and towed back to dry land. Chastised but relieved, I got back to the hostel well after midnight, burned to a crisp, shivering and utterly shattered. It took me days to recover. So much for a bit of a rest!

Those in the office dished out more scolding on Monday, but no one was able to suggest how to avoid this situation again. It was impractical to inspect the engine and battery each time we went out on a boat. But I vowed that I would at least check to see there were life jackets. In this instance it had just been one of those things. C'est la vie.

Getting back into my work, I learned that many years earlier, the Administration had established an event called an Agricultural Show. As the name suggested, these shows were held out in the open, at a sports field or somewhere similar. They usually included private sector displays of agricultural equipment, seeds and fertilisers and the like, as well as Administration stands explaining the services provided by the various departments. These Admin booths were generally rather simple and dull affairs but by the time I had arrived they were, for many, only a backdrop to the main event.

It was explained that ten years earlier, the Department of Education's Western Highlands superintendent shifted the focus from agriculture and farming to displaying the customs and social behaviour of Papua New Guineans. And now the event was described as 'a forum for tribesmen and women to share the diversity of cultures, parade their colourful costumes and celebrate their ancestral traditions with singing and dancing'.[50]

Having adopted this notion, the Administration now brought in a wide variety of tribal groups from around the country and made the event more cultural than agricultural. The title 'Agricultural Show' had stuck however, even though it was now a bit of a misnomer; after all, it was an expat initiative!

The show drew a large and varied audience and I was asked to organise our Department's stand. Focusing on what we were doing to help develop small industries and my particular area of crafts, I considered the issue of how to visually demonstrate our services. In the end, I cajoled another department to paint a large flow-chart showing the various stages from a villager making a craft to its final sale and describing government assistance available along the way.

Having just taken delivery of several sections of a rather cumbersome several metre-long timber panel diagram, I went out to the show grounds to help set it all up. I was in the midst of helping our local staff put a panel in place, when someone pointed out a shadowy cloud of dust some way off in the distance and rising over a group of tribesmen. At first, I thought this was just the usual stamping of feet for some dance or other, but then we saw a small group of people suddenly break away from the main crowd, surge out of the central arena and crash through the perimeter fence. Then, as if by magic, the riot police arrived.

Looking particularly fearsome in their black crash helmets and full body armour and with shotguns at the ready, they charged across the show grounds in somewhat ragged formation and in doing so managed to scare the hell out of the rest of the tribesmen who hadn't stampeded earlier. Eventually all the tribesmen scattered far and wide into the surrounding bush. Luckily, they ran away and not towards us and left the showgrounds deserted, and at peace.

None of the staff seemed particularly surprised. Apparently, this was not the first time. Indeed, with something like 15,000 people, from many different clans and all crowded together in a relatively small area in the unshaded, blistering heat and humidity, something was bound to give. No one knew what sparked the incident. It could have been a clan-based thing or maybe someone simply staring too long at someone else's wife.

Despite some very slight increase in animosity towards us foreigners, there was little risk to life and limb; whatever it was all about, *waitpela* was not the target.

After the dust settled on the Moresby event, and with my flow chart of services having caught the attention of the Secretary, I was asked to help organise our display at the following Mount Hagen Show. Going on previous years, a crowd of some 80,000 tribesmen was expected at that event. With probably even more different clans than there were at Moresby, it promised to be a bloodbath!

However, before going back up to the Highlands, I needed to resolve a significant problem: I needed my own transport.

The Admin car was supposedly available for business, but with only a limited number of cars available and being well down the pecking order, I usually had to resort to taxis. And, although I quite enjoyed getting around at other times by PMV, I was usually the only expat on board and stood out a bit. I soon realised that apart from the occasional hippy tourist, *waitpela* simply did not ride on PMVs. And besides, with it being sensible not to travel on them after dark, I had a problem when I wanted to socialise. Despite there being only a few hundred kilometres of roads in and around Port Moresby, the place was so spread out I just had to have my own car, so, I went shopping.

I spent ages checking out the sad collection of very beat-up second-hand machinery on offer. Being on local wages and with a limited budget, it was not easy to find a car that looked both reliable and affordable. There were a few rough old British cars around but they didn't exactly inspire one's confidence, and word was that spares were almost impossible to get. Looking more closely it was clear the manufacturers had not allowed for the strength of the tropical sun as the plastic on the dashboard and seating was badly cracked. This was only cosmetic but I also knew that the suspension, designed for smooth English roads, would have taken a thrashing and probably be expensive to repair. Eventually I homed in on a drab khaki-coloured 1959 Volkswagen Beetle. With numerous dents and scrapes complementing its dull, matt paintwork, it had obviously had a hard life. As with the British cars built for a more temperate climate, the lack of a decent shine was probably due to the UV rays of the sun rather than having been polished off by the care from its previous owners. Still, the engine sounded okay, everything opened and shut and despite its appearance, it was still a Volkswagen, a car with an excellent reputation for reliability. Besides, it was all I could afford!

Taking it out for a trial run along the bumpy coastal road to Idlers Bay, it went surprisingly well. It was noisy, it rattled and shook, but nothing fell off. I stopped and had a good look around outside and in. Behind the driver's seat, carefully concealed by a rubber mat, was a large rust hole in the floor. Being familiar with the construction of VWs, I knew it did not affect the cars overall integrity, and, if I told my friends not to be back-seat drivers and brake instinctively when they saw something I had not, I would be okay.

As it was such an ancient car, I was not blind to the possibility of some malfunction or other, but nevertheless, I returned to the dealer, parted with my $300 and took possession.

I did not have to wait long for something to go wrong. A few days after picking her up, I was cruising along the coast road at the top speed of sixty miles an hour, radio blaring, windows open and enjoying the breeze. I had just come down the hill from Koki Market and was navigating the bends of Healy Road, a couple of metres or so above the Coral Sea, when suddenly the car tilted down on its left rear quarter, the steering went light and I found myself staring at the sky. Instinctively pumping the brakes for all I was worth, I was still going forward and glancing in the rear-view mirror, I saw one of my rear wheels wobbling along the road behind me in a shower of sparks and like a child crying 'Wait for me! Wait for me!' (kidding) Fortunately, just as the wheel fell over, I came to a grinding halt, a metre or so away from a drop into the sea! Jumping out from my now slightly elevated seat, I flagged down the first car that came along, enjoyed a laugh with the driver and thanked my lucky stars I'd not gone over the edge.

My lift dropped me back at the office and I rang the manager at the garage who, apologising profusely, got the Beetle towed back to the workshop. They bolted the wheel back on and brought the car back to me later in the afternoon. They had been quick to fix the main problem, although I couldn't help but notice they had managed to create another in the process. The pick-up driver hooked my car up by the rear bumper before he had found a more suitable place to tow it from. It was essentially just another cosmetic issue and one easily fixed; I stood on the high side and jumped gently up and down until the bumper levelled out.

I later discovered the cause of this near-disaster. The rear wheel on this model was held in place by just one cotter-pin through a large castellated nut. If the pin breaks (or is not fitted in the first place?) the nut comes loose and the wheel falls off. Simple! I assume VW eventually changed the design.

Having already experienced the reality of developing-country life on Bougainville, none of this really fazed me. And now, being more mobile, I was enjoying every minute of being back in town as my social life started to develop.

Of course, the bigger challenge was at work and in making progress towards a handcraft marketing scheme my boss and I had started discussing.

My recent, and to date largely academic, exposure to management in Britain had focused on existing and usually large-scale Western-style business. But this situation, helping an entire industry sector, comprising individuals and micro-firms, in a developing country was quite a different kettle of fish and requiring a totally different approach. Nevertheless, while considering these more complex issues and contributing ideas towards a national scheme, I found it easy enough to start a few initiatives. With no assistance ever having been provided before in the country, I decided to spend much of my time focusing on promotion. Knowing the market for handcrafts was mainly expat workers or foreign visitors, I immersed myself in producing brochures and arranging publicity through various agencies, targeting them; as well as presenting government services for the locals through the agricultural shows. Although this was all fairly orthodox, one of the many challenges was that there were more ideas for promotion than there were people with the skills to put them into practice. For example, it was extremely difficult to get good-quality graphic design and finished artwork, and many a time wished I could get some help from my brother back in Britain. Unfortunately, the sheer distance and means of communication made that impractical.

While the actual planning for marketing of crafts and artefacts was tremendously interesting, there was something of a fundamental concern behind our work. As Ed had explained when I had visited the Business Development folk and Highland Weavers, the priorities of locals were different from ours. It seemed many were just not prepared to have their social lives and traditional activities (such as growing crops) organised to accommodate the discipline of work that we customarily took for granted. It was a far cry from the organised manufacturing of gaskets in a dedicated factory by people trained to work from nine to five!

Apart from this, as with the textiles, promotion, (as well as planning for marketing generally), was impossible without detailed information about the crafts that we knew to be 'out there'. And, with the only information being from the craftsmen and women in the villages, I needed to travel to often-remote parts of the country and get it myself.

As I sat and drew up my travel plans and booked my flights, I revelled in the fact that, instead of sitting in an office, at last I was now getting somewhere, job-wise and travel-wise.

Enjoyable as my work now was, it was not all that life was about. Just sitting by the bay of an evening was an agreeable experience and not something I had ever really thought of doing in Britain. Perhaps the closest thing to watching sunsets back in Britain would have been having a beer on a pub lawn at conclusion of a summer's day, but here, with the views and the smells of the sea and the smoke from cooking fires, it was all so wonderfully different. I didn't need to go far, even just by going downtown I could see a spectacular sunset. Framing this would be the promontory of Paga Hill silhouetted in the twilight, there would be the breeze on the water fussing the sea into different shades of grey and then shortly the hills would all but disappear and become dotted with the lights of Hanuabada village. This was the trigger for the cicadas and frogs, which, whether we liked it or not, serenaded us with their incessant racket. While nightfall had been a valuable crutch to my spirits on my return to Moresby, now I was in a more positive frame of mind it was something I could even better enjoy. It was breath-taking, annoying and remarkable, all at the same time.

I wasn't such a romantic as this might suggest however, and I soon found there was much more to life than just sitting and looking – the opportunity was there to participate. And after making friends with a few expats who had been in the country for some time, I was soon exploring a variety of wonderful places on day trips out of Moresby.

One popular destination was the Musgrave River, a wildly beautiful area and a great place to swim. One day, eight of us set off in a couple of cars. Mario's was an almost new medium sized Isuzu Florian sedan and the other, a much smaller Mitsubishi Colt. We drove for about half an hour, past the airport and past the

War Cemetery at Bomana, climbing up along some challengingly windy and bumpy roads, through rubber plantations, through spectacular scenery and heading on up to the rainforest on the Sogeri Plateau, 800 metres or so above town.

The views on the way up, particularly from the War Cemetery onwards, were stunning, but the road was heavily rutted. The cars often ran as if they were following tram tracks created by the drying out of the last muddy episode. Then, about three-quarters of the way there and after one too many bumps, Mario came to a dramatic halt, his view blinded by a blast of hot steamy water spewing out from under the bonnet. The fan had hit and punctured the radiator. We were miles from anywhere and despite the possibility of it being vandalised, there was no choice but to leave his lovely new car by the side of the road. Worse however was that the only way to move on was for the eight of us to cram into the Colt. It was such a tight fit we were all very uncomfortable and so decided to make a shorter trip and go to Crystal Rapids on the Laloki River instead.

Literally sitting on top of each other, we eventually passed Sirinumu dam and the hydro-electricity plant. Then, approaching the turn-off from the main road, we spent a little while, even more painfully, bumping and crashing down along the final part of the track before finally arriving at a thankfully peaceful, grassy and wooded area.

Here nature had formed the river into a complete 'U' bend, over which grew a huge old tree. Someone had conveniently tied a rope to an overhanging branch and so we spent the afternoon swinging out from the bank, jumping in Tarzan-like and floating gently downstream. Initially the river was deep and unhurried, but further along it became more urgent and we would have to quickly grab a rock to stop being swept over the rapids. Laughing and chatting awhile, basking in the shallows, we would wade ashore and do it all over again.

After the fun, there was the agony. With so many bodies in the one car, it was a slow and uncomfortable trek back to Moresby. Mario, being the chivalrous type, elected to ride in the boot of the Colt while the other seven of us sat inside. Crushed up together in thirty-degree heat we needed to have all the windows open, and driving back through swirls of dust kicked up from the road made for a pretty hellish journey; even more so for Mario. When we got back to the hostel and opened the boot, he fell out covered from head to toe with a fine layer of dust, ghostlike and half-dead.

This back-to-nature stuff was not without a few risks, but despite this latest hiccup there was never any doubt that we would carry on exploring our new environment.

Meanwhile, back at work, and as part of my gradual conversion towards the customary image of a *waitpela* Public Servant in the tropics, I modified the way I dressed. I hadn't noticed the gradual change in my appearance while I had been over in Bougainville until the day Dick had come over, all crisp white shirt etc. And, when I first started with Business Development, I had got around the office as I had over there, in T-shirt, shorts and rubber thongs. I could not help but notice that all the men in the office (there were very few women) adhered to a contemporary version of the colonial dress code. Nobody said anything about my appearance, but after a while, not wanting to be pulled aside, I conformed.

I started wearing the regulation long white socks, (neatly turned over just below the knee), decent shorts, proper shoes and a clean, and for once ironed, open-neck shirt with a collar. This was *de rigueur* for Public Servants in the offices and for going around town. Indeed, a few of the more senior guys sometimes felt it necessary to wear a collar and tie. I vowed that, I would never go so far in this climate, even in the unlikely event of an invitation to meet the Queen!

Further to wearing the right clothes and to better fit the part of a true Public Servant, the Department issued me with an official Admin briefcase. This was no ordinary briefcase but a heavy, solid, brown leather Gladstone bag, complete with the letters 'TP&NG' neatly embossed in gold on the side. Needing something for my papers, I naturally carried this about wherever I went on business. That was nothing unusual in town, but in moving around the country, calling in on a village for example, it did look a little bizarre, even by PNG standards. Occasionally, I would be sitting in a dugout canoe in my shorts, long white socks and with my Gladstone bag (with gold embossed lettering) balanced precariously on my knees. In front would be my trusty Chimbu native, paddling me down river wearing arse-grass *tasol!*

Obviously, the locals had seen all this nonsense before and, having got used to it, they didn't think the difference in our dress was anything out of the ordinary. But I would have loved to have seen the reaction of my old colleagues to my new expatriate, 'colonial' persona, as they sat in their suites, in the offices in Slough!

CHAPTER 11

CLIMB EVERY MOUNTAIN[51]

The few escapades I had enjoyed around Moresby, swimming in the sea and rivers and sailing in the harbour, had blooded me, so to speak. And while it looked like my job was going to provide plenty of travel around the country, these were business trips and often just from home to office and back. Even visiting craftspeople in their villages was no substitute for the other, more exciting opportunities for adventure I knew to be out there.

It didn't take long before I found some inspiration. While gazing down from my seat in the sky on another flight out of Moresby, I again surveyed the vast expanse of trees and rugged terrain of the Owen Stanley Range. There were more hills and valleys per kilometre as the crow flies here than anywhere else on earth, all providing plenty of opportunities for climbing. And, amongst these many peaks, stood the tallest of the lot, Mount Wilhelm.

I had read about this mountain, rising as it did out of the junction of the three provinces of Chimbu, Western Highlands and Madang, and found it owed its name to a German newspaper correspondent, Hugo Zoller. He had been in the area in 1888 and seeing a range of mountains in the distance and in keeping with the convention of the time, named them on behalf of the German Chancellor, Otto von Bismarck. There were four peaks to the range, coincidentally and conveniently matching the number of Bismarck's kids, so he named them Ottoberg, Herbertberg, Marienberg and, of course, Wilhelmberg. Zoller did not realise, or perhaps did not care to find out, that the local people, the Chimbu, had already named it Enduwa Kamboglu. But, of course, as Westerners drew the maps and the local name was far too tricky for a foreigner to pronounce, Wilhelmberg stuck – for a while at least. After the Germans ceded control to the British, it was renamed Mount Wilhelm. Whatever its name, it was eventually identified as the highest mountain in PNG and even in Oceania[52], higher indeed than Australia's Mount Kosciusko and Europe's Matterhorn.

Apart from all the history, Mount Wilhelm was just sitting there, waiting for us young Turks to climb it. So, with my latest business trip taking me up into the heart of the Highlands[53] and with a bit of careful planning, I managed to end up at a place that was ideal for the start of another adventure.

Nobody batted an eyelid at taking an opportunity to explore the country when tagged on to the end of some business trip as long as it did not interfere with one's work. So, on this occasion, after finishing my work in Goroka and Mount Hagen, I flew off to Kundiawa for the last bit of business, conveniently arriving just before another public holiday.

I would never forget flying into this place for the first time, and it still caused a heart-in-the-mouth moment when coming down on the final approach. But, as usual, the pilot nonchalantly turned us around over the 'ski-jump' drop into the Wahgi Valley, back up towards the mountains and soon had us back down on firm, if not bumpy ground, running along towards the tin shed of an airport. I got a PMV up to the Business Development office and managed a couple of hours' work before meeting up with friends with whom I had arranged to do the climb.

David and Ann Healy (both doctors) and another friend, Richard Hudson, and I made up half of our group of buddies. The other half comprised the two guys I had flown out from Britain with, Martin, who had come over from Rabaul, and Dave Clarkson who worked in the Highlands; plus, a couple of Aussies, Phillip, a dentist and Wendy who were friends from the hostel in Konedobu.

David Healy and Dave Clarkson, in planning the hike, discovered there were two recognised routes to the summit, one for mountaineers and one for hikers. They also found that, while Kundiawa (where they both worked) was close to Mount Wilhelm, it was a fair way across difficult terrain to get to where we could actually start climbing. Considering our lack of any kind of mountaineering experience, there was really no choice and so focused on the route for hikers. This was described by those who they had asked as being 'an easy to moderately difficult climb' in an area of 'untouched vegetation, rivers and magnificent landscape views'.

This route started some way further up to the north, at a little place called Keglsugl, too far away from Kundiawa for us to walk it in the time available. We had to either drive or fly. Dave C managed to score a Land Cruiser from the provincial office of his department, but with all the gear, there was only room for four, so we split into two groups. Dave C, Phillip, Martin and Wendy, would drive up, and, we others, David H, Anne, Richard and I, would fly. So, while the others went off to get their gear and the Toyota, we went and met up with our pilot.

Eventually, after cramming us four and our pile of mountain gear into the tiny cabin, the pilot raced the little Cessna along the grass strip until we practically fell off the end at the ski-jump. With that certain lightness in the stomach we dropped further down towards the Wahgi River before picking up enough speed and lift to start the climb back up towards Keglsugl.

Flying up the valley, we saw what by now I knew to be a typical rural scene. A few gardens and huts scattered around steeply sloping, scrubby grasslands, contrasting with the wider backdrop of rugged and undulating hills and mountains; a few tendrils of smoke from cooking fires proved human inhabitation, but not much else.

Probably because of the more remarkable terrain and scary approach and take-off around Kundiawa, I had become a little blasé about other PNG airstrips. So, as we approached Keglsugl, although it was high up, at around 8,300 feet above sea level, I was happy to see there were no rivers or valleys or sheer cliffs in the immediate vicinity to worry about. Nevertheless, just to test my confidence, the pilot touched down and then immediately hopped us back up in the air for a couple of hundred feet or so before finally landing and running us along a strip that proved to be only marginally better than a ploughed field.

With silent sighs of relief all round, we jumped out, dumped our gear on the ground, and before we knew it, the pilot revved his engine, waved a cheery goodbye, taxied around and took off back to Kundiawa. The four of us stood there in that moment of peaceful silence one gets standing in the middle of a field, at the foothills of the mountains and in the middle of nowhere.

It didn't last long. With the noise of an aeroplane in such remote areas heralding some sort of occasion, a bunch of animated villagers soon surrounded us and, seeing our camping gear, knew exactly what we were after. When Dave asked who would be interested in acting as our porters, all hands quickly shot up in the air. Everyone said 'Yes', even the naked *pikinini's* who could barely carry a water flask. These kids knew they could climb mountain paths faster than any of us old whiteys and were keen to help, just for the fun of it.

We singled out a few of the hardiest-looking characters and struck a deal. No one seemed too sure as to exactly what it was that we had agreed to, but the cost was so trivial, it didn't matter. Negotiations over, without further ado, the gaggle of robust and somewhat scary-looking natives and some snotty-nosed, round-tummied *pikinini's* grabbed our gear, and off we went on our climb.

I had planned to make this trip for some time and had equipped myself with a decent rucksack and boots. However, except for a bit of work at Kuraio, swimming and an occasional round of squash back in Moresby, I had not really done much by way of physical exercise. I was not very fit and even though the porters carried the heavy stuff, I now found it tough going. And of course, it got harder as we got higher. Having already started at 2,500 metres and now heading up towards 3,000, it was not so steep, but the rarefied atmosphere (Actually: lower atmospheric pressure) meant breathing faster and deeper than ever before, and, despite the colder climate, I was soon dripping in perspiration.

We had started by a crossing over a small tributary of the Gwaki River and then entered thick upper montane rainforest. By now we were hiking along steep, roughly cut pathways, sometimes with the small luxury of broken bark laid down by the local villagers who used the route themselves. We walked heads down, checking for a safe footing, climbing up through dark shadows and the blinding contrast of sunlight through the trees. Then, on and up through the jungly rainforest, until gradually we found the sparser nature of the vegetation allowed a glimpse of the hills beyond.

After a couple more hours we broke through the tree line completely at around 3,000 metres and emerged onto alpine-like tundra and grassland. As we reached the lower part of the Pindaunde Valley and in the higher mountain air, we noted an even harsher edge to the climate and quite a different landscape. Here, sprouting out of pale, yellow green tussocky grasses were widely spread-out stands of tree ferns and countless tall cycads. We had been told there would be a large variety of habitats up around the lakes near here and that it would likely be home to quite a few species of mammals and other animals. It was also the haunt of some of the exotic Birds of Paradise for which the country was so famous.

Even though we could not identify much of the flora, we were certainly aware of its variety and abundance because we could not avoid battling our way through it! Sadly, our bashing and crashing didn't exactly encourage the wildlife to make an appearance. And, rather than trying very hard to spot any fauna, we focused more on the more mundane activity of keeping our footing. Cursing the effort and wondering how much longer the agony would last before we could make camp, we struggled on.

Abruptly, during yet another rest, the spokesman for the carriers told us this was as far as the deal went. He said that only a few more kilometres and up over the next brow the track was so clear we could easily manage the rest by ourselves.

We didn't know if the carriers decided to stop here because they had had enough or perhaps simply thought we were crazy to be going to where they knew altitude sickness or exposure ended people's lives. Maybe they would not venture into another tribe's territory, or they were in fear of some malevolent spirits? It was probably because it just was not worth the money. Whatever the reason, they had done their job and so we paid them off, kitted ourselves up with the extra gear, (which seemed to have mysteriously increased in size) and set off for what was the last and hardest stretch.

Before they had gone, the porters told us the path was reasonably safe, but that we should be careful about one particularly steep slope. Only a year earlier an Australian Army sergeant[54] had fallen down a crevasse there and died. And with several other climbers having also died on this track, there was to be no underestimating the dangers for our expedition.

Apart from this warning, we soon knew the real reason the porters had given up. Just over the next brow, the path became exceedingly steep, and it was now agonising under the additional load. The porters knew this all along and made sure they did not exert themselves any more than necessary. We had been helped, but we had also been gently had!

Carrying our own gear vastly increased the effort of the slog, which in turn required even more cursing and blinding to ease the pain. Eventually, when words alone were not enough, we took a break, collapsed on the nearest grassy bank and again disturbed the tranquillity and any wildlife with our rasping breath and rustling clothes.

Thankfully, we had made decent progress and were now within spitting distance of our destination for the day. We could just see, a little way above us, the lower lake, Lake Piunde (female), where we were to camp and then, further above that, the shadowy waterfall feeding into it from the upper lake, Lake Aunde (male). Somewhat dauntingly, we could also see the very steep, rugged and rocky path beside the waterfall through which we were soon going to have to clamber to get to the peak.

Finally, we reached our planned campsite. Here, steep grassy slopes rose a few hundred metres on either side of us, formed by glacial activity many aeons ago. The shadow from these slopes turned the lake surface pitch black and, combined with the rock face and the cascading waterfall, produced a vaguely amphitheatre-like setting: the lake was the watery stage and our camp site the stalls, the best seats in the house!

My hopes of having a roof over my head for the night rose for a second when I spotted an old wooden hut away in the distance. This was the research station for the Australian National University, but, tempting as it looked, David assured us he knew it was strictly out of bounds to climbers. Instead, as planned, we made do with setting up camp on the ground on which we were standing.

The climb of this first day had taken us a little under four hours, including a few stops to catch our breath and for our carriers to have a *smoko*. Certainly no big deal for seasoned hikers, but we were office wallahs and I for one certainly felt the effort. Despite that, after taking a bit of a breather, we set about putting up the tents and importantly, got the Primus going to make a desperately longed-for cup of tea. How British!

I went off to fetch water from the lake and found even this to be a bit of a challenge. Instead of the usual well-defined bank, the lake was full to overflowing making the water and the ground around it both on the same level. The only way to scoop up a kettleful was by wading into several metres of soggy, grassy weed. I got the kettle of water and wet feet, but managed to avoid wetting my pants.

Even setting up the tents proved tricky. All around us were half-metre tussocks of grass interspersed with small patches of relatively bare, flat ground. It was impossible to find an area large enough and flat enough to lay the groundsheet. We ended up putting the tents wherever we could and later wriggled around in our sleeping bags between the grassy tufts to get comfy. I thought again of the old wooden hut and doubted if anyone would have ever known if we had stayed there. However, the bumpiness of the ground proved of little consequence; after all the effort of climbing and the rarefied atmosphere, none of us had trouble sleeping.

Before turning in for the night, we agreed that next day three of us would set off for the top while one would stay back to care for the camp (and make sure nothing went missing) and wait for the other party. I drew the short straw and next morning at four, the others woke me when they went off to conquer the summit. I happily stayed in bed and dozed off again. I was relatively cosy in my sleeping bag and tent and dreamed of how I hadn't regretted not going with Chris and Stewart in climbing Mount Balbi; they had slept in the bush without even these simple comforts!

Later, by way of something to occupy myself, I climbed up the southern most of the steep grassy sides of our valley. The lower part of the slope was in the shade and was cool, but as I climbed higher and into the full sunlight, it again became hot and hard work. It was worth it, there was a magnificent view from on top of the ridge and I could see the serried ranks of other peaks for miles around. I simply sat and lazed and enjoyed the moment. As the morning progressed the shadows came off the lake and the sky and clouds gradually turned it into a giant disc of blue and white. Then the wind got up a little and rustled the grasses and, getting chilly, I skidded and slid back down to camp.

No sooner was I back than Dave, Wendy, Phil and Martin arrived with cries of excitement and now-familiar exclamations of exhaustion (as if I didn't know already). Then, as they were setting up camp, and with perfect timing, David, Annie and Richard returned from their climb to summit. They had all got there of course and prattled on excitedly about the tremendous view.

According to them, neither the effort involved nor the 'rarefied atmosphere' was such a big deal. But, apparently, the lower atmospheric pressure at this altitude, resulting in less oxygen taken in with each breath, could be a serious health issue and, as a worst-case scenario, could even lead to death. With two medicos in the group, I figured the 'no big deal' was partly your typical British understatement and noted all three complained of mild headaches for hours afterwards.

Next day, it was my turn and this time five of us set off for the top. After a supposedly healthy (but quite disgusting to taste) breakfast of porridge, we left the base camp around four-thirty to make sure we got to the summit around daybreak and hopefully before the clouds came in.

We made the first slog up through the rugged rocky passage from Piunde to Aunde in good time to see moonlight and misty clouds swathing the waters. Then, although not considered a 'technical climb', once past Aunde it really did become quite hazardous. With loose stones and slippery rocks in many places, we needed to watch our footing; I muttered to myself 'Keep your eyes on the ground, Nicholas!' However, walking in single-file through narrow rocky pathways, I must admit the hypnotic rhythm of Wendy's swaying backside, atop those beautiful tanned legs (ending somewhat incongruously in chunky climbing boots), sometimes distracted me. A diversion from Mother Nature!

Shortly before daylight, after much huffing and puffing, we could see the lights of Madang twinkling away on the coast, a hundred or so kilometres to the north east. We climbed and climbed and worked hard for what seemed an eternity; I couldn't recall ever having exerted myself for so long before. But then, gradually, after panting and scrambling our way even higher, cloudy mist started eddying around us. Soon a dark grey fog obscured our view beyond a few metres, and then almost as quickly thinned to a ghostly haze, then back again to a dense, impenetrable cloud. We now needed serious concentration to stay on track and find our way.

We took another short break at the glacial passage known as Saddle Camp, then soon after we came across patches of snow. As we got closer to the top, it became even colder and the snow even thicker, particularly on flat surfaces. Fortunately, it was not so slippery; we were more intrigued by the novelty of there being any snow at all, because we were only 500 kilometres from the equator. But there again of course, we were now also several kilometres up above all that steamy tropical heat.

We survived the clouds, the cold and the exertion and finally, after something like a four-and-a-half-hour slog, made it to the summit at 14,793 feet (4,508 metres) above sea level. With the airstrip at Keglsugl at about 8,000 feet, we had managed to climb the last and loftiest 7,000 feet of it all.

Thankful for the chance to rest, we simply sat and enjoyed the peace and beauty of the craggy place and watched the spectacular sunrise unfold. With the colours of the clouds and the sky enhanced by the more rarefied air, we laughed that their brilliance was because we were now just that much closer to heaven!

The view was terrific and, for a short time at least, we could see about two hundred miles in all directions. We looked towards Karkar Island in the north, Wapenamanda in the Enga Province to the west, the Markham Valley in the Morobe Province eastwards and Kikori in the south. Of course, although we knew these places were there, we could not categorically identify each one, so we just turned to face the points of the compass.

But now in full light, and looking again to the north-east, we could at least pick out the silver thread of the Ramu River. And, as earlier in our trek, we could also see the lights of Madang, still burning brightly, a hundred kilometres or so away up on the coast.

For a short while the view was clear and far into the distance, but sure enough, the clouds started coming in again, and quickly too. It was time to go, if we did not want to miss the path. We hurriedly formed ourselves into a group, took the obligatory photographs, signed the book and started jogging back down before we could lose our way.

The author and friends, Mount Wilhelm, 1973

Just above Lake Aunde, in the better light of our descent, we saw a few bits of aluminium, wreckage from a F-7A Liberator that had crashed there during WWII. Apparently, the plane took off on a photo-reconnaissance from Nadzab, south-east of here, in May 1944. Crashing into the side of the mountain after getting lost, all eleven crew had perished. Being slightly more fortunate, we got back down to our base camp and crashed in a sweaty pile of exhaustion.

The spectacular scenery, the waterfall, the forest, the mountain ridges, alpine grasslands and the view of the coastline from the summit had all been quite wonderful. It was definitely worth the effort and the mild headaches. Secretly however, being a bit of a lazy fellow at heart, I was glad it was over. It was all too much like hard work for me!

We relaxed and soaked up the beauty of the place without the distraction of excessive physical effort and camped for another night at Lake Piunde. Next day, we all walked back down to

Keglsugl together, and while the others found their Toyota and set off to drive back, my gang rendezvoused with the pilot as arranged. All muddy and smelly, we crammed back into the same tiny Cessna and flew off, back down to Kundiawa.

After booking into the Chimbu Lodge, all eight of us intrepid hikers enjoyed a second, lazy phase of recovery and later that evening, a celebratory dinner. Happy and exhausted, that night I swore a regular bed had never felt so good.

The following day Dave H and Ann went back home and Martin flew back to Rabaul, while Dave C, Phil, Richard, Wendy and I stayed on. Almost fully recovered and fighting my inherent laziness, I joined these others on another excursion. We were in the area anyway and the opportunity of hiking the Chimbu Gorge presented an appropriate conclusion for our climbing expedition.

Although the terrain around Kundiawa is as steep and rugged as that around Mount Wilhelm, this time we mostly stayed on the level. We set off along the dirt road out of town and up the right branch of the gorge, with the Chimbu River rushing alongside and beneath us[55]. We were looking out for some caves we had been told about that were once burial sites for local warriors.

Initially we saw nothing but a patchwork of neatly planted gardens covering the hillsides above us, but then Phil spotted a cave a little way up off the road and we all went to have a quick peek. It was not particularly deep but, hearing that it was the habit of some tribes to place their deceased sitting up instead of lying prone, we thought we should find the skeleton of someone sitting around. We must have got the wrong cave; there were a few stalagmites and stalactites, but other than the dank smell of bat droppings, disappointingly, there was not the slightest vestige of any warriors, sitting, standing or even hanging around. It was not a particularly pleasant place and so, with nothing else to keep our attention, we made a hasty exit.

Later, walking in single-file and further along the now shady path, we came across a perilous-looking wire bridge over the Chimbu River. Just at that very moment, a rather nasty little snake slid out of the hedgerow and onto the path right in front of me. Coming to a sudden stop, Dave bumped into me and swore loudly, thinking I was going to chicken out over the bridge. But then, seeing the snake slithering away, he chided me saying, 'It's only a little snake!'

The wire bridge over the Wahgi River

We enjoyed the rest of the wild scenery walking back along the path without any further excitement, conveniently arriving back in Kundiawa just in time for a sundowner.

For Phil and Wendy, the expedition was over the following day. They flew back to Moresby, but I stayed back with Richard and Dave. That evening, at the club, retelling the events of the past few days to whoever would listen, we soaked up a few more beers and whiskies, and watched the Aussies gambling away at Two-Up. We learned that soldiers in the First World War had played the game extensively and now they played it on ANZAC Day out of respect and to mark a shared experience with Diggers through the ages, and, of course, just for the fun of it.

Subsequently, I flew back to Moresby with Richard and Dave, having just enjoyed a couple of the most exhilarating weeks of my life.

But then I fell sick!

I'd had a good run, but ironically I was knocked out by the 'London 'flu'. I had come all this way to the other side of the world to cop this! Apparently, I was lucky. This type-A virus caused many deaths, which confusingly, were mainly in North America. I endured such a debilitating combination of headache, backache, runny nose, sore eyes, sore throat and fever that I was wiped out for a week. Must have been something in the water! Rubbing salt into the wound, so to speak, I wasted money on medicines and doctors' fees that made absolutely no difference. And, worse still, I later found I could have gone to the hospital and got it all for free, because I was employed on local terms and conditions.

Eventually I gained enough energy to get back into the swing of work, and by mid-year I was happy to hear the news that I was not going to Goroka to manage Highland Weavers after all. Ed had found another volunteer for the job. It would have been an interesting challenge, but I was relieved. The Department wanted me to carry on the marketing work at HQ, something that comprised far broader socio-economic implications and, more importantly for me, far greater opportunities for travel.

Margaret and I had probably gone as far as we could with the technical and marketing issues for the woven goods for the time being. It was now a matter of putting the recommendations into practice, getting on with training of weavers, improving quality and producing the goods.

While all this was in play, I started having some nagging concerns about the overall nature of our task. I was more than comfortable with the encouragement of selling so-called real ethnic carvings, but felt private enterprise, not the government, was already doing the actual selling quite effectively. There were quite a few shops in Moresby and other towns around the country doing what looked like a reasonable trade. My overriding concern was that neither the government nor the private sector should allow the debasement of these crafts and production of tourist rubbish, which appeared to be a real possibility.

By now I'd had a good look around and seen a fair amount of both artefacts and handcrafts. Even Blind Freddy could tell the difference between Western-style tourist items (pottery, woollen

Wood carver at work

blankets, wooden bowls, etc.) and the items of ethnic origin (shields, food hooks, Mwai masks etc.) commonly referred to as 'artefacts'. They were distinctly different and suited different uses and interests of buyers. But just to make it a little trickier, many of the so-called artefacts were also obviously tourist items and there again, some were like items of museum quality[56].

Arising from all this, some fundamental differences between Hovey and myself in how we should proceed came to the fore. On the one hand, he wanted us (the Administration and me) to encourage the manufacture and marketing of contemporary carvings based on traditional designs. On the other hand, and quite justifiably, there was pressure on the government to preserve local culture.

Encouraging the use of traditional designs in Western-style crafts was okay by me. Indeed, both Margaret and I agreed on incorporating local patterns into the blankets. Unfortunately, Hovey was the sort of person who thought plastic flowers were wonderful and wanted to go one step further. If he could get people to produce traditional masks in great volume, he would. And that was certainly not okay by me. However, he was the boss and to put his idea into effect he imported a sophisticated (and costly) pantograph duplicating machine from Germany. He set this up in the Small Industries Development Centre, hired an operator to make a wooden Sepik mask master and then started trials to copy it. I, and others were horrified. This machine could, potentially, churn out thousands of replicas, and what that would do for local craftsmen did not bear thinking about. Fortunately, for one reason or other, the machine never worked properly and it was eventually left to collect dust, sitting idly in the corner of the workshop.

I realised that even replicating a carving for money, rather than its original traditional purpose, was a diminution of the culture. But at the same time, I wholeheartedly agreed with encouraging locals to participate in the economy and enjoy a better quality of life. However, while I had any sway in the matter, all the crafts were to be made by artisans using their traditional skills in as authentic a fashion as possible. And I was determined to stand my ground on the issue.

Then there was the other important point of difference between my boss and myself over the nature of government assistance to the sector. I felt very strongly that the government should only be involved in encouraging individuals and businesses to make and trade handcrafts. I never believed the Administration should get involved in buying and selling commercially. Of course, it was always going to be necessary to buy a few handcrafts and commercial artefacts for photographs to help promote the industry, or as samples to show to prospective purchasers, but not to buy and sell them as a business. Awkwardly, my boss believed the government should buy and sell.

Around the time my boss and I were debating all this, the PNG Government was being urged to set up a national council[57], to 'formulate a programme for the preservation and development of all aspects of culture and the arts.' With so much influence on PNG society from outsiders, the anthropologists who were knowledgeable about such things were sensibly concerned for the future of the customs, songs, dances and other means of artistic expression. This admirable drive for cultural preservation included traditional artefacts. The big question then was, what artefacts should be preserved as part of the culture and what could, or should, be encouraged to be made and sold as a handcraft?

This difficulty in definition involved considerable debate and resulted in a degree of antipathy between those wishing to protect and Business Development wishing to promote. Those involved in setting up the council were worried Business Development would spoil PNG's culture by encouraging commercialisation, while we at Business Development thought those setting up the council were creating an unnecessarily high hurdle for Papua New Guinean craftsmen to participate in the economy.[58]

These discussions went on forever, but even though I was aware of it all, I just carried on with my marketing efforts and planning for the means by which Business Development could encourage the handcrafts sector more comprehensively without upsetting the culture or us getting involved in trading. And, so, in line with this implicit understanding, I continued my fact-finding work in marketing and went up to Wewak and Madang on another exploratory hunt for handcrafts.

For some reason best known to the airlines and maybe because of the weather, I ended up flying from Mount Hagen to Wewak via Lae, zigzagging east to west. This long way around for not much more than a one-hour flight, perhaps two at the most, ended up taking me all day. I spent most of the time kicking my heels around airport lounges wondering if flights would ever leave!

I finally arrived in Wewak, the last largish Papua New Guinean town just before the city of Jayapura over the border in Irian Jaya. It fascinated me that Indonesia was so close but still essentially out of reach, at least while I was travelling on business, and I aimed to visit that side of the island one day.

Meanwhile, after eventually checking into my fancy hotel and having yet another lovely meal, I decided to relax for a while. Despite not having done much all day, I was weary from the stress of flying and figured I deserved a break. I went and sat on the low cliff overlooking the bay and enjoyed another idyllic scene, a bonus no level of wages would ever rival. The ubiquitous palm trees in the distance, starkly silhouetted in the moonlight, a thin stream of smoke from a cooking fire on Mushu Island just across the water, the hint of frangipani on the still, warm evening air… truly magical!

Next day, I spent time looking around the town, photographing and recording details of the large variety of handcrafts available: masks, drums, bilums (string bags) and wood carvings etc., but because of my delayed arrival I did not have enough time to capture all the details. I would have to come back again to do my investigation justice.

I flew back east again, back to Madang. As well as having an attractive name (and certainly much less of a mouthful than the original of Friedrich-Wilhelmshaven given by the Germans), this was one of the oldest established towns in the PNG and probably one of the most beautiful. Even before I arrived, seeing the many plantations up and down the coast from the air, all so neatly laid out, Madang looked pretty. The presence of such an enormous number of palm trees reminded me again of Kuraio. Just offshore, on Kar Kar Island, there were even more palms. Apparently, this one island produced half the copra of the entire province and most of the cocoa. They were lucky, as being just a little way off from the mainland, getting their produce to market would be far easier than from Kuraio.

Wandering around Madang, I found the place to be full of parks and waterways, grassy pathways and of course the ubiquitous palm trees, some so old they were slanting at such impossible angles to the ground they made good playthings for the *pikinini's*. The town was on a peninsula jutting out into the Bismarck Sea, and I saw the waters had formed a couple of lagoons, one of which came almost into the centre of town. Then, out at Kaliboro Point, I came across the ninety-foot Coastwatcher's monument. To me it looked to me a bit like a concrete spaceship but I discovered it was in fact a fully functioning lighthouse. And I read that it had been unveiled in 1959 as a memorial to the Allied servicemen and locals who sacrificed themselves in protecting the country by providing intelligence from behind enemy lines that lead to the sinking of enemy ships and warning of impending air attacks during the Second World War.[59]

Despite the poignancy this engendered, what with the sea on one side, jungle on the other and the general layout, Madang was a delightful oasis. Although I was only there for three days, I felt I could easily have spent thirty or more.

The following day, getting back to work, I explained to the Business Development OIC that I was there to investigate the crafts in the area and that my boss had said I should look at the pottery in particular. Being a bit surprised, he said that, in addition to pots, he knew of villagers who made drums, wooden plates, bark belts and many other things and that I should also look at these. I insisted that as I had found a similarly large variety of crafts in Wewak, but had insufficient time to capture details of everything, I would have to come back again, but this time I would focus on the pots. Accordingly, he allocated a local driver and a Toyota for the day and off we went, a couple of kilometres inland to the little village of Yabob.

Here I met up with the headman, who, with the help of my driver/interpreter, told me how his people came to be in the area. He said they had moved there when they'd had to abandon their original village, just offshore from Madang, after the Japanese destroyed it during their invasion. After the brief history lesson, he then went on to tell me it was the women (here and in the twin village of Bilbil) who produced the pots. They had made them for their own use, from time immemorial and used them also as a form of currency in bartering for food and for various goods. Indeed, reading up about this later, I found this had formed part of a vast trade network spreading from the Siassi Islands of Morobe Province to Kar Kar Island in the north.[60]

As we talked, the headman called one of the women over to show me how they made the pots by hand. I was surprised to see that, instead of being thrown on a wheel she took a lump of clay, a little larger than a cricket ball, in her left hand, patted it into an egg shape and then, plunging her thumb into the top, gradually twisted the clay around, some fingers on the inside and others outside. She slowly formed the wall and the distinctive

Yabob woman making pot by hand

sharp ridge about a third of the way down and then smoothed the surface by patting it with a wooden spatula. No machinery involved.

The headman told me, after allowing time for pots to dry in the sun, they then painted them with a dark yellow slip and baked them on an open wood fire. Care was necessary here to ensure the surface was not burned, as this would leave it with a dark smoky blemish. But, if successful, the reaction of the heat to the slip made the pot a pleasant reddish ochre colour.

The pots were attractive and certainly distinctive and I thought they would sell well, but being earthenware, they were not particularly strong so careful and effective packaging would be necessary when shipping to other markets and for them to arrive in one piece. I bought a couple as photographic subjects for use in promotional material.

Having done with the demonstration and rather peremptorily dismissing the potter, the headman then hurried back into his hut and brought out a superb blackwood bow and set of arrows. He carefully explained how the arrows were each made to suit a different purpose. Pointing to one with a series of multi-serrated tips, he said it was for fishing and the serrations were there to stop the fish from slipping away. Another arrow sported a stub-end, specially designed to stun a bird of paradise rather than pierce its skin and have the blood ruin the feathers they used for ceremonial headdresses.

Clearly, he wanted me to buy the set, and of course I just could not refuse. So, carefully loading bow, arrows and pots into the Toyota and thanking the headman, we set off back into town.

When I got back to the hotel that evening, I thought word must have somehow got around there was a *waitpela* in town interested in handcrafts, because a couple of local craftsmen came over and laid out their wares in the lobby. But it was nothing to do with me at all – this was the way they usually made sales. Many craftsmen preferred to sell direct to the public, rather than having their price bargained down by a local dealer. By now I knew that many of the best woodcarvings and handcrafts came from Madang and the Sepik and these locals had certainly brought along a fair cross-section to sell. There were some beautiful necklaces, smallish, 20-30 cm crocodiles carved of wood, other decorations of polished seeds, more bows and arrows, and some male and female figures, purportedly of ancestral heroes, again carved from wood. But there were no drums, wooden plates or bark belts!

I bought a couple of items that looked representative of what I had seen around town to add to the other examples of artefacts and crafts I had bought earlier. My collection was growing and now included a yam mask, a food hook, a small crocodile, the bow and arrows, two kundus, a fierce and frightening Sepik mask and a stone axe, as well as a one and half metre-long wooden carving of a Kamanggabi spirit. As the Business Development Officer had told me and as I was now beginning to discover there was a huge variety of craft and artefacts made. However, I decided this would be enough for the moment because there would be quite enough work to go on with in researching the background of each item, have them photographed and then develop and print promotional material for each item.

Back in Moresby, before I could do all that, I needed to deal with another, more urgent, task. Before I had left on this trip, I had been working on a brochure to promote the hand-woven products. I had asked the government printer for finished copies by the end of July to coincide with the launch of the new range of woven items Margaret had developed and in time for the Hagen Show. Part of this exercise had involved a modelling shoot and, after having managed to persuade the government photographer and one of the prettiest local girls in the office to help, we drove over to a nice spot we knew would provide an appropriate backdrop. In the process of unloading and readying his camera equipment, Alistair, the photographer, who was a bit of a supercilious braggart, told us that his Hasselblad gear cost more than the car we had just driven over in! Thinking of my second-hand 35mm Pentax (without an exposure meter) I feigned being impressed and got on with the job of directing the young lady in what to wear and how to pose.

On completion Alistair had captured plenty of photographs of each of the ponchos and wraps worn by the young lady, and so I had left him with the request to develop and print the best for the brochure. That had been some weeks earlier, but when I got back to Moresby, Alistair still hadn't even printed the proofs! I hurried round to sweet-talk him to meet my deadline and thankfully, he obliged. But now I was starting to realise that nothing much happened in my area of work unless I did it myself or kept nagging those others I had asked. I supposed this would be the same in the Public Service whether in PNG or Australia. People worked to their own schedule, and urgency was anathema to them. Why should they hurry, when the job was near enough for life?

Then, just before going up to Hagen, there was another disturbance in POM. After the skirmish at the Moresby Show earlier, I thought it unlikely that we would see another; things had settled down, and we all hoped it had been a one-off, cause unknown. However, it was not to be. Whoever was in charge had selected a rugby team from the New Guinea Highlands to compete against a team of Papuans for the annual play-off in Port Moresby. This was a remarkably bad decision, as the animosity between the Papuan coastal people and those from the Highlands was well known. Many Papuans were upset because they believed Highlanders had settled in their area and stolen their jobs. As it had been with Father Peter on Bougainville, there was a degree of racial prejudice and it didn't help that Highlanders had distinctively different physical features from Papuans and were easy to spot around town!

On this occasion, it seemed an off-hand remark by a female Papuan spectator at the game caused an initial scuffle. Although it was quite localised, it unfortunately brought this underlying tension to the fore. The fight[61] quickly developed, and the mob broke out of the sports grounds and spilt out along Waigani Drive just as my mountaineer mate Richard Hudson was driving in the immediate area. He was quite animated when he got back to the hostel.

"Wow guys, that was a bit hairy!" he said. "I was driving slowly through the crowd of locals and it looked like I was okay. But, then, part way through, someone threw a bloody great rock through my windscreen. Bastards! It will cost a fortune. I'm okay, but it was a bit scary, there was glass everywhere!"

"What's it all about, Richie?" I asked.

"Well, it was the footy match for sure. We expats weren't targeted specifically and I'm sure it was nothing personal."

"Are you really sure? If only they knew you!"

We all agreed that it was not he, as a white expatriate, who was the target, but that he had just been in the wrong area when feelings were running high.

Richard went on to explain that he had seen a few other cars and buses also caught up in the fuss. He had heard they also had their windscreens smashed and a few people on board the buses were hurt. We all hoped it would settle down and soon be over, but the next day, emotions flared up again. There were more scuffles between Highlanders and Papuans in Koki Market and a few other places around town, and someone even went to the trouble of cutting down telephone lines (why that was no one seemed to know). When it looked like the situation might become serious, Secretary Matane said for the women in the offices to go home. By mid-afternoon, he told all other workers in downtown Moresby to go.

As far as I was concerned the whole affair was a big nuisance as it further delayed my work for the Hagen Show. But I left the office around two-thirty anyway, and then, rather than going back to the hostel, I drove around town with my camera to see if I could get some shots of the action. I soon came across a gaggle of university students, some of whom were very drunk, half-heartedly blocking the road and shouting and yelling obscenities. With so many police around and with the students obviously not considering me a target of their anger, they moved over and let me drive through. However, I didn't push my luck with the camera when I recognised some might not take too kindly to being photographed.

I went back to the hostel and heard later that the situation was still serious in some areas. Moresby was on edge, so I decided not to go out again for a little while. No one seemed to know anything except that the whole affair was a coastal Papuan versus Highlander thing. After a couple of days, it all fizzled out, and peace settled over town once more. It could have been worse.

And, despite there being little chance of any of this news finding its way into Britain and to be on the safe side, I wrote home to Mum to say there was nothing to worry about.

After all this excitement, and having finally got my brochure printed, I went up to Mount Hagen to undertake two jobs: preparing for the official opening of our Small Industries Sericulture Centre and helping organise the Department's exhibit out at the Kagamuga showgrounds.

The Department had built the Sericulture Centre to demonstrate the viability of growing silk and as another way for Papua New Guineans to participate in the economy. It had been operating for a few months to sort out any teething problems and was now ready for the official opening. With Chief Minister Somare officiating and all the press invited, this was a carefully staged event, to help raise the profile of the efforts of our Department.

But, before attending to this, I decided to check out our stand. To get there, I first had to navigate rows of chanting and spear-thrusting Huli tribesmen lined up on either side of the muddy road leading into the showgrounds. With their faces painted in bright yellow ochre, 'Pirate Hat' wigs on top and bark belts and 'arse-grass' around the nether regions, they certainly made for a colourful lot. But with the bone through the nose and bodies glistening darkly in the sun from all the charcoal and pig grease, they also had quite a sinister appearance!

I ran the gauntlet believing they would not dare attack an expatriate and assured myself that their chanting was nothing personal; it was just their warm-up act and show of strength for the main event. Nevertheless, they were quite an intimidating looking bunch and I hurried on past the tips of their spears, being careful not to upset any of them.

Getting to the stand I found our local Department staff had already done an excellent job. Everything was displayed well and in good order. We were selling woven goods from Highland Weavers, but it did not totally contradict my aim that the government should not get involved in trading. As it was a one-off event and with prices set at the same level as the retailers in town, there was no hint of undercutting. Plus of course, it did help reduce costs.

As the staff didn't need my help, after a bit of a chat and confirming that they had everything they needed and were happy to look after things, I left them to it and went back the way I had come. The Huli were still chanting and thrusting in full force, but now, with greater confidence, I lingered awhile to take photographs before running the gauntlet again.

Getting back to the silk centre, I focused on arrangements for the grand opening. I had to make do with what I could get hold of; it was all very basic. Firstly, as Somare was not a particularly tall fellow I thought I would get something to help set the scene,

Huli Tribesman – Mount Hagen

make him stand out a little. I borrowed some table-tennis tables from a local club, cajoled some concrete blocks out of the Public Works Department ('You must return them afterwards!') and set up a simple dais for him to stand on whilst he made his speech.

The bronze plaque proudly announcing that the Chief Minister had opened the centre on such and such a date, had already been fixed to the wall by the time I arrived. But, then according to the usual protocol, it needed unveiling. I really wanted one of those little drawstring curtain affairs, but with no such luxury to hand I had to improvise, and quickly. I managed to find a decent sized national flag, fixed one corner firmly to the wall over the plaque with a thumbtack and then, very lightly, pinned it up at the opposite corner.

Just before the ceremony, I whispered to Somare to pull gently on the right-hand side of the flag and simply let it go at the appropriate moment in his speech. I prayed the pin would not come out and hit him in the eye. The other worry was that the whole flag would fall on the ground, which would be embarrassing! Thankfully, Somare pulled with a suitable amount of force, the flag draped away nicely to one side and, with his words of encouragement, the centre was officially open.

Somare opening Silk Centre, Mount Hagen 1973

Somare and I shared a few pleasantries after the speeches, but before we could talk of anything of consequence, his minder whisked him away. Nevertheless, I was pleased to have met the man, even if it had been very briefly.

Later, after the show, I heard our Department stand had taken lots of enquiries for handcrafts and sold over $1,000 worth of blankets, ponchos, floor rugs and other hand-woven items. This was excellent, especially considering that our target market was predominantly resident expats and the few tourists from Australia and New Zealand. The icing on the cake was that our display, set up by our local staff, won first prize in the Departmental Exhibits category. I really had little to do with it, but I was pleased to know that my boss and Matane were happy with the outcome.

Come August and September, Moresby was again brown and shrivelled up. I had seen the place turn green after my return from Bougainville in February, but now there had not been decent rain since April, and the hills were looking quite ugly. Their natural drab straw-coloured sides were scarred with ragged black patches where any remaining grass had burned off, probably ignited by the sun on broken beer bottles. The fire brigade was often busy preventing houses from getting caught up and incinerated in the grassy blaze.

Although it was 'the dry' and the temperature only hovered around twenty-eight Celsius or so, it was still tiringly humid in the day. It cooled down in the evening which was a relief and by early morning the temperature had dropped to just ten degrees or so. It was quite cold!

And, so, apart from the chilly night air, the constant chirruping of crickets, the howling of dogs, a couple of riots, having my car damaged by some rock-throwing *kanaka* and the fact that the

Leader of the Opposition suddenly upped and died, all was well in the world. The sad demise of a politician had no effect on my daily life, and I managed to fix the problem of the temperature at night with a Highland Weavers blanket, naturally! But the various hassles at the hostel were getting on my nerves. I had been trying to find somewhere else to live for quite a while and finally, in late September 1973, I managed to get an Administration leave house a little way out in the suburbs. The leave house arrangement was popular amongst expats because it was reckoned to be safer to have another expat stay in the house when away rather than to let it lie empty and give anyone the opportunity to break in and steal things. Indeed, because break-ins were commonplace, some expats had developed a particularly repulsive method of deterrence. They would get their *haus-boi* to put their pet dog in a sack and then beat the poor thing with a stick. The dog would then naturally associate Papua New Guineans with a potential beating and growl or bark, or even attack, when any *kanaka* came near the house. Luckily my leave house did not come with a dog; although it did provide me with the luxury of an excellent stereo, a massive deep freeze and all the mod cons one could think of. Now I had both a fantastic job and accommodation that was far superior to anything I had ever enjoyed in England - including the family home!

Whilst I was now more comfortable with my living arrangements life also seemed to get even better at work. After I had given a talk about my work at a Department meeting one day, I came to the attention of the big man himself. The Secretary of the Department of Business Development, Paulius Matane[62] (later to become Governor-General) came over and invited me over to his place for a drink. As a mere Technical Officer (Grade 1), I didn't usually aspire to communicate directly, let alone socialise, with heads of departments, so I felt both honoured, and a little intimidated. I was not sure why he had invited me. Was he just being friendly?

As it turned out it could not have been more informal. Paulius and I sat side by side on the front steps of his house, drinking SP[63] out of the bottle. We chatted away for some time about the problems and prospects for socio-economic development while his two beautiful kids played around in the front yard. Never being one to shy away from an opportunity, I gave Matane my two-bobs' worth, even if it was from the perspective of a newcomer with only a superficial understanding of how administrations worked or the real social issues of developing a whole country. However, this time I felt the meeting was of value. I was able to talk about my ideas for small industries and crafts development with someone in a position of authority and hopefully contributed something worthwhile; very different from my meeting with the very condescending Administrator! After getting back to my fancy leave-house, I then wondered what, if any, consequences there might be from my meeting. As with all his discussions, I am sure Matane took on board whatever he thought was appropriate and discarded the rest. But there must have been a reason for him inviting me over in the first place. I hoped I had not said anything untoward, and supposed only time would tell.

So, now, on top of the move to more up-market accommodation, I was getting to meet, albeit on the fringe, some important and smart people. The British High Commissioner had invited me for drinks; I had chatted with the Administrator; I had briefly met the Chief Minister, and now I had enjoyed a few beers with the Departmental Secretary. Things were definitely on the up!

CHAPTER 12

WE NEARLY DIDN'T MAKE IT

Just to bring me back down to earth, so to speak, and remind me of my mortality, my next adventure involved a bit of a scare.

Come October the adventure drug had kicked in again and I set about planning to climb another mountain. Mount Wilhelm had been both agony and ecstasy, and despite the effort involved, it had been great fun and I wanted more.

A couple of the friends with whom I had climbed Mt. Wilhelm, David and Anne Healy, had transferred from their original project in Kundiawa to Mendi in the Southern Highlands. Coincidentally, this happened to be in the foothills of the second highest mountain in PNG, Mount Giluwe. So, naturally, having climbed the highest, this had to be next.

I rang David and discussed the idea, and he said that with

the township of Mendi located at 1,675 metres above sea level and with Mount Giluwe rising to 4,368, the climb would still be over 2,500 metres. We knew our trek up Mount Wilhelm had effectively been only a little over 2,000 metres, so we were both a bit surprised when David said he had been told we did not require any camping gear because we could readily get to the summit of Giluwe and back in a day. Apparently, it was still not mountaineering stuff, but it did seem an awful long way for a one-day hike. Anyway, whatever the distance I was game to give it a go, and arranged to fly over and stay with David and Anne for a couple of days.

Bright and early next morning I was down at Jacksons to catch the six-thirty flight for Mendi. Climbing aboard I saw we were a full complement of six with the last seat for me right behind the pilot. We taxied out, took off, banked around to the west, and gradually started climbing. I had taken some comfort from the pilot's careful pre-take-off checks and the fact that this was a Beechcraft Baron, a twin-engine plane, my theory being that if one engine was to fail, at least there was another to keep us going! With so many small planes zigzagging around the country we were all aware of PNG's reputation for scary flying. Indeed, with the frequently stormy weather I had already experienced plenty of heart stopping bumpy rides!

Whilst pondering all this and watching the clouds roll away beneath us, we gradually got up to around 10,000 feet and levelled out. Suddenly, the propeller on my side came to a spluttering stop, right beside me. The engine had cut out!

My first thought was how clean and shiny the steel of the propeller blades looked, but even before I had had time to think further, lo and behold, the port engine did the same thing!

Simultaneously we started dropping, not in a dive, but the whole body of the plane started fluttering clumsily down like a falling leaf. There was not the slightest hint of gliding. No one said a word. Everyone's face was pale, and I swear I saw the hair on the back of the pilot's neck stand up on end! I looked around in the cabin and, silence, we all knew we were going to die.

Now it was totally grey outside as we fell through the clouds. I knew the mountain stood at over fourteen thousand feet, and here we were falling from ten thousand. Where was the mountain? Visibility was zero. We couldn't see any land. Death would be very sudden!

The next few seconds passed like hours. We continued falling awkwardly in a stomach-churning erratic descent, while, despite his evident fear, with all due credit, the pilot calmly went through his routine of checking switches and knobs and then, somewhat nonchalantly, pressed the starter button! To our sweet relief, the right-hand engine coughed and, with a little puff of smoke from the exhaust, the propeller rotated and disappeared into that wonderful, reassuring blur. The pilot did the same for the port side engine and got that started, and we gradually stopped falling. After dropping a couple of thousand feet we resumed normal flying attitude, we levelled out and started to gain altitude again, flying under power.

I regained a degree of equanimity as the intense aura of focus gradually faded. But it wasn't over yet! No one said anything as we flew on towards Mendi, all of us simply sat there stunned, wondering if the engines would stop again and compel us to crash. It was dreadfully unnerving.

Eventually, on approaching Mendi, and still in thick cloud, the pilot started to descend. But then, after circling around a couple of times, to everyone's dismay, we climbed back up again. He couldn't see the airstrip (or the mountain) because it was clouded in. We still could not land!

The pilot then flew us on towards Mount Hagen to find out if we could land there, but clouds also obscured our view of the airstrip there. After an eternity, we flew south again and now, seeing the coastline through thinning clouds, the pilot got his bearings and finally returned us to Moresby. It had been three hours since we had set out on a one-hour flight. All the time we had been in the air and with no one game enough to talk to the pilot about the engines, we had been living in a state of fear. A truly horrible experience!

After we landed, the pilot (who I now saw was about my age, perhaps even younger) explained what had happened. He said it was standard safety procedure to take off with the engines fed from auxiliary fuel tanks, then, sometime later, in flight and after gaining altitude, to switch over to the main tanks. He said he thought he had switched over but failed to do so, and both engines were starved of fuel. He quickly added in his own defence (although it was of no comfort to us) that there had been some accidents caused by mistakes in using the Baron's fuel management system, even though the one on this model was simpler than others. Learning all this after the event was all well and good, but not knowing about it at the time meant we had all endured an almighty and long-drawn-out scare.

Nevertheless, still determined to get to Mendi and climb Mount Giluwe, I boarded another aircraft and left POM for a second try. This time it was a Cessna 402, which somehow felt much better. I decided I did not like Beechcraft Barons, even if they did have two engines. This was quite irrational because, apparently, although requiring some skilful piloting, the Beechcraft could maintain height on one engine at full power. But there again, they cannot glide any significant distance without any power, which was our scenario, and it was highly unlikely that they could maintain height. We had been lucky!

Eventually, I got to Mendi and was met by David, who naturally wondered why the delay. The emotional rollercoaster and the protracted journey had exhausted me. I realised again that there really was a bit of danger involved in this travelling lark.

Over a meal later that evening, David, Anne and I, somewhat perversely, entertained each other by telling stories of disasters and near misses. One such tale was that of the fate of a Short SC7 Skyvan 3-300, operated by Ansett Airlines. Just over a year earlier, the pilot was flying this plane over to Mendi from a little place called Minj, when, at 9,000 feet, clouds obscured their view. At that altitude and in this known terrain, the pilot should have ascended, because there was unlimited visibility above 10,000 feet. But he did not and sadly they crashed into Mount Giluwe at 10,250 feet, killing him and his three passengers.

David went into town next morning to get someone to guide us up the mountain, but soon came back with more bad news. There had been a robbery at the Mission Station and the police would not allow anyone, including potential guides or carriers, to leave town. I could not believe it. Having gone through all the drama of getting here, I was frustrated that our climb was to be thwarted by some petty crime.

We bemoaned the situation for a little while, but with nothing else to do, we eventually decided to try to find the track up the mountain by ourselves. As with many things in life, this proved easier said than done, and despite our best efforts, we did not get terribly close to the mountain. Instead, we trekked for a couple of hours up to a lookout called Clancy's Nob (named after a well-respected District Commissioner) but still quite a few miles from Mount Giluwe. Agreeing that we really did not know where we were or which was the right way to go and not wanting to vanish into the bush, we turned back. On our return, as a welcome diversion, we came across the bed of a shallow watercourse, one of the headwaters of several rivers that cross the province. The setting was like that of the river above our watering hole in the Tsinamutu where I had splashed around with the others a year or so earlier: crystal clear water, meandering gently and shallow over smooth-worn pebbles, all in dappled shadows and sunlight. With a few large bugs flitting here and there amongst sunlit creepers, and an abundance of other vegetation, the rustle of the breeze and the occasional call of an unseen bird, it was a truly enchanting place.

We walked upstream looking out for wildlife, taking photographs as we went. I caught a glimpse of what I thought was a Bird of Paradise, although I couldn't tell the actual species. We saw many other less striking birds and a few pretty butterflies. Neither of us was quick enough to get a decent photograph; by the time we spotted a bird, focused and clicked, the little devil had always flown away.

Eventually we got back to the house and agreed that our session with nature had been most enjoyable and compensation enough for not seeing the world from the top of the mountain, and what is more, it certainly required far less effort.

Next day, David and I spent a few hours strolling around Mendi town. Located in a long, lush green valley, surrounded by an imposing vista of rugged limestone peaks and already close to 2,000 metres above sea level, it was a most agreeable environment. There was a market down beside the Lai River that runs past the town, and not far from David and Anne's house, a few trade stores lining the dirt main street, the post office and a bank, including, of course, the *haus sik* where David and Anne worked.

Coming closer to the hospital, we bumped into a friend of David's who, yet again, reminded us that the route was so simple that guides were not necessary. Well, yes, we said, but we had missed it anyway and still had enjoyed a great day. Dave and I agreed that after climbing the highest mountain in the country, the second highest would just have to wait for another time.

Later, we heard they had caught the thief. Apparently a *haus boi* at the Mission had pinched some cash and the local cop had locked him up in the calaboose for a few days. After recognising that the crook was genuinely remorseful, the local padre, being a naturally compassionate man, reprimanded him and told him not to do it again, and let him out. He had ruined our chances of climbing the mountain, which was much more serious than the theft in my eyes, but he was not to know that!

CHAPTER 13

ON THE SEPIK

Recovering from the dramatic flight and somewhat anti-climactic adventure, I had just one day back in the office before I needed to travel up country again. This time it was to Lae for the Morobe Show. I stayed at the sumptuous Melanesian Hotel, hired a car for the week and everything was terrific. My work was easy; the hotel was luxurious, the car was nice and nippy compared with my old VW, and best of all, Lae was yet another beautiful town to visit.

Then, immediately on my return to Moresby, I was introduced to Bill Schulz. I knew Hovey was contacting aid agencies to get assistance on the production side of the project. What I did not know was that he had found a UN expert or that he had arrived in the country. But, now here he was, sitting right here in the office. Communication was a bit of an issue!

In his late fifties, Bill was, in my opinion, one of your archetypal ugly Americans: tall, loud and full on. He had an overly firm handshake, a broad Yankee drawl and a habit of flicking his mop of greying, gingery hair out of his bespectacled eyes. Even more apparent was a very pronounced swinging gait; a car crash some years earlier had left him with a gammy knee. Now his right leg was practically one long limb, straight from the hip down, and he had to swing this forward and back with every step. It would be quite an impediment for him, particularly in getting in and out of aeroplanes and dugouts.

Putting all this to one side, we got down to business. While I had been learning about what marketing assistance might be appropriate for our, as yet, embryonic, national plan, I also found we needed a better understanding of the production side of crafts. So, after discussing the various issues, the three of us agreed more fieldwork was necessary. We decided to investigate and focus on what from now on we would refer to as 'handcrafts' (not handicrafts, crafts or artefacts), to get a better understanding of what was being made and how. The study would identify what items were of traditional design but would sell as 'handcrafts' rather than 'artefacts'. Armed with all this and with Bill's experience from his work in other countries and my marketing input, we could then better evaluate what the Administration would need to do to encourage the sector overall.

To get the required information, we decided to focus on a section of the Sepik River where the villages were known for their craftsmanship and I immediately started planning an achievable schedule of visits and the places to stay en route. Although there were apparently no issues from the point of safety, the area was still remote. And, to get there involved flying to Ambunti via

Mount Hagen before travelling along a stretch of the river to Angoram, the central town in the East Sepik Province. And, after all that, flying back to Moresby via Wewak and Lae. While hardly groundbreaking exploration, it was still going to be quite a trip. So, disregarding any concerns lurking in the back of my mind about crashing and ending up torn to pieces or lost in the jungle somewhere, I made the necessary bookings, and in early November 1973, Bill and I flew to up Mount Hagen en route to the start of our expedition.

We had gone first to Mount Hagen because Ed Hankin from Goroka had organised a weaving workshop there. He had asked me to talk to the local would-be craftspeople about what the government could do for them now and how we planned to assist in future.

I arrived at the venue on time, well prepared and ready to speak. Unfortunately, only half the number of those invited turned up to listen. Nevertheless, I got on with the job and spoke for half an hour or so to the small gathering of bewildered-looking villagers. Bill said he thought my talk went down well, but for me, it seemed wasted. I knew organising anything for the locals was hard. Papua New Guineans did not share the same imperatives when agreeing to something, or perhaps they just did not like saying no. As well as this, even though I now spoke reasonably good pidgin, I was not sure much of what I said went in.

I was beginning to see that the locals viewed us expats with a fair degree of ambivalence. They wanted us there because they could see some benefits, but at the same time they did not really want us interfering with the traditional routine of their lives. At the end of the day I wondered if my audience had learned or even understood much of what I had been saying anyway. It was all a bit frustrating, but I did the best I could.

After the talk we refocused on our primary mission. I had already learned from my desk research that the Sepik people had been making various articles for household, spiritual and defence use from time immemorial: pottery, canoes, musical instruments, funerary items, weapons etc. Indeed, since the first European contact in 1885 and well before us Public Servants came along, many foreign explorers had already discovered and exported a lot of these artefacts. Consequently, many Papua New Guineans became used to trade and, encouraged by the money, were now making certain items specifically for sale. Some of these were of artistic merit and as such considered to be of cultural value, suited to museums or for preservation for ethnographic reasons. But some of these were the sorts of things we were after, items we now chose to class as handcrafts and hoped to encourage tourists and other folk to buy, to help promote economic growth.

With all this in mind, we set off for Ambunti. With no direct flight we first caught a plane to Wapenamanda, then another on to Wewak and yet another to Hayfields and finally to our destination for the day.

With four take-offs and landings in one day it was all pretty tiring stuff, and we needed a break before we had even started! But when we arrived on the doorstep of District Officer Laurie Bragge's place late in the day, it was clear he had received little warning. Although I had gone through the right channels and signalled ahead, the Department had not provided a proper explanation of our purpose or even mentioned that we wanted to stay overnight. Laurie said he 'sort of' knew about our being in the area, but was not sure about our movements or even why we were there. He made it clear, quite justifiably, that his home was not a guesthouse. He also emphasised that, as he was responsible for the territory, it was customary to send him word about any planned expeditions well in advance. There had obviously been another breakdown in communication somewhere. Naturally Laurie didn't offer quite the usual warm hospitality that expats living a relatively isolated existence in the bush were known for and I don't think our gung-ho in your face Bill helped much in the diplomacy stakes either.

After a very basic meal, Bill and I were allocated a spare room and turned in for the night. Meanwhile Laurie, having regained a degree of affability, set about overcoming our poor planning and organised transport for our trip on the river. Luckily for us he saved the day and, getting up early the following morning our native boatman met us with a cheery smile and explained how he was to take us downstream. Loading our gear into the dugout, this time with the luxury of an outboard motor, and feeling glad to get away from the slightly chilly reception, we set off northeast for Pagwi.

The middle Sepik River. Ambunti is about thirty kilometres as the crow flies to the west of Pagwi. (Map copyright © Carolyn Leigh, 1996-2011; used with permission – http://art-pacific.com)

It was not a particularly comfortable ride for either of us. Being very narrow craft, dugout canoes do not allow for a great deal of body movement, so it was a bit of a torment, especially for Bill with his stiff leg. We both needed to fidget about to keep the circulation going.

Mainly it was tedious, just sitting there, skimming across the greeny-brown water, staring at the rather dull scenery and listening to the drone of the outboard. The close horizon was mostly thick with tall reeds and then, further south in the distance, the shadowy mass of the Hunstein Mountains made an abrupt end to the vista. We worried that the dark clouds were going to break and give us a soaking, but it stayed dry, and with very little breeze over the water we instead baked in a blanket of soporific heat.

The area was apparently home to many species of wildlife, but discounting the billions of mosquitos, all we really saw were birds. Every now and then a few herons flapped up out of the reeds, their composure broken by our outboard; and then occasionally, a cormorant, a darting parrot or two and a few other unidentified birds. On narrower reaches, passing by the river's edge, we would peer through the tangle of vegetation into some mysterious and steamy-looking swamp where the waters of this already languid river were taking an added break, and there, in the sunlight, would be a hazy cloud of even more bugs.

We had been told to watch out also for a dreadful type of sand fly that infested the muddy banks. If disturbed, these would apparently give a bite far worse than any mosquito and an itch that would get ten times worse if scratched. Our trusty boatman avoided getting us closer to the river's edge than was necessary and luckily (if that is the right word), our bites were only from mosquitos.

Of greater concern was the *puk-puk*. These four-metre crocs (*Crocodylus novae guinea*) were plentiful on the river and the dangers reported about them were no exaggeration. Even though they usually retreated into the swampy areas if disturbed, we needed to be vigilant, because they were known to turn as quick as a flash and take a human snack now and then.

After a long and uncomfortable trip surviving these few natural pests and the cooking heat, we finally arrived at Pagwi. Here, a river truck and another local boatman had been organised by Laurie. Although considerably less glamorous than a dugout, this flat-bottomed aluminium craft, complete with a 40 hp outboard, was far more practical and provided greater comfort, particularly for Bill. After transferring our stuff, we set off on our journey proper.

We had decided to track along a route like that of the famed Swiss anthropologist Paul Wirz, who had been collecting artefacts here in the 1950s. Our quest was more of a commercial than a cultural nature, and while we did not pretend to aspire to his ethnographic efforts[64], we nevertheless hoped the outcome of our work would still be of considerable value.

Continuing our cruise along the river, I couldn't say the scenery was any more spectacular than the first leg from Ambunti. The riverbanks varied from brown-grey mud to mangrove swamps. Over the low reedy horizon in the closer distance, we could now see the backdrop of impenetrable jungle and still the hazy blue foothills of the far distant mountains. Occasionally, the river narrowed and we glided between overhanging vegetation with trees and forest on one side and the ubiquitous reeds on the other. When the banks again turned muddy, the suddenly close presence of a slumbering crocodile momentarily fuelled the imagination of an alternative outcome to what was simply a hot, dull and rather uneventful journey.

Finally, breaking the monotony, we made our first stop at a little place called Nyaurengai. Here, we had been told, the villagers had a reputation for carving wooden hooks, used to protect food from being eaten by rats. As we arrived, instead of the usual crowd of inquisitive folk I had grown to expect when visiting villages, just one *lapun* (old man) came down to greet us. Our boatman explained to him who we were and what we were after, and the old man apologised that everyone else was out in the gardens. Just to continue to impress Bill with my pidgin, I told him, '*Olsem, mi no wari*' (I was not worried). We had not really expected a welcoming party.

The old fellow walked us up from the river and showed us into the smoky interior of a large hut, pointing out a few food hooks and some other poor-quality carvings scattered around. I was disappointed with the numbers, but the old guy told us, '*Em tasol*' (that's all). That was it; they just did not have many crafts to show us. They were actively carving but a collector had been through the previous week and bought up much of what they had made.

Later, moving on a little way to the village of Kandangai, we found they too had food hooks, along with some small figurines. These were more in line with the sort of thing we were after, but again were disappointed with there being so few. We duly took notes and photographed everything there was for our records.

From Kandangai we travelled on to Korogo and then on to Kanganaman. As we journeyed along, we found only a small volume of handcrafts available and figured the collectors had been busy. As an aside, we observed a pattern in the style and location of the villages. They were commonly set well back and strategically out of immediate sight from anyone travelling on the river. However, I guessed that the original purpose of their siting, as defence from enemies, was no longer so important as there had been no attempt to hide smoke from their cooking fires, which would alert anyone to their presence. After having visited the fourth village, I noted a commonality also in the layout of all the buildings. There would be a scattering of thatched *Pandanus* walled houses on stilts, a metre or so off the ground, surrounded by a neat and tidy area of beaten earth, encircled by grass. In a couple of villages there was also a large and dramatically styled meeting house, the *Haus Tambaran*. I had read earlier about the importance of these houses to traditional community life, and how they were also used as places for initiation ceremonies and ancestor and spirit worship. More relevant to our present purpose, we also knew that this was where we could expect to find traditional artefacts, and hopefully, even more contemporary handcrafts. Of more immediate and somewhat more practical importance, we knew that by tradition, only initiated warriors were allowed inside. Foreigners such as us were barred from entry, apparently under pain of death! However, when arriving at the *Haus Tambaran* in Kanganaman, yet another *lapun* met us two white apparitions walking up from the river (one with a dramatic loping gait) and soon waived the tradition aside. He had seen a few foreigners like us before and probably knew there could be money involved. So, before he could change his mind, we took the opportunity and walked quickly in.

As our eyes adjusted to the dark, and in contrast to our previous stops, we could make out quite a few artefacts lying around as if casually discarded by their makers. Here, illuminated by rays of sunlight penetrating through cracks in the walls, was a wonderful variety of crafts: there were Mwai masks of woven fibre, (used by young men in the coming of age initiation ceremonies); ancestral figurines, food hooks and crocodile figures and over in one corner even a large, ornately-decorated orator's stool. It was a treasure trove. Noticeably, there was also a few smallish stools gathered around a few dying embers. It seems the menfolk, who would have been sitting around gossiping by the fire (while their women were no doubt out tending the gardens), had quietly left on our arrival. I suggested to Bill that they would probably have decided to go and do something rather than be bothered by our questions.

We asked our guide about the numbers of men involved in carving, took notes and photographs and made our way back out of the murkiness. After thanking our host, Bill and I joked that we had been fortunate to both see their artefacts and lived to tell the tale!

Then, rather than leaving the village immediately, we paused awhile to look back at the impressive building. Having seen a few *Haus Tambarans* before, I had noted the common theme of their design to be a tall, narrow triangular prow like a gable at the front, rising perhaps twenty-five metres or so from the ground and then sloping gradually forward a metre or so from the vertical at the peak. The fascia of the gable itself was usually decorated with designs peculiar to the Sepik, and then, down at ground level and to one side, there would be a small doorway. Behind the gable, the ridged roofline then usually flowed gradually down twenty or so metres away to the other end of the building, ending just a metre or so from the ground. Here at Kanganaman however, the *Haus Tambaran* was of a different style. This one had an elevated floor, supported by elaborately carved tree-trunk sized posts and accessed by a stepladder to one side. Unlike most of the others, this one had a tall prow-like gable at both ends and a horizontal ridgeline in between. Indeed, we later learned, this one was so important in its design that the government declared it National Cultural Property a few years earlier.

Haus Tamberan, Kanganaman

Later, we realised that many of the items we had seen so far, although made recently and specifically for sale, could also be described as artefacts. Here was the difficulty. As they were not of museum quality the question arose as to whether we were comfortable in classifying them as handcrafts and include them in our count. It was an issue that we could not fully resolve. We saw other, older items that were apparently been made for their original traditional purpose and, because they were clearly outside our definition of handcrafts, and out of respect for the people's traditions, we ignored them. Nevertheless, the issue of what exactly was cultural property was something we suspected we would have to revisit.

Continuing with our journey, on and through the unrelenting blanket of humidity, we eventually spent the night at the Kapwaimari Catholic Mission. The missionaries were welcoming, and helpful and readily provided us with a room for the night. Of course, by our spoilt standards, it was basic, hot and stuffy, but just when we thought the heat was all we would have to endure, we found also that it was infested with bugs. Indeed, as we travelled along the Sepik, Bill and I talked not so much about the hot and steamy weather but the mosquitoes! We never really got used to these little blighters, and on the Sepik in particular, they nipped and bit whenever they could. But there again, in Kapwaimari it was not only the mosquitos and other bugs but again, the frogs! I assumed that their incessant croaking carried on all night, but I was so exhausted from living in a pressure cooker, even they could not keep me awake.

We were up early next morning, and after a wonderful (!) breakfast of porridge and black tea, we had just started loading up our gear when the heavens opened at last. We had been lucky thus far, so this sudden drenching downpour was a bit of a shock to the system. Nevertheless, pushing on with gear and clothes now sodden and quite uncomfortable, we still got away by eight. Gradually, as we headed on towards Chambri Lakes and on to Wanbun, we got to the stage where we could not tell the difference between being rain-wet or the usual perspiration-wet.

Eventually, now dry enough, we lingered at the next village, Aibom. Here we examined the distinctive pottery typified by grotesque, ochre painted faces, moulded in high relief. With their obviously human characteristics, this was an entirely different type of pottery from that I had seen in Yabob. And even though they were clearly more rugged, they shared the same problem – how they could be successfully transported.

Travelling on, we visited Kamindimbit and then Mindibit. Here we were pleased to find an even larger variety of crafts. There were the usual woodcarvings of food hooks again but also fight shields, wooden and fibre ancestral masks, figurines and ever more pottery. There was a good mix of articles; some looked to be of museum quality artefacts and some the sorts of handcraft items in which we were particularly interested.

After one more hot and sticky day we stayed overnight at another Catholic mission, this time at Timbunke, near Tambanum. Here, we were a bit taken aback by the reception. In contrast to Kapwaimari, we were not particularly welcome, and were rather dismissively told 'You can sleep in the library'. Then, quite begrudgingly, we were each given a bowl of rice and a bit of meat for dinner. No one was interested in talking too much. And while I had always thought people in such remote places would be happy to have some company, I recalled the District Officer in Ambunti saying they would probably think we were just using them as a convenient place to stay, which, of course, was true. It had not crossed my mind also that they might be running low on food, and how deliveries of any more supplies could be delayed because of the often-atrocious weather. Probably the main reason was that they just saw us government types as a nuisance; after all, theirs was a mission quite different from ours.

We supposed the frosty welcome was justified, but apart from the mood and again the terrible insects, it was at least somewhere to stay out of the wet. We bade them a polite farewell next morning and left the place as swiftly as possible.

Overall, we had found that the crafts varied greatly in use and style and that each village and community had its own unique designs and, often, a focus on certain items. But, thus far, we had been a little disappointed by the low volume of handcrafts compared with the relatively greater number of commercial artefacts. But then, on arriving at Tambanum, we were somewhat relieved to find what we had been looking for at last. The villagers here were far more productive. Indeed, it was perhaps the most fruitful of all the places we had visited so far. There was a huge quantity of good-quality woodcarvings, figurines, drums, masks and other items. They still numbered in the tens and not hundreds, but at least they were all still very much handmade. With no hint of mass production, Hovey would be disappointed!

Over the three days, we had travelled two hundred kilometres or so along this broad, languid waterway and finally ended up at Angoram. And, as the crow flies, we were now a hundred kilometres east of Wewak where we had started and still around fifty kilometres or so from where the river flowed into the Bismarck Sea. Despite its relative isolation, here, to my relief, we found all the mod cons I had missed over the last couple of days: government offices, traders, a post office and, most welcome of all, even though it was a little rudimentary, a hotel!

The uncomfortable nights we spent at Laurie's and the Catholic missions reminded me of Bougainville and the resolve I had made to never put up with those sorts of conditions again, not for any length of time at least. So, the hotel was a pleasant relief indeed and we enjoyed lazing around recovering with the help of a cold beer or two.

Flying back to Madang the following day, just to keep me on my toes about a rather important thing called my life, the pilot miscalculated his position or speed or both in attempting to land. Knowing he was clearly going to overshoot the end of runway, he throttled up, banked around and tried again. I guessed in the overall scheme of things it was all a bit commonplace, but, nevertheless, knowing PNG airstrips had limited room for error, I was happy when we were actually back on the ground, even if it had been an extremely hard landing.

From there, Bill and I split up. Bill went on back to POM to talk with others involved in the crafts industry and write his report, while I stayed back in Madang and wrote up mine.

There was another reason I stayed on. I had only just scratched the surface of the crafts that I saw here the last time (because of delayed flights) and besides, I rather liked the place. Also, coincidentally, I knew some of the volunteers working in the area, so this time I took the opportunity to look them up.

After finishing my report, but before meeting up with my friends, I spent the next day (a Sunday) enjoying the relative comfort of the Smugglers Inn and simply wandering around town. I liked its broad, tree-shaded streets and the well-maintained expat houses with their wide verandas and lovely manicured lawns. In fact, it was the sort of place that explained why some expats were reluctant to encourage independence or be in any hurry to leave. Their lifestyle was probably not that far removed from the old colonial days in India, still enjoying plenty of assistance from the natives!

Instead of dreaming about the halcyon days of the Raj (for the British that is) and by now having developed a thirst from wandering around in the heat, I went over to Hotel Madang and sat on the veranda with a beer. Looking out towards the Bismarck Sea, I marvelled at the sunset...., the stunning view of the harbour with its numerous islands dotting the calm waters...., the last rays of sunlight burning the clouds into red and orange and then, finally, the glowing embers dying away into the charcoal shadow of night....Clearly having had more than enough to drink, I concluded my séance with nature, wandered back to Smugglers and arrived just in time to hear the beat of the *garamut*[65] announcing that it was time for dinner.

Next day I met up with my VSO friends, and as I had already told them of my new work interest, they had very thoughtfully gathered up a whole variety of handcrafts for me to inspect. I spent a while chatting, taking photographs and recording details, while they told me of their concerns about illegal trading of cultural property. By coincidence, they suspected something was happening right now, as we spoke. So, always ready for a bit of excitement, we jumped in the car and drove down to the wharf.

But now, feeling a little less self-assured when faced with the actual situation, we hung around trying to be inconspicuous and just watching as a whole lot of apparently museum quality artefacts was unloaded from a boat and put onto the back of a truck. Not having any evidence that what we saw was unlawful, or authority to do anything about it, we didn't make contact. But shortly after, we drove over to the Customs people to report what we had seen. The officer at Customs said the boat had just come in from the Siassi Islands, off West New Britain, but he was not particularly interested in our concerns about anything illegal going on. Instead, he brushed us off with a casual 'Okay, we'll go and look' sort of attitude.

I figured that it was either all above board or, for various reasons, Customs did not want to confront these people; or perhaps they simply did not want to make any extra work for themselves. I left them to deal with it, whichever way they chose. However, I recalled that around a year earlier (June 1972) Dirk Smidt, the Museum Director, had closed all Papua New

Guinea's ports over one weekend and instigated a search of all the freight that was due to be shipped out of the country. During that process, Customs found a huge cache of artefacts that were subsequently deemed to be National Cultural Property. They were confiscated, donated to the museum and eventually became known as 'The Seized Collection'. Those responsible (perhaps the very same characters we saw?) were well-known collectors but were never charged and apparently carried on their activities for some years, potentially flouting attempts at the protection of culturally valuable artefacts.

Meanwhile, I needed to get on with my job and justified my lack of action by having no authority in the matter. I didn't want to go making a fool of myself in confronting potentially legitimate dealers or, conversely, angry and treacherous wrongdoers.

As if to underscore my concern over possible danger, we had just heard of the recent murder of a kiap up in Kerema, just five hours northwest of Moresby. Apparently, the Assistant District Commissioner, Des Murphy's cook boy, had attacked and killed him. This was reminder enough that the environment we were working in could sometimes be quite risky. Apart from the sad loss of his life, this event was a big deal because ADCs were the bosses in their territory. Indeed, Murphy had played a major role in helping develop PNG. He had been involved in the exploration of new territory in the Gulf District and in helping pacify neighbouring tribes that were in conflict with each other. It was a great irony that he was killed by one of the very people he had no doubt been trying to help! There was no suggestion that the motive was anything other than personal, but his murder conjured up the negative aspects of our old imperialist ways. And, whereas it was a bit of a stretch to connect his murder to my concerns over smuggling, it did highlight one of the hazards expats faced. There was often a fair amount of money at stake and some very unscrupulous types involved in many aspects of trade.

There was often chatter about these various dangers, about riots, cannibalism, the tribal fighting, and stories about the cargo-cult, of the Tambarans and *puri-puri*. Then there was the occasional attack or (even rarer) killing of an expatriate, or word of an aeroplane crash or near miss. But despite all this neither *kiaps* nor the government said much about it officially.

It was also understood (and by default, accepted) that the media played down this sort of news, so as not to stir up undue ill feelings between 'us' and 'them' and we just got on with our work. Indeed, it was par for the course that no further detail was forthcoming as to the motive for Murphy's murder, or what happened to his assailant.

CHAPTER 14

WORK AND PLEASURE

Thus far I'd had quite an exciting time in my quest to travel and see the world. There had been the problem over the boat at Kuraio, then with Dick's car and the wheel falling off my own. I had been stranded offshore for nine hours, had a terrifying flight, seen a bit of rioting and now witnessed a possible smuggling operation, and I had only been here a year!

Against this somewhat exhilarating backdrop, in late November of 1973, my boss asked if I would like to carry on in my job for a while longer and if I would be interested in a contract with the Administration. It suddenly clicked that my chat with Matane a few months earlier had not been purely social after all. He must have been assessing my ability to fill a transitional posting and to help teach something to the locals and, I had obviously come across as 'OK'.

My immediate reaction was to go for it, but then I paused to consider the pros and cons. The big plus in staying on for a couple more years was in continuing with the work I found so interesting, but now on expatriate terms and conditions. I had left the prosaic world of selling gaskets a lifetime ago and more recently, wrestling with the idea of running a boat and the reality of greasy equipment in the heat and humidity of Bougainville. I had eagerly embraced the far more interesting world of artefacts and handicrafts and especially the relative comforts of city life. It was all quite remarkable how things had panned out, far better than I had ever dreamt of in my original, relatively simple ambition to travel (and do something useful!)

Hovey said I could still work out my obligations to VSO, but there was an important issue over timing. The whole process would take a few months to organise because Admin first had to create the expatriate position; then the Public Service Board (PSB) would have to approve it and then, if all went well, they would have to gazette it! The problem for me then was that the position would be open for all to apply and of course there would be no guarantee that I would get it. If all went to plan however and they accepted my application, I would start my contract in July 1974. But if someone else came along and was awarded the position, I would be out of PNG quick as a flash, back in the UK with no job and nothing to do! Should I start making enquiries about a job in Britain now, as a fall back, or just let it happen?

I certainly was not keen on returning to my old life and work. I had been well and truly bitten by my now reasonably adventurous life in the tropics and felt that I had only just started exploring. And then, of course, there was the generous pay, far more than I could ever expect to earn back in the UK.

The only other concern of any significance was the potential effect on my career. If I stayed any longer in PNG, would I still be able to pick up where I had left off when I did eventually return to the West? I thought about all this for about ten minutes and decided – Go for it! How could I refuse!

Part of the deal involved me returning to the UK for a break before coming back as a fully-fledged Public Servant. So, when discussing all this, and pushing my luck a little, I suggested to Hovey that, if I were successful in getting the job and while I was on that side of the world, it would make sense to do some market research to evaluate export demand for PNG crafts.

"It's a possibility. Why not?" he said. "It would have to remain a bit tentative at this stage. But, in the meantime, think about what you'd like to do and I'll suggest it to Matane."

Then, warming to the idea, he added, "We could probably get the Australian Trade Missions to help organise visits, so come back with a plan and I'll sound out Foreign Affairs and Trade to ask the Australians to arrange some people for you to meet."

This was too good to be true!

I drew up a schedule of countries it would be best to visit, those with some prior connection with Papua New Guinea made sense (the U.K., Netherlands, Germany and Switzerland, sprang to mind). I checked out some likely sounding businesses using an old copy of Kompass and figured out roughly how long I might need in each country.

In the meantime, of somewhat greater importance, Papua New Guinea was readying itself for self-government. As Hovey tried to tell me on my first week of joining, the Papua New Guinean and Australian administrators had been working for many years to form political parties in readiness for this moment. The process had not been an easy one, because it emerged that those local individuals with an interest in politics did not necessarily have the same level of interest in forming a party as did we Westerners. However, they had eventually formed parties[66], and just before I had arrived, three had contested the country's first general election. And now, as we all knew, they elected the head of the Pangu Party, Michael Somare, as leader and Chief Minister.

Thus, on 1st December 1973 and with the country in a state of readiness (but with considerable debate over the degree to which this was true) the Prime Minister of Australia, Gough Whitlam, declared self-government.

By design, only a few low-key events were organised to celebrate the occasion, with larger celebrations reserved for when the country would achieve independence. From this moment on, Australia gradually transferred the functions of government to the interim Papua New Guinea Administration, led by Somare.

With the bureaucracy preoccupied with these affairs of state, it took its time to approve the one expat position of importance and I had an anxious time worrying as to whether there would even be a job I could apply for. With no choice but to wait, social life and the various events around Christmas were fortunately a good distraction.

As well as enjoying the musical magic of Led Zeppelin and others, there was the swimming, sailing, bushwalking, riding motorbikes and of course, the pretty girls. There was just so much going on!

Rock music was just *there*; it was a natural and important part of our lives. But the motorbikes, apart from being useful in getting around town, were, I soon discovered, essential for other thrills. I had bought a Honda trail bike a little while earlier and although it was not very powerful or very fast, it was great for visiting places a car couldn't go. Some days, a group of us would take our girls off on rides along dirt roads, usually at crazy speeds, to places like Shell Bay, to swim and snorkel. Then, with the wind in our hair and the kick of adrenaline we would ride back to someone's place and relax listening to *Stairway to Heaven*[67]. It was just brilliant! Although we managed to annoy the neighbours with our bikes and the rock-music, there was never any malicious intent; it was just the way it was.

Motorbike riding was great fun and even though racing each other on a loose dirt road was crazy, there were other dangers. Despite knowing it was foolish to ride on one's own, I succumbed to the temptation. One day I took off up into the hills above Port Moresby and rode up to the Sogeri Plateau on and up past the Bomana War Cemetery. At the start of the Varirata National Park I left the road and went out into the bush, aiming for the views over Port Moresby and out to sea, somewhat ironically to enjoy the peace and quiet.

Initially I had a great time exploring the area, but in aiming for higher ground, I found myself riding up and down a series of small and particularly steep hillocks. Suddenly, the bike just didn't have the power to make it to the top of one small hill. I lost my balance, fell off and dropped the bike on the rocks. As well as being a bit shaken and bruised, somehow, the front end of the bike was also a bit damaged. However, wobbling around a little, I managed to nurse the bike and myself back to Moresby and eventually got home in one piece.

Telling friends about my folly prompted the usual scare stories. Someone, they said, had a similar accident but had not been so lucky. He had cracked his skull and, by the time they had got him to hospital, had picked up some dreadful bug and died shortly thereafter! I was convinced that solo riding was not such a good idea and didn't go trail bike riding on my own again.

There was really no excuse anyway. I already had several bike-crazy friends with whom to ride. One guy, Andy, a rather distant and eccentric sort of fellow from Canberra, rode a noisy Yamaha around town like a madman. His most attractive girlfriend, Ligouri (a tall, willowy, girl with a big Afro hairstyle, great sense of humour and a laid-back nature) was one of only four girls who rode motorbikes around POM. There were two Papua New Guineans and two Europeans: Ligouri and Molly, Elizabeth and Sue. Molly was John Mason's equally attractive girlfriend (Miss PNG Beauty Queen 1972) and in contrast to Ligouri had a vivacious and bubbly personality. Then there was Sue and Elizabeth. Elizabeth was the Australian girlfriend of Richard, the manager of the Honda dealership, and both she and Richard were really only acquaintances (he had sold me my bike); and Sue was an adventurous and pretty Pom with an aquiline nose and no-nonsense manner, partner to Malcolm, another Pom, who I had met briefly at a party sometime earlier.

Sue, Malcolm, Ligouri, Andy, Molly, John and a few other characters comprised my circle of bikie friends, and were in some contrast to my VSO mountain-climbing gang. We were not leather-clad bikies; we just enjoyed riding - and loud music!

John was a mad Australian daredevil character. We all enjoyed the various toys that money could buy but he not only had a super-fast Kawasaki S3 but also a Zodiac inflatable dinghy complete with a powerful outboard motor. This he used for scuba diving and although I always meant to go diving with him after my experience in Rabaul, I knew it deserved professional training and I was not too sure I trusted him and, at the time, I was just too busy with my work. But one day, round at his place and seeing the Zodiac sitting on the trailer behind his Ute, I couldn't resist the opportunity to enjoy the next best thing and so asked to borrow it. Being the generous fellow he was, John immediately agreed and before he could change his mind, I jumped in his Ute, drove down to the bay and took the Zodiac out for a spin on the harbour.

Seeing very few other craft around and being a bit gung-ho, I yanked the throttle to maximum, screamed out onto the water and had a great time, skating sideways, this way and that, amazed by the craft's manoeuvrability. Suddenly the nose of the dinghy leapt up in the air and the horizon disappeared! With an instinctive yell, I let go the throttle and came back down with a splash. Knowing the dinghy had next to no draught I had assumed I wouldn't need to worry about the depth of the water, but as luck would have it, I'd cut right across the top of the only sandbar in the bay.

Having scared myself with these unplanned aerobatics, I marked time for a while, worrying that I had damaged John's precious boat. But with no water coming in and still fully inflated and still afloat, I whizzed around some more before calling it a day.

Later, back at John's place, in the excitement of relating how impressed I had been with his dinghy's performance, I somehow overlooked telling him about the sandbar experience. But then, a few days later, John complained about how the tropics were so tough on things and how quality was not what it used to be. He explained (to my feigned surprise) how the strips over the bottom seams of the dinghy had already come off. I felt a little better when he explained Zodiac provided a repair kit for such eventualities and he soon had it mended. I was never sure whether John suspected that it was something I had done that caused it. He was too nice a guy to say anything and hopefully, being a fatalist, simply thought 'Shit happens'!

John and I enjoyed a rather strange relationship. We were good friends, but we were each quite different in character. He was very much a gung-ho Aussie type, adventurous to the point of dangerous, while I was more reserved, although rapidly adjusting to living life to the full, he had had a head start on me and was already what Aussies called a bit of a larrikin[68]. I am not sure how we met, probably through another friend, maybe Andy. Andy was a bit more like me, but there again a bit unusual in that his conservative appearance (short, well-kept hair, smart slacks, ironed shirt etc) belied his love of the quite avant-garde music of Frank Zappa.

One hot day, Andy, John and I were sitting on the veranda at John's place, enjoying a beer and overlooking his rather sparse front lawn. I was not sure if it was the beer or the sun or both having an influence on his brains, but John suddenly decided he wanted to beautify his garden. After chatting briefly, he thought the best way to do this would be to plant some trees (Andy and I agreed, just to humour him). That would at least make the lawn a little more interesting and provide some much-needed shade. However, as it was an Admin house, John was not keen on spending any money on plants from the local nursery and suggested instead we go and dig up some saplings from the bush on the outskirts of town. It made sense, as they would be free. It would be hot work, but it was an excuse for an outing and we knew there would be plenty more beer later to ease the pain.

We jumped into John's Ute and set off along a dirt road until we were some way out of town, eventually stopping at a likely looking spot at the edge of the bush. With shovels at the ready, we rambled off into the thicket. It was a bit of a trick wrestling with the undergrowth of roots and creepers, but after foraging around, we managed to find a few suitable saplings, dig them out, chuck them into the back of the Ute and go back for more.

I had just bent over to clear an area to start digging out another likely looking specimen when, quick as a flash, a little black scorpion ran down the trunk, arched its tail, plunged its stinger into my finger and scurried off again, back into the undergrowth! The sting was barely noticeable. It was more of the psychological shock than anything; well, everyone knows scorpions are lethal.

I shouted out to John and Andy that a scorpion had stung me and rushing over and without further ado, they bundled me into the Ute and we tore off back into town and to the General Hospital. John and Andy hurried me up to Emergency and called out for help. The doctor on duty looked at me, peered into my eyes, checked over the slight swelling that had appeared on my finger and asked if I was in pain. It was a bit uncomfortable, but I could hardly call it *painful*. The doctor said that if a *deadly* scorpion had stung me, I would either be in excruciating pain or I would be dead! He told me to go away and stop wasting his time. None of us realised that only a few scorpions have a sting that is life-threatening. The pain and swelling were no worse than that of a common or garden nettle. I was relieved and embarrassed at the same time.

We'd got enough saplings to go on with anyway, and although

I had ended the tree-gathering mission, we all enjoyed a good laugh (at me), went back to John's house and started digging. Still, I thought, you never know - better safe than sorry!

Parties, swimming, day trips and other similar activities normally took up much of our leisure time. One trip in particular involved checking out the possibility of walking the Kokoda Trail. The Trail was well known as the site of some terrible and fierce battles between Japanese and Allied (mainly Australian) forces during World War II, with our side having incredible support from the Papua New Guinean 'Fuzzy Wuzzy Angels'. My office friends said walking the Trail was a must, as a pilgrimage in memory of those who had fought and those who had died protecting us from invasion by the Japanese. More than anything, we all knew it would be a significant test of physical endurance.

Simply looking at the end of the Trail could not answer the question of whether we thought we could manage it, but we decided to go and have a look anyway. It was an excuse for a bit of exploration, so we drove the fifty kilometres or so out of town, north-east of Moresby and up to the southern end of the Trail at a place called Owers' Corner.

The Trail was a serious hike, 160 kilometres or so up hill and down dale through hot and sticky jungle and mountainous terrain. Apparently, it took around five days to complete, which naturally meant camping gear. Also, with the Trail ending up near the village of Kokoda, on the northern side of the Owen Stanley's, and with no one crazy enough to suggest we should walk back and do it all over again, it meant having to fly back to POM.

After some discussion, and having looked at the lie of the land at Owers', my friends decided they would do it. But the length of time required meant it would have to be over the Easter break. Fortunately, or unfortunately as the case may be, this clashed with my return to the UK, the dates of which I had just about finalised. I was (sort of) disappointed to miss out, but I was not so keen anyway. The trip up Mount Wilhelm taught me the extent of my comfort level when it came to strenuous exercise, and that was in the far more comfortable climate of the Highlands. Kokoda would be in the full heat and humidity of the tropics. I agreed to join them if there was any change to my program. But even though I was still waiting on my flight details, my research appointments in Europe and the confirmation of a job, I knew it was unlikely I would have to face this self-inflicted struggle, and so breathed a quiet sigh of relief.

Around this time the Department Secretary and the PSB were discussing whether to send someone to a UN Small Industry development seminar in Geneva. My boss thought that if I got the job I should go, but the rule was that only Papua New Guinea nationals could attend overseas events such as this. Eventually, with no understudy in sight, my Department boss was over-ruled, and no one went, such a waste really. If I got the job and approval of the research, I could easily be in Geneva at the right time, plus there was no charge. Too many 'ifs' perhaps, but here was an unfortunate example of the virtue of essentially free assistance being overridden by the reality of Public Service rules. In my book, the bureaucracy was out of kilter.

Now however, the time of year determined that we needed to organise our social life. Christmas was fast approaching and, having been born on the 24th December, I had so far always managed to avoid going to work on my birthday, and I was not going to start now! Even though Christmas Eve was not a public holiday, I treated myself to the day off and went sailing with Pete Latty. The weather was far too beautiful to sit in the office!

Pete was a mid-30s, tanned, scrawny and somewhat taciturn sort of fellow. And, with his long hair and a beard down to his navel it meant some people mistook him for a hippy. But there was nothing airy-fairy about him. He was another CUSO and a serious and diligent architect with the Public Works Department. More importantly, he was an avid sailor. A year or so back he had been looking for a solid boat that he could sail back to Canada. He eventually heard of an old pearling lugger moored down in Samarai on the eastern tip of Papua. He had flown down to inspect it, found it met his needs and then sailed her back to Moresby.

The *Norseman*, as Pete named her, was a 37-foot gaff-rigged ketch, built around 1944. Although sound of hull, she needed considerable work to make her habitable and seaworthy. So, he moored her on the inner reaches of Fairfax Harbour and started living on her, doing her up and making her ready for the big trip home.

I had been out with Pete a few times already and contrary to my earlier marine adventures, I found sailing on a yacht a thoroughly enjoyable experience. The *Kiriaka Aro* had always been about getting from A to B, and as well as the need for care with navigation it was usually a smelly, dirty and uncomfortable affair. Sailing on a yacht on the other hand was all about the journey, and depending on the weather, was a far more peaceful sort of experience.

This day Pete had asked me to helm so he could check out the rigging and a few of the things he had been fixing. It was excellent weather, just enough breeze to enjoy the moment, without having to worry about anything in particular (excepting that sandbar!) It was only a quick trip and we were back on the mooring by midday. Thanking Pete for the pleasure and thinking I was glad it was he that had to look after the boat, I then went over to Ralph Elms' place to chat about the party we were going to hold the next day.

I had met Ralph at the hostel. He was another serious fellow: conservative, pipe-smoking and quite intense, characteristics that fitted well with his work as a scientific officer with the Department of Agriculture. As he had been born on Christmas Day, we shared some commonality with our birthdays coinciding with the anniversary of someone almightily more important than either of us.

After spending three years at Ranuguri, Ralph desperately wanted to get out and, at last, had a house allocated to him. It was basic, a fibro (cement sheet walled) donga a few kilometres out of the CBD, a little way up a steep and shady dirt road. Ralph and I agreed that now was the perfect time to hold a party to celebrate his escape from the hostel and a Christmas, birthday and housewarming party all in one!

So, on Christmas morning, after a quick swim with a few other friends down at Idlers Bay and then picking up the ice, I drove back up to Ralph's place. We had only just managed to finish setting things up when people started arriving already. In the distraction of fixing drinks and chattering away and not being sure whose friend was whose, it took a while for each of us to realise our visitors included a rag-tag bunch of other individuals who neither of us recognised. Some were friends and then there were friends of friends, but then there were others who were complete strangers to both of us and our friends -

gate-crashers - people neither of us knew. I recalled how Stewart said this was the way it was with expat parties, but I was not mad about the custom!

However, with a whole gang of folk now filling Ralph's new donga to bursting point, we spent the rest of the day and night shouting at each other over the brilliant music[69], drinking, eating, dancing and generally enjoying a loud and boozy time until some dreadful hour of the morning.

Come Boxing Day (and feeling surprisingly well considering the amount of grog I had consumed) we saw the start of a quick succession of yet more parties. One was just drinks at a fancy leave-house a friend managed to get for a few months and which he wanted to show off (fabulous view, furnishings, rooms etc., making us all aware as to how, relatively speaking, some of us were still roughing it!).

After that, it was over to watch a movie. Gary Kildea, the filmmaker with the Department of Information Services, asked a few of us around to get our reaction to a movie he had just completed. It was about a traditional pig kill held by the Chimbu people up in the Highlands and documented the progress of rituals undertaken on such occasions. Gary demonstrated how the ceremony provided an opportunity for different tribes to get together, to share and exchange food, perhaps help identify potential leaders in case of the death of an existing chief[70] and to give young people the chance to get together for courtship.

With the ceremony including lots of dancing and singing and plenty of music, even across the cultural divide, we could see the parallel with our previous night's party. Nevertheless, it was very different. Apart from the nature of the people involved, it was full of scenes of the gory killing of pigs. I was pretty sure our own primitive behaviour of the night before had not identified any potential leaders, or killed any pigs, but there had almost certainly been some courtship involved!

Gary then projected some of the remarkable 35mm colour-slides he had made. I had taken lots of photos of similar subjects myself on my travels and was frustrated to see his were so much better than mine. He explained that only five per cent of his photos were any good and it was the five per cent that he was showing. Plus, after all, it was his job, he was a trained filmmaker and photographer.

Shortly after the Christmas festivities, it started belting down with rain. This was a bit of a contrast to the excellent weather we had been enjoying and a bit of come-down, but it was a good excuse to take a break and stay inside for once. I needed to recover!

Around this time, my VSO friends and I were saddened to hear that our Field Officer, Dick Bird, was leaving PNG. He had done his two-year stint and decided to return to Britain. Almost singlehandedly he had looked after 120 or so VSOs across the country. This was quite an achievement, particularly when considering that some volunteers (who shall remain nameless) had caused a few headaches and extra work, and certainly so when compared with another volunteer administration service which employed three people looking after just sixty volunteers! All my volunteer colleagues and I thought Dick had done an excellent job and we knew he would be sorely missed.

However, Dick's impending departure did not delay our excursions. Life went on, and soon after Christmas with the weather now improving, three carloads of us friends headed up to the Sogeri Plateau again. This time we were aiming for a smallish man-made lake that some friends told us was a beautiful place to swim. The lake had been created by an increase in the size of the Sirinumu dam on the Laloki River, and as part of the development of hydroelectric power for Moresby. Coincidentally, it was close to the place where Errol Flynn enjoyed the company of Tuperselai, a beautiful Papuan girl, as his autobiography relates: *"We let ourselves be carried down by the current of the stream and, on the shores, in a secluded nook of shade, at last, we made love. I can only say that I don't know when again my heart pounded so..."*[71]

Although I had something similar on my mind with my current girlfriend, I somehow doubted I would enjoy circumstances similar to *'a secluded nook of shade'*, as there were twelve of us in our party!

We had been told to look out for a bush shelter close to the lake that provided protection from the sun and rain and was an ideal spot for a picnic. After thirty kilometres of rumbling along dirt roads, we spied the turn-off and drove down the narrow and increasingly rough track. With undergrowth catching the side of the car and the ruts giving the springs a good work out, I slowed down for the sake of my poor old car. With the four of us on board, the suspension bottomed out several times, but thankfully, the exhaust, always a bit of a worry in these conditions, survived. Then, as the other cars arrived, we busied ourselves carrying the picnic food and coolers over to the grass thatched sanctuary, and clambering up the few rickety steps, we spread ourselves out on the open-sided deck.

The area was visually spectacular, but to call it beautiful was a bit of a stretch. The surrounding wilderness was as good as nature had made it, but despite it now being the wet season, grey grass still covered the hills, dotted with a few scrubby bushes here and there. It was a little austere to say the least. The lake was quite different. The water captured by damming the river had flooded a valley that had once been home to a copse of trees. And, now, just the top halves of hundreds of dark grey, leafless trunks stuck up through the surface. The stark, dead trees, piercing the black and static water, presented an unsettling spectacle; and the leaden sky, and air pregnant with humidity, made for such an oppressive atmosphere we could hardly breathe.

Despite this disagreeable environment, we set out the picnic things and made ourselves as comfortable as possible. We were just discussing whether or not to go for a swim before or after eating, when it started raining. A moment of indecision: should we stay or should we wait for it to pass? We were going to get wet anyway.

But then nature decided for us. Suddenly a bright blue bolt of lightning hit a tree, barely a hundred metres away to our left, and immediately an almighty crack of thunder rent the stillness. Standing up as one, we saw the tree explode in a flash of red and a huge section of trunk break off and crash into the water. None of us had seen lightning strike anything before (and certainly not so close by), so it really was one hell of a surprise.

With only a thin trickle of smoke coming off the remains of the blackened stump as evidence, it was literally all over in a flash. Although we soon settled back down, with some concern over further strikes, we decided to defer the swim and have an early picnic instead.

The rain stopped eventually and despite lingering concerns that another lightning strike could fry us all, we traipsed off down to the lake. Contrary to its reputation as being a suitable place for swimming, we found it almost impossible. Broken tree trunks, vegetation and other debris lay just below the surface at the water's edge, making it difficult to wade out to any depth. We spent much of our time trying for a safe footing before taking the plunge.

Thus, with some having stripped off for a skinny dip, we mostly stood around in the shallows, feeling both vulnerable and nervous. With the guys peeking at the girls and the girls checking out the boys, one or two daredevils eventually made it out into water deep enough to splash around. But most of us, myself included, decided it was all too difficult and dangerous. The presence of thunder and lightning in the still air made for a very unsettling sort of atmosphere; we could feel the electricity.

So, it was back to the shelter and we spent the rest of the afternoon simply lazing, drinking and chatting. Nature had provided us with yet another dramatic experience, and although we all had a good laugh at our reaction, at the end of the day we packed up our gear and drove home in an uncharacteristically sober mood.

A positive feeling soon replaced the thundery downer of our trip to the lake however and, by the first week of February 1974, there was so much happening I wasn't sure if I was coming or going.

CHAPTER 15

SO MANY GOINGS ON

So far, I had spent time with the Secretary of the Department chatting about my ideas on handcrafts marketing. I'd just heard I'd been accepted as an Associate Member of the British Institute of Management; I'd recently initiated a meeting between Business Development and Foreign Relations and Trade and got agreement over responsibilities for handcrafts development and, now, on top of this, Matane had approved my market research in Europe, in principle, should I get the job.

The biggest news, however, was that the new expatriate position of Handcrafts Marketing Officer had been approved and gazetted by the PSB, and now all I needed to do was to apply. At the same time, I found another understudy position was created for the Department. The position I had initially been hired for and was now vacating was for a national, but the

Department wanted to have two Papua New Guineans trained up and working towards the process of localisation.

The creation of the expatriate position had taken many months, and now the only thing was for the PSB to approve *my* application. Being a cautious sort of fellow, I knew there was many a slip twixt cup and lip, and hoped like hell that no other better-qualified individual was lurking out there waiting to steal 'my' job. I just had to get on with things and tried not to worry about it.

In the meantime, as some sort of entrée, as it were, I also managed to escape from the dreaded Ranuguri Hostel, a place that had become a torment for so many. Ralph asked if I would like to share his accommodation and as we seemed to get on quite well together and his *donga* had a spare bedroom it was convenient. Even though I was not mad keen on sharing with another guy, it would only be for a short while and almost anything was better than the hostel. I had been told that if I did get the job, I might also be eligible for my own accommodation some way down the track, but, being single, I shouldn't hold my breath. Houses were in short supply and families got priority. In the meantime, I took up Ralph's offer and moved in as soon as I possibly could.

Of far greater importance than the goings on in my little world, this was a particularly hectic and rousing time for the city of Port Moresby. Preparations were underway and they were tidying up the place for the first-ever visit of Her Majesty Queen Elizabeth II, scheduled for the 22nd to 27th February 1974. Somewhat cynically, my friends and I thought Her Majesty's visit was a consolation prize because she hadn't attended the declaration of self-government in December. However, we also knew that, if she had, it would then have been contrary to the aim of keeping the transition to self-government as low-key as possible. Now, we heard the Queen was going to visit to celebrate the decision by the new government to become a member of the Commonwealth of Nations. This would then lead up to Independence, the specific date of which was still yet to be announced.

We were then a little surprised when we found the Queen was not planning to be here for the Independence celebrations. After all, it was not exactly an everyday event and, in our view, (i.e. that of my relatively small coterie of colleagues and friends) the occasion deserved representation by the head of the Commonwealth. Instead, Prince Charles was to do the honours, acting as Her Majesty's special representative. We could not know if this was a scheduling issue, with the Queen having promised to attend other functions; or maybe it was a protocol issue because PNG did not rate highly enough in the Commonwealth of Nations hierarchy? There again, perhaps it had been designed as a training session for the Prince?

Whatever the reason and whoever was to officiate, the effort of smartening the place up for the Queen's visit at this time was considerable. There was feverish activity in road surfacing, white lining and painting of signs, cleaning and refurbishing venues, checking flags would not stick halfway up flagpoles (which could easily send the wrong, rather ominous message). There were invitations to be sent to VIPs, transport of dancers from around the country to be organised and a million other things. A fair bit of this was cosmetic, but there was also a good deal of genuine civic pride.

Despite the new-found bonhomie and expectation of finally being put on the map, and after all the tarting-up, Moresby still looked a bit like the broken-down outpost it was. There was only so much one could do for the place. There again, perhaps it was never a good idea to appear to be too prosperous!

Being preoccupied with yet another field trip, I didn't get involved in any of the arrangements. I had to continue with the identification of what handcrafts were available and from which area. This time I was to visit Popondetta in the Northern District – not so far from Moresby – and then travel from Oro Bay to the village of Wanigela and return to POM a week later. After three days in the office writing up my reports, my plan was to go off on another trip. This was to be to West New Britain, to a place called Hoskins[72] (well known locally for its oil palm plantation) and after that, on to Kimbe and Talasea, etc. It was such a hard life!

For my Oro (Northern) District tour I first flew to Popondetta, where a Business Development Officer with the rather apt name of Tom Popp met me.

Driving over to the office together, we enjoyed an immediate rapport, a huge contrast with the *kiap* at Ambunti. Tom suggested that as the hotel accommodation left a lot to be desired, perhaps I would like to stay overnight at his place? Even though this was only a moderately remote posting, he said he and his wife would enjoy a bit of company.

In swapping the usual expat chitchat of 'Where are you from?' he told me his great-grandfather had emigrated from Germany many years earlier and that he and his wife were originally from South Australia but came to PNG simply for a bit of adventure.

Then, arriving at the office and after the usual warm greetings all round from the local staff, we got down to business. Actually, I mostly sat and nodded at Tom's suggestions as he telephoned around and arranged meetings and all the local transport, I needed to put me on track to discover the district's crafts. Then, with no other business of importance, we walked over to his place a little way out of town.

As we passed rows of tidy expat houses, and hearing my appreciative comments, Tom explained, "Nick, the reason Popondetta looks so neat is because it's only been here for about twenty years. It was set up as the new admin headquarters of the Northern District when Mount Lamington erupted in 1951. That was a pretty dreadful event. It killed about five thousand people would you believe, and totally destroyed the former township at Higaturu."

"Incredible" said I, "It all looks pretty neat now. But is there much else to the place?"

"Plenty," he said. "The town's actually behind us, and, having travelled around the country, I'd say it's one of the more attractive and comfortable places in PNG. We are lucky here. There's a solid resident expat population, you know, government workers, planters, tradesmen, missionaries and the like, and with that lot there's enough demand to support most of the things one needs. There's the hotel you might have stayed at – although I wouldn't hurry there – banks, a hospital, churches, schools and stores. We've even got a cinema and a golf course. You name it, we've got the lot really."

Tom's home was also complete. Although it was a standard Government *donga*, as soon as I entered it was clear there had been a woman's influence. Pretty cotton curtains covered the louvre windows, bright cushions scattered here and there; all quite an improvement over the usual male bachelor surroundings I was familiar with and certainly more homely than any of those

I had been into so far. Also, rather surprisingly, I saw a pale blue miniature dining table and chair set up beside the full-size version.

Tom introduced me to his wife Janet and then to Sam, their chatty five-year-old, who for some strange reason took to me like an uncle! That evening we ate our dinner, with the boy, like a mini-adult, sitting down to eat besides us grown-ups at his special table chatting away partly to mum and partly to himself. We shared a bottle of wine (excluding Sam, whose mother soon had him packed off to bed) and had a great time talking about PNG.

Echoing the feeling I had developed towards the country, Tom and Janet explained life was, paradoxically, both satisfying and frustrating. They both loved the place, the relaxed working conditions and the sociable and tight-knit expat community. Janet helped in the *haus sik*, and said the assistance provided by a Papua New Guinean in the housework and nannying for Sam was a godsend. Perhaps somewhat surprisingly, they both loved the climate, and, being right on the coast I realised a decent sea-breeze mitigated the humidity. Also, contrary to what some others had told me before, they didn't consider personal safety to be an issue and said the rare event of any violence was usually between the locals and, often, caused by drink. No, the main frustration, Tom explained, was with succession. While he had a reliable understudy and good staff, the problem was in getting someone who was half capable of taking over his job. The locals were keen and tried hard, but there were a few years to go before he could feel confident that they could help others to anything like the necessary standard. But then, as we both agreed, that was what we were here for. It was all just a matter of time, and we were patient.

Next day, after Tom had confirmed my travel arrangements, I jumped up onto the back of a truck and set off on the hour-long drive down to Oro Bay. As the locals had already been alerted indirectly, via bush telegraph, my arrival at the village of Eroro brought forth a few of the local big-men eager to meet me and see what it was this latest *waitpela* wanted. I explained (again) who I was, which section of the Department I was from and what it was I was after. Then, shortly, after a bit of to-ing and fro-ing, some older *meri's* came over and showed me what crafts they had been making. It was mainly shell jewellery, necklaces and bangles, all quite acceptable, easy to transport and usually quite saleable. However, the few examples I was shown were of quite poor quality. The fishing line used for threading was too thick and tied too tightly, making the shells so jumbled up against each other that they could not fall nicely around the neck. I gave some basic advice in pidgin as my guide translated into Orokaiva. Then, after asking how many people were involved and how many items they made, I think I understood, (never something I took for granted) that even if they improved the quality, the quantity available would be quite insignificant. It would be a long time before any volume of items would be available for retailers in town. However, there were good prospects for active encouragement.

I was a tiny bit disappointed, but now, being more familiar with the situation across the country, I was not surprised. Giving thanks I made my farewell, boarded the local banana boat[73] Tom had organised, and set off on the long trip down the coast to Tufi. Towards the middle of the day, as we approached the Cape Nelson peninsula (so named by John Moresby after the one and only Horatio), I was fascinated to see many inlets, penetrating deeply inland, along a lengthy stretch of the coastline. With the usual rather limited vocabulary, the boatman pointed and simply said "fjords". Although thinking fjords were more of a northern hemisphere characteristic, I didn't believe him, but didn't argue either. I later found out I was right, but for the wrong reason. Apparently, although having a similar appearance to fjords, these physical indentations were river valleys. Volcanic activity and rising sea levels had submerged the rivers aeons ago, rather than the land having been carved out by glaciers; and so they were not fjords but in actual fact were 'rias'.

Putting my fascination with the lie of the land to one side, I eventually stepped ashore at Tufi. Thanks to Tom's organising skills and the mysterious workings of bush telegraph alerting them to my arrival, villagers appeared from out of nowhere, right on cue. Then, with the usual big red betel nut-stained toothy smile introductions done, the welcoming party took me a little way up from the beach to a neat little Pandanus hut. Here I was proudly shown a (rather sad) display of the coarse fibrous Tapa cloth Tom had told me about. With everyone seeming to talk at once, I listened carefully as my trusty boatman-cum-guide, interpreted the method by which they made it. He said the local's harvested strips of bark from the paper mulberry tree, which they then soaked, scraped and pounded flat with a special wooden tool until it was relatively soft and pliable. After drying it out, they then used plant dyes, ochre, charcoal and other earthy colours to decorate the material with various designs, some of which, I noted, resembled the traditional tattoos I had seen on a few of the women's faces.

My boatman interpreter continued, saying the resulting material had originally been made for clothing but now, with

Western clothes being so readily available (and certainly more comfortable than bark cloth), it was mostly for tourists as decorative wall hangings and table runners. I had already seen it as one of the more frequently available craft items in the shops in Moresby and believed it had good potential for encouragement, not only because it was lightweight and easy to pack but also above all because of its distinctive designs were so characteristic of the country.

Sadly, the Tapa cloth they had available was (again!) of poor quality. Apart from a few pieces hanging from the walls there was only a small pile on the floor and that was about it. There just was not much there.

"Was this all there was?" I asked my interpreter.

"*Olsem, man e kamap long Mosbi, na e baim planti gutpela tapa, na lusim rabis! Mi sori tumas.*"

He was saying he had recently sold all the good stuff to someone who had come up from Moresby and who had left the rubbish behind. I was not surprised. With a local population of perhaps only a couple of hundred folk, the quantities were always going to be rather small. I was concerned also that if they encouraged production, they were also going to have to ensure the on-going cultivation of the Mulberry trees that provided the bark.

On asking about prices, I found they expected about the same dollars for each item that I had seen it retail for in Moresby, reinforcing my belief that government should not be involved in trading. Locals knew the government had deep pockets and had bumped up their prices as soon as they knew I was '*Ofisa bilong gavman*'. There was no point in haggling. There was nothing worth photographing anyway. I knew a private dealer would come through again sometime after they had made some more and would pay reasonable prices for decent quality.[74]

I thanked my contacts, jumped in the boat and on we went to the next, thankfully much shorter trip, on down to Wanigela. We stopped off at a couple of villages en route but didn't see any other handcrafts. I was really at the mercy of the boatman, and even though I trusted he had taken me to the most likely villages, I did not have enough time to find out what mysteries might lie up many of the rias defining the coastline.

I resigned myself to believing that the rather poor-quality jewellery and the commercially interesting Tapa were the sum of crafts in the region. I thought I had seen all there was to see. But then, on arriving at Wanigela, I found the best had been saved for last! On this, my final stop, my guide took me up a little way into town, to something he said I would find interesting. Here I was quite excited to find many examples of a most attractive thin-walled 'Lapita' style pottery. The old *meri* I spoke with said she had made the pots I saw on display and, pointing out the larger ones, said these were for cooking and called '*baitab nokwat*'. My interpreter explained that pots like this had been made here, in the Collingwood Bay area, for generations. As with Yabob and Bilbil at the other end of the country, they commonly bartered the pots surplus to the needs of the cooks, for things such as canoes, hunting dogs (really!), bilums, mats and even Tapa[75]. The pots were most attractive, and although of a wide variety of designs and sizes, they all shared a distinctive style of consistently repeated, lightly indented patterns over their surfaces. I thought they had tremendous potential and would fetch excellent prices if made available to appreciative buyers in Moresby.

Of course, being very thin-walled their fragility (as with most pottery), presented real difficulties, in the short term at least. Special and effective packaging would be vital. This would take time to organise, and even good packing could still not guarantee safe arrival. It was something more our plan for assistance would need to consider. Nevertheless, it was certainly an item deserving further support. I bought one beautiful 30 cm diameter dark 'fire smoke brown' pot as an example and carried it carefully on my lap on the flight back to POM so that a professional photographer could produce illustrations for promotional material.

Even though I had not had much to do on my travels other than look, chat and be a passenger on the boat, the journey was tiring. I had been in the sun all day and, while the sea breeze ameliorated the heat somewhat, it was still there.

I completed my survey work and then, with a day before my flight back to POM was due, I happily took a break in Wanigela. Tom said he would try to arrange for me to stay at the Anglican Mission, which coincidentally happened to be right next to the airstrip.

Before leaving me and returning to Popondetta, my boatman and very useful interpreter, took me over and introduced me to Helen Roberts[76], the sister in charge. Fortunately, she had got Tom's message and I avoided the embarrassment of arriving unannounced.

We sat and chatted away for quite a while, about Mission life generally and handcrafts in particular. Naturally, I had to share my initial experiences in Kuraio with her. We both agreed Mission life could get a bit tedious, but Sister Helen said her duties kept her busy, which meant time would fly. As Coordinator of the Anglican Medical Division, she helped to ensure the training given to local medical workers was in line with government requirements (amongst other tasks).

Fortunately, she knew all about the pottery and Tapa cloth and had been helping the locals to sell their crafts over the years. This was great news. We needed a contact in the area, someone other than Tom, who was too far away up the coast, and Sister Helen's experience, knowledge and inherent reliability, would be invaluable for any assistance we might introduce in future.

Then, somewhat surprisingly, after chatting a little while longer, Sister Helen explained that I was to spend the night in another building, a few hundred metres across the other side of the airstrip. Arming me with an old kero lamp, she pointed to a little bush guesthouse, close to mangrove swamps and the sea, and bade me goodnight.

It was now dusk and the on-going staccato 'peep-peep-peep' of lapwings, feeding on the grass runway, kept me company. And later, the gentle sound of the waves sloshing around in the mangroves lulled me off to sleep. After Kuraio and the trip on the Sepik, I realised that if the conditions were reasonably okay, I could tolerate these forays into the bush, for a short while at least.

Next morning, after bidding farewell to Sister Helen and with the lapwings scattering as my own bird swooped down to collect me, I was soon back in POM. Just in time to see the Queen.

Amazingly, nothing untoward had happened on this trip. I didn't get sick; flights and boat rides were all on time. Most importantly, I had identified and recorded a few good handcrafts, some worth promoting immediately and some worth encouraging down the track. As a bonus, I had met some lovely people, including my trusty boatman who had carried me leisurely down the coast in a banana boat, while I balanced my briefcase (with gold-embossed lettering) on my knees and I'd enjoyed seeing some of the most breath-taking scenery on this planet. Such good fortune!

I did not get to meet the Queen of course. I hadn't done anything to deserve such an honour, and after all, I told myself, she did have a hectic schedule. However, in chatting with my other volunteer friends, the consensus was a feeling of disappointment. There was such a large contingent of VSO volunteers countrywide (as well as volunteers from other Commonwealth countries) all doing a lot of good work, so we were surprised Her Majesty had not invited even one representative to meet her. This was especially so as the Queen was Patron of the British Council, the overarching body of VSO, and the Duke of Edinburgh was Patron of VSO itself.

However, to an extent, the invitations to the 'Civic Reception', assuaged any disappointment us Vollies felt. And, fortunately, I found myself in the grandstand sitting just a few metres behind *Missis Kwin*. She was clearly feeling the heat and looking like it was all a bit of an effort. And, with her in her best quality stylish Western clothes (including the usual lovely hat), and the native tribesmen dancing around in their largely plant-based traditional gear, it was also quite bizarre. The contrast could not have been greater!

Port Moresby was basically an ordinary, hard-working administrative centre, and even though it had been tarted up for the occasion, it didn't really have much time for ceremony. But on this occasion, some folk enjoyed themselves. Indeed, Paulius Matane was pleased because the Queen invited him to have dinner with her on the Royal Yacht *Britannia*.

The Queen in Port Moresby, February 1974

Not long after the Queen had left PNG, in late February 1974, and having given Her Royal Assent, Somare made changes to the various ministry portfolios. He renamed us The Department of Commerce and Industry and, at the same time, allocated us a new Minister. There was a small welcoming party for Ebia Olewale on that Friday and I, along with everyone else in the Department, got to meet him. Judging by what he said, he was a more practical man than his predecessor. Molar had supposedly never visited the Department or even issued a directive over the last year.

With the Minister whisked away by his minders and advisers the Assistant Director elaborated on an issue of great interest to us servants of the public, the much-anticipated move to new offices. The increase in the scale of Australian government assistance to PNG (i.e. more Public Servants) meant we had outgrown the old offices (it had certainly been cosy at the meeting) and, yes, we really would be moving to a brand-new building, he said. "But don't hold your breath – it won't be until sometime later in the year."

I wasn't too fussed about the delay. Although it was hot and crowded, I was enjoying having my own little office and working in the CBD and besides, it might be quite academic because I was not sure I would be coming back to PNG anyway.

CHAPTER 16

BACK TO BOUGAINVILLE

After the Queen left, and the dust had settled from the Ministerial changes, we got back to refocus on our development work. Over the last several months my boss and I had discussed the various issues about encouraging the handcrafts sector and had concluded the best course of action would be to establish a separate national marketing organisation. We had drafted a Cabinet submission to this effect, but it was still work in progress. So, while Hovey hurried to incorporate the issues identified by Bill Schulz from our trip down the Sepik and to meet the deadline imposed by Matane, I carried on gathering further information.

From various field officers we knew there were still quite a few areas where they were making crafts but even though we had few details, the field officers also said the quantities were too few and the people were not yet ready for assistance nor for us to spend time on research. However, we also knew of one or two other crafts that were popular amongst expats, and these we just had to investigate. One such item was the 'Buka basket'.

I had heard the folk in the leper colony in Torokina, close to Kuraio, on Bougainville, were making baskets, although the Buka basket was not from there. Rather curiously, it was also well known that the so-called Buka baskets were not woven in Buka either. In fact, they were made further south on the island. So, at the request of my boss, my next trip was to resolve this little mystery and visit the towns and villages of Buin, Kieta and Arawa to find out more information about them and where they really were made.

This trip was planned to be close to Easter, and because of the flight schedules, it meant, quite conveniently, that I would have to come back via Rabaul. Luckily, I could take a few days' break there to catch up with some friends.

This was all scheduled for just a couple of weeks before I was due to *go pinis* as a volunteer. And if I didn't get the job as an expat, I would really '*go pinis olgeta*' – I would be back in the UK for good, and this really would be my last visit to Rabaul.

So, early in April 1974, I flew from POM to Kieta where the area Business Development Officer, Gary Ray, met me. With field staff always keen to know first-hand what was going in Moresby, we chatted about the Queen's visit, the change of Minister and other various developments at HQ, who was in favour and who was out.

Then, driving into town, with the Pacific Ocean on one side and dense green jungle on the other, I had a strong sense of déjà vu, a flashback to my Kuraio days. It was just jungle, just as it should be, green and dense. But this side of the island, as well as having a tarmac road, it looked different, somehow prettier. Perhaps being more exposed to the unfettered expanse of the Pacific Ocean affected the plant life? More likely it was my imagination. With the better circumstances, the style of travel and quality of accommodation, things had changed and the issues I had faced before no longer clouded my temperament. In contrast to my first visit to the island, I felt privileged to be coming here on official government business, and well cossetted too!

Gary and I continued our discussions about handcrafts and business opportunities generally, and he told me not to get too excited about the numbers of crafts being made in his patch either. Indeed, he was a bit surprised that I had come all the way over from Moresby just to see baskets. But he was a little more comfortable about my being there when I described how we, the Administration, was planning to make a major drive to develop the crafts sector.

Later, having checked into the Davara Motel and then relaxing in the bar after my meal, I wondered if I was starting to get just a little bit too fussy about accommodation. The hotel was quite pleasant and the meal okay, but the place was dreadfully cold. They must have turned up the air-conditioning full blast. I was getting used to the tropical heat and more comfortable in the daytime temperature – and getting picky!

Next day I caught yet another flight, this time on a light utility Britten-Norman Islander, and flew further south, down the coast to the little town of Buin. This was one of the places where the baskets that had earned such a reputation for their excellence were made. We were only a little way across the sea from Choiseul, the northernmost island of a different country altogether, the British Solomon Islands Protectorate, a little part of Britain.

As with my yearning to visit Irian Jaya when up in Wewak, I would have loved to find out a little more about the place and see the contrast between the Solomons and Bougainville, but that wasn't to be; I had to make do with the wartime history Gary gave me instead. He explained this was close to where the commander of the Imperial Japanese Navy and architect of the Japanese attack on Pearl Harbour, Admiral Yamamoto, had met his maker. In 1943, American P-38 Lightning's operating out of Guadalcanal, shot his G4M1 'Betty' bomber down and it crashed just 15 miles or so from Buin.

However, back to business, and regrettably, for the same reason I had been warned off going to West New Britain and, as already explained by Gary, there was little to see. There were only half a dozen or so finished baskets to inspect, and one of these was very lopsided! However, I chatted briefly with a couple of locals who knew all about the baskets and gleaned as much information as I could about the numbers made and how many people made them. After recording all this at Buin, I got a lift over to the other basket-making village at Siwai. But, again, there was nothing much to see.

Although somewhat disappointing, I did learn something useful. The shortage of baskets was due to the price of cocoa! When the price of cocoa was high, weavers made fewer baskets because they were too busy tending their crops. It meant that if individuals who made popular crafts were also involved in cash crops, (or other competing activities) we would have to train more people if we wanted more of that craft. All obvious in hindsight and important to understand, but this was the first time it had really registered.

Despite the low volumes, these baskets were one of the most appealing crafts I had seen to date, and like Tapa cloth, they would enjoy good demand. Although quite bulky, they were light and easy to pack and ship, and if the prices and quality were right, they would certainly be worth encouraging.

Importantly, we learned that apart from being very expensive, there were not even the basics in place to arrange for a supply. We supposed we could set up a cash float in the Business Development Office, but this then got government involved in trading, which was contrary to my principles. Another alternative was to organise supply on consignment, which was a possibility down the track, but this would be less appealing to the makers, and with no baskets available at this stage anyway, it was all a bit academic.

My visit was not entirely in vain. I had gathered valuable information that underscored another fundamental issue about developing the handcrafts sector, and something Bill and I had suspected on other visits. It was as much to do with being able to get regular supplies of good quality crafts as it was to do with marketing and promotion. Further refinements to the nature of the work within our proposed organisation were necessary.

I took the short flight back to Kieta and Gary met me again. He immediately apologised that I was no longer staying at the Davara Hotel (because it was booked-out, not because it was too cold!) However, not to worry, he said he had found me a room at the Arovo Hotel. He warned me that I would probably find the service poor, but as it was only for a couple of nights, I should be okay. 'Oh, and by the way, it's on an island,' he added. Not knowing one hotel in the area from the other, I was not too fussed.

Gary drove me along the peninsula out of Kieta and down on to the wharf and put me and my bags on to a speedboat. Then, with a cheery 'See you in the morning' I was whisked away to my new accommodation.

As we crossed the short passage, I could see the hotel, resting quietly in the sun atop the lovely little island of Arovo. It seemed a bit of a mirage really: a hotel with a foreground of a pristine white coral sandy beach, shimmering away over the brilliant ultramarine blue waters of the Pacific Ocean, and with the backdrop of rain forest and palm trees. I didn't yet know about service levels, but it was certainly one of the prettiest settings for a hotel one could imagine.

As we arrived at the jetty a smartly uniformed local welcomed me, helped me off the speedboat, took my things and led me along the pathway through luxuriant shrubbery and into the hotel. I was amazed at the place. It was lavish! No expense spared, and to me it looked like it had been designed as an executive retreat. The beautiful facilities masked any suggestion of a chequered past.

Making myself comfortable in a cane chair and sipping a gin and tonic from the mini-bar, I stared out over the ocean and back to the main island. I could easily put up with poor service just for the view. The gin got me dreaming about how neat it would be to be living like this all the time, being rich and famous, mollycoddled to the nth degree. Or perhaps one of those Michelin people, going around rating restaurants according to some set criteria, and awarding stars… or not. This was dangerous gin thinking and, besides, what I was doing now was far better and more valuable than such a decadent life. I vowed never to forget my recent past, slumming it on the other side of the island, with Calimo serving tinned *pis*. Now that I had landed on my feet, I must not forget my good fortune. I especially thanked my lucky stars as I went along to the restaurant and, somewhat perversely, had a fabulous *pis* based meal of prawn cocktail, baked barramundi and pancakes. For this I would have awarded at least one Michelin star!

In the end, dinner was excellent, breakfast next day was great and it was clear that they had resolved the poor service issue. Everything was just fine.

Next day was a Saturday and free time at weekends was observed on field trips as if at home. As no self-respecting expatriate, or indeed any Public Servant for that matter, could visit Bougainville without seeing the mine, Gary took me up to Panguna. We drove along the access road, winding our way up through the Crown Prince Range of mountains, past utilitarian housing and administration buildings before finally arriving at the site.

They had begun full commercial production here a couple of years earlier and it was now one of the largest copper and gold mines in the world. As I had never been anywhere near a mine before, large or small, and seeing the size of the hole in the ground, it certainly looked large to me.

Gary said the Central Government in Moresby owned a fifth of the operation and the revenue from this alone represented nearly half of PNG's economy. It was incredibly important in helping to develop the country. However, for some reason, the island of Bougainville, with an estimated population of around seven per cent of the population of the country[77], received, at best, a little over one per cent of the profits. Obviously, the size of the share was a point of considerable controversy.

Gary introduced me to Doug, a hard-hatted toughie and my guide for the day. Explaining the operations in lay-man's terms, he said mining here essentially involved blasting ore out of the ground, trucking it to a massive crusher (using some of the largest vehicles in the world[78]) and then transporting the crushed rock along several kilometres of conveyor belting to grinding mills. Here, they broke the ore down further in vast, ten to fifteen-metre diameter, steel drums until it became a fine slurry. They then scraped off the froth containing the metals and piped this nearly twenty-five kilometres down to the coast. Finally, they dried it and finally shipped it out to smelters which then separated out the various metals.

After giving me the run-down, my guide told me there was a blast scheduled in half an hour and we should go and see it. We jumped in a beat-up utility, drove for fifteen minutes or so away from the site offices and stood on an outcrop of rocks to watch. Now, about a kilometre away from the blast zone, we looked out over a barren landscape of flattened, dark yellowy-brown clay, entirely devoid of any trees or remnant jungle. Shortly a warning siren went off and a few minutes later we were treated to an amazing spectacle: twenty or so huge spouts of dirt and rock shot up in the air, followed instantly by an area of land the size of two or three soccer fields rising a few metres off the ground before immediately slumping back down again, all followed by an almighty rumbling, muffled 'whumpf'.

Thinking back on my one previous observation of blasting, with Stewart and his tree roots on the other side of the island, I recalled how he had used dynamite. Here, according to my guide, dynamite was just the detonator for the real charge. The material that did the heavy lifting was massive amounts of ammonium nitrate packed into many 20 cm-diameter holes, each of which was around fifteen metres, or three or four car lengths, deep.

I went back to the hotel incredibly impressed by the scale of the operation and in the knowledge that nature's mineral deposits contributed so much to the development of the country and people's welfare. After Panguna had become fully operational in 1972, mineral exports had risen to comprise over half of the country's total export earnings.

Following on from this, on the Monday and after a luxurious, lazy day of rest, I was ferried back to the mainland, met by one of Gary's staff and driven the ten kilometres or so up to the Arawa office. Here, I was introduced to some folk who were starting up a handcraft shop and we chatted about how the Department could help them get supplies of crafts from other parts of the country.

Afterwards I went and looked around the various stores here, and again up at Panguna. With all the comings and goings for mine operations and with so many expat workers wanting to take home a souvenir, the handcrafts scene was quite active on this side of the island. Retailers already enjoyed a good deal of demand and, with freight and transport frequent and plentiful, it would be easy to expand the market by facilitating the supply of crafts from other parts of PNG.

So, come mid-April '74 I was again sitting in a trusty Fokker F27 Friendship and, having just finished writing up my report, I was enjoying a well-earned drink. I had taken off from Hoskins in West New Britain, and after this leg of the trip I would have flown from Port Moresby to Kieta, thence to Buin and back, from Kieta to Rabaul, on to Hoskins and finally back to Moresby. It had all been great fun and very productive, but now I was glad to be on my way home.

One of the good things about the Friendship was that its wings are high up on the fuselage, offering a clear view of the terrain below from each window. So now I could again see the volcanic hills, the ubiquitous serried rows of coconut palms of the plantations and then the jungle of wild trees as we crossed over the island of New Britain. Heading west for the mainland, we were flying over cotton-boll clouds, over an endless expanse, first of the green of the jungle and then of the remarkable blue of the sea. A brief glimpse of a few more islands in the distance presented itself as we crossed the northern part of the Solomon Sea. This was far more enjoyable than flying higher in a jet where there was rarely anything to see other than blue sky or grey and white clouds. Another trip was nearly over and the drink helped me reminisce about the last few days in Rabaul I had tacked on to the finish of my business trip.

Rabaul was still as beautiful as I had remembered, but I recalled how at my last departure fourteen months earlier my feelings had been dreadfully mixed. On the one hand I was relieved to be leaving, but, on the other I was sad to think it would be the last time I would see this beautiful town. I never dreamt I would be back again, least of all on a stopover while working for the government.

Again, I contacted Martin and later, joined by a few of his friends, we all went to have a drink to celebrate having survived PNG thus far. After the consumption of several beers, and in a bit of an alcoholic haze, we agreed that, next day, just for fun, we should go for a climb in the hills. We knew there was any number of peaks and craters around Simpson Harbour[79], but we picked Mount Kabiu because it was the closest to where we were staying. This dormant volcano, more commonly known as The Mother, was only seven hundred metres or so above sea level and we figured it would be an easy climb.

The evening carried on with some serious drinking and of course, by the next day it was a real struggle even to get out of bed. By the time we had got ourselves organised and set off it was already mid-morning. But we walked anyway. We climbed, we got hot and we got even hotter. The sun rose brassily over us until we'd been almost cooked alive, so much so, dehydration quickly manifested itself in the shakes. Only a few days earlier in Kieta, I had thought I had become fully acclimatised to the tropics and had graduated to being more like my gung-ho, do-anything Aussie friend John Mason. Now I knew I had underestimated how much energetic exercise I could undertake and I was seriously uncomfortable.

Fortunately, less than halfway up, someone (not me) said 'Sod this! All too hard!' and, as one, and without any argument, we called it quits, turned around, walked back down and collapsed in the relative cool of the house.

In justifying our retreat, we knew The Mother was the highest of all the peaks and very steep sided and we all agreed that as with any mountain, climbing it is much harder than it appears to be from a distance. We joked that at least she had not blown her top!

Later, in relating our half-hearted attempt to other friends, they told us we had been foolish to even try. Not only because of the heat and humidity but also because of The Mother's reputation. They explained that Rabaul had been built on unstable tectonic plates and surrounded by volcanoes and volcanic hills and frequently experienced earthquakes, tsunamis and volcanic eruptions[80]. I recalled the *guria's* I felt in Bougainville and had to agree. Indeed, only a few months before we had arrived in PNG, in July 1971, as a report put it:

'Two massive earthquakes, twelve days apart, rocked Rabaul and its environs, each causing damage and followed by a tsunami. From the Vulcanological Observatory on the hill above the town came warnings that another volcanic eruption was likely. Evacuation plans were drawn up and emergency procedures trialled.'[81]

Even after hearing this I found it impossible to imagine the impact such another event would have on the place.

CHAPTER 17

WHAT'S NEXT?

By the close of April 1974, despite all the excitement, I was looking forward to going back to Britain. After the initial roller coaster of emotions followed by a year or so of exploration through my job, I realised I had grown to love Papua New Guinea. I loved my work and the casual lifestyle; I enjoyed the company of my friends and I had even learned to love the climate. But now I needed to get back to the cold for a little while. And naturally, I wanted to share my stories with my family.

For the last few months, I had been concerned about my job. Sure, the PSB had approved the position, but there was still no guarantee I would get it; I was on tenterhooks. But then, just after I got back from Bougainville, Hovey came around with the good news. The PSB had responded and to my relief had awarded me the job.

The conditions of employment were way beyond my expectations. At twenty-eight years of age, I was to become a Senior Technical Office, Grade 1, with pay nearly five times as much as my last job in Britain! With such a low rate of tax, low cost of accommodation and with three months leave every couple of years, it was all bloomin' marvellous!

Now, my plan was to finish my voluntary service with VSO, go home to the UK, carry out the research in Europe, return to PNG and carry on as usual, but now as a fully-paid expatriate Public Servant with the Australian Administration. I was on a roll!

Shortly after this, the Australian Department of Trade sent me a schedule of appointments they had made for me with businesses scattered across the UK, The Netherlands, Germany and Switzerland. It all sounded appropriate for the job at hand, but I knew I would need a break after all that, so I planned my journey, quite logically, to end up in Italy. Despite feeling my work was close to being on holiday anyway, I made sure I was going to stop here awhile and have a real one!

Meanwhile, over the past few months, Hovey and I had become convinced that support for the handcrafts sector was as much about supply as it was about stimulating demand. We had to ask the question: even if I found strong interest from Europe in buying our crafts, could we deliver? We had come to realise that a significant issue with the whole exercise was the relatively low level of dedicated involvement of Papua New Guinean craftsmen. They were mostly village folk whose focus was on living their traditional lifestyle and it was hardly surprising that many people only produced crafts when they felt like it or in their spare time. Also, with the introduction of cash crops, it meant craft making would only ever be a secondary, or at best a cyclical activity. Left to their own devices, this would probably be the case for many years to come.

Also, of concern was the apparent shortage of locals involved in the business of trading crafts. Even though Papua New Guineans were running a variety of businesses, few, if any, appeared to be very interested in buying and selling handcrafts or artefacts. And, although many of the expatriate dealers employed local staff, they were essentially assistants and probably some way off being capable of managing the business. Even knowing these private sector people were a good and existing conduit to the market, the Administration could not be seen to be helping expatriate businesses, so our relationship with them was (unnecessarily in my opinion) quite distant.

There was one local guy we thought was involved in the artefact trade. He was a young man, destined to be a tribal chief. Unfortunately, he also had a reputation for being a bit radical in his anti-colonial sentiments. His political aspirations clearly came first, but even if he was not directly involved in trading, we knew he was keen to ensure all monies made from artefacts and crafts ended up in the hands of nationals, which was fair enough. But, probably because of his known attitude, our conservative section of the Administration simply could not pursue a closer working relationship.

While I found these aspects of the project frustrating, I reminded myself that I was currently only *contributing* to the planning for development of the crafts industry with my focus on marketing. Most of these bigger worries were common to the overall process of localisation and they were for my boss to handle. Nevertheless, I was keen to progress the crafts development plan we were devising and looked forward to doing that on my return later in the year.

I started preparing for my big trip in Europe. I needed to tidy up a lot of loose ends: pack away things I was not taking with me, sell my car (I could not leave it out on the lane unattended at Ralph's place where it would most likely be stolen or vandalised) and confirm my flights. And, then, just when I was busiest, at the very last minute, something else came up. Two friends, Alan and Di, had been a couple for a long time before I had met them in Moresby and we were all happy to hear they were going south to get married. I had always found Alan to be a bit of a morose bore, but I liked Di. She was a complete contrast, a green-eyed, freckle-faced redhead with a kind, chatty nature.

Suddenly, one afternoon, Di turned up at my place, alone, a crying wreck. Through the sobs I heard that right at the very last-minute Alan had just packed his bags and flown back to Brisbane, on his own. He had got cold feet and left her almost literally standing at the altar! She was a mess.

It seemed far too soon for her to plan sensibly, but between sobs, she said she was now going to travel in Europe to get over it all, before returning home to the UK. I was even more surprised when Di asked me if we could perhaps meet up in Europe somewhere. I was a bit preoccupied with my own affairs, but without really thinking about it I said, "Well, sure, of course. I will be in Switzerland in June, why don't we meet there? How about in Zurich?"

"Wonderful," she says, "see you there!"

Knowing how emotionally unsettled she was, I really didn't expect anything to come of the arrangement, but I gave her my hotel and the dates and left it at that.

I left Moresby in late April 1974, and after enduring a long, tedious and readily forgotten series of flights, finally arrived back in Britain. Peering out of the window as we taxied towards Arrivals at Heathrow, the first thing I saw was that all the baggage handlers were white men. I had become so used to Papua New Guineans doing these sorts of jobs, it looked most peculiar!

Catching the train down to Bath Spa and then the big green double-decker Number 48 bus to Winsley, I was soon travelling through the beautiful Limpley Stoke valley, with its railway line, canal and river (overlooked by Brown's Folly), then down the very tight turn off the A36 just before the viaduct and subsequently up Winsley Hill.

How bizarre it all was, compared with a day or so earlier in Moresby and the tropics! I had this urge to talk to someone on the bus and tell them where I had just come from. They would have moved seats!

Finally, I arrived back at East Hill, and after travelling halfway around the globe and switching so abruptly from one culture to another, there was Mother, standing in the doorway. She looked much older than I remembered and even clumsier on her walking sticks (she would not use crutches). We embraced awkwardly.

"So glad to see you, my dear. Did you have a good trip?" I had a tear in my eye.

Then the huge comfy armchairs that enveloped you; the same old pink carpet ('It's a Wilton, you know') in the living room... all so strange.

After the initial euphoria, more hugs with Mother, and sitting in the living room and chatting over a cup of tea, it felt like I had just been down the road to Bradford-on-Avon and back. Having lived in such a different environment and now coming back to where I had started produced a most disconcerting feeling. I had changed and was restless; I could not wait to get up and go somewhere again, anywhere. I had missed Mum of course and England, but my feelings towards the country had changed.

Hearing Harold Wilson had recently formed a minority Labour government did not help much. Being a staunch Conservative, this was not good news to my ears and promised little hope for an economic turnaround from the recession I had left in 1972. And, despite all this, Winsley was precisely the same quiet, safe place it always had been: quiet, safe and boring!

I made myself at home as best I could and thought briefly about looking up a few of my old friends. We had not been great letter writers and as it was such a long time since we had last communicated, I, rather curiously, just did not feel like seeing them again. Apart from the fact most of them lived a hundred and more miles away in Buckinghamshire, even though I had enjoyed their company in the past, I knew they would either be married or still living their own standard British lives. I had left all that behind a long time ago, and now, while I had certainly never intended it to be so, that way of life in Britain was now somehow so... irrelevant? I never dreamt of considering myself to be in the same league as a missionary, but it was of some consolation to hear they also go through a 'no home' experience when they transition back out of service from a third-world country.

To counter all these unusual emotions, I occupied myself with doing my duty with family and preparing for my research. As luck would have it one of my Mum's sisters, the quintessential maiden aunt, phoned to say she was coming over to stay with us at East Hill 'Just for a short while'. While there was some foreboding expressed between Mum and me, the upside was it saved me the long drive over to her place. She lived in the charming, very British and very upper-class village of Midhurst in Sussex, but it was on the other side of Britain and there was no direct road from Winsley.

Although I had not got on with Aunt Mary (Mother used to say she was a real trial and Dad said she was 'horsey' and once joked he'd buy her a saddle for her birthday), she was undoubtedly the most intellectual of our family, on mother's side at least. She had developed a career in education and was Headmistress of Londonderry High School for Girls in Northern Ireland from 1962 until late in 1973. Indeed, she had only resigned after they had found a .303 bullet embedded in the oak panelling behind her office desk! Everyone knew The Troubles affected a lot of people, and being a Protestant from England didn't help her situation. She got the message and decided it was time to go. While many of us found it a bother that Mary was usually the boss, she had her points. She was the only one in the family with whom I could have a reasonably in-depth conversation.

And so, one sunny afternoon, we were sitting on deck chairs in the quiet of the back lawn, while I told her of my recent visit to the mine on Bougainville. She immediately picked up on the damage the mine must be causing to the environment and asked what I thought about that! Quite honestly, I had not thought about the environment at all and thus had not formed an opinion; I had focused instead on the benefits the mine was bringing to Papua New Guineans and the economy.

She asked whether I had read the book *Silent Spring* by Rachel Carson[82] (I had not) and then proceeded to summarise the issues the author raised regarding environmental damage caused by man. Mary explained that while Carson was mainly concerned with the indiscriminate use of pesticides, many of man's other activities were causing serious harm, and mining was one of them. I reluctantly agreed with her, and recalled seeing the white residue on the foliage of bushes resulting from the widespread spraying of DDT around Moresby and supposed I had been a little concerned. But everyone knew malaria was a big killer and with the government Anti-Malaria Unit going around spraying houses to kill off the mosquitos, we all assumed DDT was safe. I believed the advantage of keeping down mosquitos and malaria outweighed any possible downsides. Besides, not knowing anything about any side effects from the processes involved in mining, I didn't think it was of such significant concern. The politicians and technocrats no doubt understood the issue of environmental damage (assuming the mining companies told them all they knew), and both were obviously effective in playing it down. The attention of Papua New Guinea's Ministers (and Australia's as well) was more focused on the wealth the mine generated for PNG. My take on the situation was that the benefits brought to society of the revenue and the minerals themselves, used in so many products, far outweighed the negative impact on the environment.

I left Aunt Mary as I usually did, in a somewhat disagreeable frame of mind. It was not that I thought she was wrong, it was more a matter of her raising a problem and me not having thought about it, or caring, even though I knew I probably should. I had my adventure to live, and I was carrying on with that. My interest was more (like Cicero) to do with the reality of finding practical solutions to problems today, rather than a perhaps futile search for the virtuous ideal.

After staying with Mother for a week or so, I made a quick trip down to Plymouth to see my other aunt, dear Aunty Joan, the one who had travelled all the way up to farewell me at Heathrow. I stayed with her for a few days and from there visited my brother, his wife and their children, who lived around the corner in Saltash.

Joan was always my favourite. She had lived a totally different life from Mary. She had been in the Queen Alexandra's Royal Naval Nursing Service based in Alexandria in Egypt during the Second World War, and by all accounts, somewhat ironically, had enjoyed herself! We could relate. Latterly she had been and still was, walking miles around Plymouth every day visiting her patients as a district health nurse.

After getting over the usual chitchat about PNG and what I was doing, it appeared her main concern was about my health and she said I needed to come back to Britain and a cold climate as the tropics 'thinned the blood' – I didn't argue.

It was also good to see and talk with Richard again and hear (and see) how his interests in aesthetics, as a commercial artist-cum-graphic designer, had evolved. Somewhat like Dad, he seemed to spend an awful lot of his time making physical improvements to his house.

I found it a little bizarre to realise that I was now an uncle to his two kids. Seeing how much they had grown, without warning, made me wake up to my age and my still unmarried status. Of course, brother, wife and kids also provided a captive audience and even though I bored them silly, I had to tell them all my tales of the tropics. Different worlds!

Family duty done, I drove back up to Winsley and realised I still had itchy feet. There was only so much to keep me amused in this little village. I kicked my heels around Bath, visited my friend

Paul Green, who ran a hi-fi business selling fancy stereo systems and decided on the one I would buy when I actually got paid.

I also visited a few of my other old haunts, including the Hop Pole in Limpley Stoke. This was my Dad's favourite pub and he had been such a regular the landlord named a drink after him, a 'John Brown'. I discovered later this was just a gin and bitters or a pink gin, a common tipple, but I liked to think my Dad started the trend.

Then there was the Seven Stars in Winsley, where I had spent many an evening boozing with my friends before I had left home. Revisiting this cosy 18th century stone-built pub, I found that all my old friends had now left the village, and I ended up drinking on my own. A dreadful bore. On top of that, the beer was warm! Now I pined for PNG as much as I had looked forward to the UK when I was there. Talk about unsettled!

So, as planned, I left Mum again, not thinking too much about her welfare. I hard-heartedly thought she could look after herself as she had all along since Dad died ten years earlier. With my suitcase full of handcraft samples, I set off on my travels to find out what potential buyers thought about them.

Earlier on, while planning for this research, Hovey and I decided it would be a good idea to take orders for specific items to test the market at the same time. We figured that if I got some actual orders, it would provide a better indication of genuine interest. Otherwise, the answers to my questions of 'Would you buy?' 'How much would you pay for.....?' etc would be hypothetical and the whole exercise could be quite academic.

My first guinea pig, when I started off in London, was very welcoming and fascinated to hear my story about what we were doing to encourage small industry in such an unusual part of the world. She said parts of Africa and South America, Asia even, were well known for their crafts, but the mention of Papua New Guinea drew the same sort of response I had shown originally – 'Where is that exactly?'

On closer inspection she thought none of the items we had to offer were either useful or works of art, but somewhere in between. Even the wooden bowl was too elaborate to be of practical worth, and 'far too expensive'. It was obvious she would not be buying.

This partly reflected a mismatch with the nature of their business, but then again, I realised visitors to a country, expat workers or tourists, did not necessarily purchase items to suit the reasons of utility either. Indeed, they usually bought them as decoration and a memento of their time in that country. And, of course, if they had not visited PNG but maybe just seen the item in a shop in London, for example, a large part of the reason to purchase just was not there. But there again, I supposed this same argument applied to all third-world crafts.

I wasn't particularly surprised at her response. The crafts I was evaluating just did not fit her type of business. She did not believe sales would justify the effort of sourcing the few items that might sell from a country she and many others had never heard of, particularly as the prices suggested would make them far more expensive than comparable crafts from other countries. But surely, there had to be a market for them somewhere?

After a few more visits in Britain, I set off on the European leg of my tour. Arriving in Amsterdam, my first appointment was with the manager of a curio shop. Following on from a few awkward pleasantries and fencing around the language barrier, I found he had started focusing on prices. I was not sure if he was giving me some bargaining spiel to get a better price, or was simply playing a game, but after more disjointed discussions, I realised, to my surprise, he was genuinely interested in buying, so we started talking detail. In the end, he placed a large order for a trial shipment! With my spirits up, I realised Holland's past involvement in Indonesia and that part of the world helped, and had also provided a useful clue for further promotion.

After Holland, I went on to Germany and stopped first in Hamburg. My reception was a replay of what I had found in London. I took it all on board and noted the comments. I was getting good feedback. I saw there was a fair degree of uncertainty over the question of who would be interested in buying PNG crafts in Germany.

It also became apparent that a few of the businesses the Australian Consulates had arranged for me to visit were quite inappropriate. One was a store selling German souvenirs to foreign tourists. A handcrafted item from Papua New Guinea was not really the sort of thing a foreign tourist visiting Germany would expect to find, or be particularly interested in buying. It seemed at least some of the businesses we should be targeting were those selling items to the local population for decoration in their own homes or offices.

Moving on, I experienced a dreadfully bumpy flight from Hamburg to Stuttgart and had my equilibrium additionally impacted by the faulty sound system. The muzak tape machine, (switched on to calm our nerves during take-off, descent and landing) had such a severe case of wow and flutter, it sounded like a strangled cat and succeeded in doing quite the opposite!

After all that and the hassle of getting to and from the airport, I realised flying was quite unnecessary anyway. The German rail system was so good I could more fruitfully have gone from centre to centre by train and have seen something of Germany in the process. As it was, I saw plenty of airports and insides of planes, and nothing much else.

I had better luck with my research in Stuttgart. Although my respondents were not quite as enthusiastic as in Amsterdam, I received lots of advice and another sizable sample order.

With my spirits lifted yet again and my business visits done for the day, I was now determined to see something of Germany. From a brochure in the hotel, I read about the Neues Schloss, an 18th century baroque style palace in the centre of town, so I went to have a peek. Although the Allies had bombed the place in the war, the stone façade had survived and they had recently completed rebuilding the remainder. It was now home to the Ministry of Culture, the Baden-Württemberg State Government and the Treasury. It was an eye-catching honey-coloured building, which positively glowed in the afternoon sun. The architecture was so attractive, I thought I would take a photograph, and to do so I walked back across the Schlossplatz to Konigstrasse to get it all in frame. I had barely positioned myself to take the shot when a man came up and stood right in front of me, hiding the building and filling my viewfinder. I moved to one side, but the guy moved in front of me again and this time started shouting and gesticulating wildly. I tried one more time and the same thing happened again, but this time he started walking towards me! Concerned that he was aiming to physically attack me, I turned and ran to the nearest building and literally bumped into a group of smartly dressed, big, beefy business types coming out of the doorway. I hurriedly garbled my predicament in English, with a few words of German thrown in for good measure and, as I turned to point out my would-be attacker, my new acquaintances and I just managed to glimpse the fellow. It was enough, and on seeing my bodyguard, he turned his face to one side and pretended to be part of the crowd.

There was the distinct possibility my new acquaintances thought that maybe it was I who was the crazy one, but fortunately not so. They formed a protective circle around me and after an initial 'Kommen Sie mit uns' and 'der Verrückte' (the crazy guy) one of them said suddenly, in perfect English, "We're catching a tram back to our hotel. Why don't you come with us and we'll give this crazy the slip?"

I gratefully hopped on the tram with these guys and travelled a little way out of town with them. Having recovered from my scare, I thanked them, jumped off and walked back to my hotel. The light was still strong enough to reflect off the tram tracks winding down the hill, but the sunny brightness of the day had gone and taken my carefree mood with it. Now I felt vulnerable and rather lonely. As I wended my way through other pedestrians on the street, all minding their own business, the mood gradually passed. But it did seem a long walk back to the hotel, and now, also with the light gone, I had missed out on getting a decent shot of the Schloss!

Next stop Basel. By this stage, I was beginning to worry about the overall response to my research thus far. It seemed only a few of those I had spoken to were very interested in PNG handcrafts. I had certainly got a few sample orders, but I also got the impression most were doing me a favour just to meet with me. They were fascinated to hear about PNG, but no one was terribly interested in the crafts. Hoping things would change and that I would find some greater enthusiasm, I prepared to meet my next survey respondent cum potential customer.

I had found from my research back in PNG that the Swiss had an excellent collection of primitive art in their museums. In fact, as we had discovered before our trip down the Sepik, the Basel Museum der Kulturen held a vast collection of items from Papua New Guinea. I hoped some of this interest in primitive art might have rubbed off on the population in general. It was not to be. Again, I was given the sweet talk and told 'Thanks but no thanks'. My samples all looked 'sehr interessant', but not interesting enough to buy, not now, nor in the future.

From Basel I moved on to Zürich, the commercial centre of Switzerland. Surely, they would be interested, and maybe they would even place an order?

As I arrived, I could not help but notice the majestic skyline of the Alps contrasting with the towers of the Grossmünster church and other wonderful buildings in the foreground. Zürich was an attractive city, but I soon came back down to earth when, unbelievably, I found the Australian Trade Mission had booked me into a grubby, poor-quality hotel! There were photographs and a cheap tapestry on the walls hiding stains and torn wallpaper, and wardrobe door handles that didn't match! This was a surprise. I had enjoyed far by better accommodation in the back blocks of PNG and now I was spoiled, I guess. Either the Trade Mission was getting low on their budget or my status in a third-world country, even as a *Senior* Technical Officer did not warrant anything better in the eyes of the Trade Mission.

As something of a counterbalance to the tatty hotel, I found the Swiss to be far friendlier than the few Germans I had met.

Maybe it was a personal thing, but they far were less dismissive and more sincere in their manner.

I also discovered that while my very basic German (limited vocabulary, non-existent grammar and questionable pronunciation) was quite useful for ordering a coffee, it could also be quite inconvenient. The differences in pronunciation between the Germans and the Swiss did not much help either. Thus, while I felt most people I spoke to understood me, a taxi driver I had asked to take me to one particular address certainly took me for a ride. I had asked for a place on Wührestrasse, but unfortunately for me (but not for him) he heard 'Wuhrstrasse' and dumped me a full thirty kilometres away from where I had wanted to go! How many other visitors had been conveniently misunderstood by this taxi driver I wondered? To make matters worse, when I eventually got to the right address, I found it was a retail shop selling cotton yarns, buttons and cloth by the metre. They would not sell PNG crafts, or anyone else's crafts, in a million years. Such a waste of time! The Australian Trade Mission was supposed to have checked out the places I had given them as suggestions for my research, but it looked like one or two had slipped through the net.

After leaving my last visit of the day, I needed some fresh air and relief from the by now somewhat predictable responses to the questions about our crafts. I spent a bit of time wandering around Zürich and confirmed my initial impressions that it was a lovely old town. But, as the evening progressed however, it seemed winter had come early. There was no real snow, but with flurries of fine powder running across the tops of the cobblestones and without appropriate clothing, I felt the bitterly cold breeze off the Alps. I prayed it would be warmer down in

Italy. Continuing to shiver, and seeing people scurrying around to get home from work and hunched over against the cold, the old chestnut of an expression 'the Gnomes of Zürich' came to mind. Walking around the backstreets of the Rindermarkt and Seilergraben area, I found little cobbled alleyways going hither and thither. Bordered by shops and houses of all sorts of shapes and sizes, it seemed all quite picturesque and appropriate as homes for gnomes!

Despite the poor quality of my hotel I hurried back to be out of the cold and then, surprise, surprise, who should I find waiting in the lobby but Di, my friend from PNG. She had been in such turmoil I had not really expected her to keep to her plan. And meeting up with someone I had known in one context and who now suddenly appeared in another produced a very strange sense of *déja vu*, a 'past-life' experience.

But anyway, here she was, as planned, travelling to get over her broken heart. She was still very emotional and I could quite understand when she again, quite tearfully, recalled the events leading up to her being alone. I rather reluctantly became her shoulder to cry on and continued to empathise, but explained she would have to look around town by herself while I finished off my work.

Finally, I completed my last few visits. I now had all the information I needed, plus a few sample orders to practice with as a bonus. Very broadly, I had found potential buyers wanted either standardised products aligned with a fixed price list showing unit cost, discount for volume, all the usual commercial terms, or alternatively, one-off museum-quality artefacts. When my contacts realised the individuality of PNG handcrafts, their interest dropped. They were spoiled by crafts, supposedly made by hand, from places such as the Philippines, which had succumbed (as my boss had wanted) to being commercialised and standardised. Ours were not for everyone. Indeed, for many businesses, they were too hard to order, stock, promote and sell. Nevertheless, getting the sample orders was of great value, because it showed there was at least some real interest. The proof of the pudding would be the rate at which these buyers would sell on to the public and then provide repeat orders (which, if I had my way, we would channel through the private sector). It was a start.

I finished off my report, faxed it and the orders back to Hovey and left it to him to action. I reckoned I had done quite well and definitely earned myself a vacation. It was time to relax!

I had found Di's companionship to be a nice change from the last few days. And, so now, with us both champing at the bit to go and see the sights we caught the train down to Lausanne and on to Geneva. We stopped there for a while and explored the city, and sat and ate lunch beside Lac Léman in beautiful crisp sunny weather. We went over and took a quick look at the Palais des Nations (boring) and a few other local sights and then later, travelled on to the pretty little town of Ascona. Located on the northern shore of Lake Maggiore and right on the border between Switzerland and Italy, it was such a lovely spot we just had to linger. After wandering along the lake promenade, with its street cafés and all the local bustle, we stopped for a beer and enjoyed the lazy, soft and golden afternoon sunshine. We were still in Switzerland, but the place was much warmer than Zürich and with a definite Latin air about it – a primer for Italy.

We carried on by train down to Milan and then, on entering the massive and spectacular Duomo di Milano (the building of which started in 1386 and was not finished until 1965), we found, to our surprise, attendants allowed us right up on the roof. There, we stood in thrall of the myriad marble statues, each on its own smaller spire and displayed against the backdrop of the city. We learned that the statues were there to *'provide an image of Paradise: patriarchs and prophets, martyrs and saints indicate (ing) our eternal destiny as people redeemed by the sacrifice of the Cross, guided towards heaven by the Virgin Mary'*[83]. These truly were artefacts, and works of art!

Running back down the many stairs until our knees wobbled, we hiked across town to the magnificent 15th Century Sforza Castle. Built by the Duke of Milan on the remains of an even older fort, it included a wonderful collection of art and artefacts. Here I realised the chasm between their culture and that of the people of Papua New Guinea, something that had existed even so many centuries earlier.

After a couple of days in Milan, we took the train on down to Venice. We did the obligatory St. Mark's Basilica, the Square, the Bridge of Sighs, (so appropriate, although for a different reason!) before again taking a train down to the serene town of Padua and eventually all the way down to Florence.

We swooned together over the many famous works of art in the Uffizi and one item I would never forget, Botticelli's huge *'Nascita di Venere'* (Birth of Venus). Magnificent! And then, an even larger example of truly outstanding art and craftsmanship, the statue of Michelangelo's David in the Galleria dell' Accademia. What a dream!

But suddenly it was all over. Di went back to Britain to hopefully get over her sorrows and I moved on to Rome to catch my flight back to PNG. But I was happy. I had enjoyed a pleasant visit back home, a successful business trip through Europe and a wonderful holiday in Italy with the added pleasure of some female company!

During this sojourn I had been able to reflect on my aspirations and my career. In the process of fulfilling my dream to travel and doing my duty as a volunteer, I realised that I had been caught up in a new way of life. Originally, I'd simply wanted to see the world, but in having done so, I had found there to be so many issues of importance.

The influences of PNG were entirely different from those in Britain. I'd swapped a prosaic office job on Slough Trading Estate for an exciting one in a hot, sunny and wet (or dry and dusty) vibrant tropical environment; a job with travel, flying, fancy hotels, the occasional dugout canoe trip, a totally different culture, social expectations etc, the informality of Australian working conditions, the 'us and them' mentality of expats and the locals (not in a derogatory sense, simply the undeniable reality). Britain was now too quiet, too unexciting and, somewhat strangely, too big. In Britain, I was just one of too many millions of people striving to make a living. In PNG there was a sense of excitement, because what we were doing was of national importance – we were doing it for a whole country, and I was part of the action.

More importantly, during this time I had developed not only a new interest in small business but an understanding of the needs of others in a different society; a concern over inequity and inequality. And now I had to pursue it all. I had achieved a level of commitment to PNG and having been back to Britain, I had seen the country from an entirely different perspective. It was a strange feeling, as if in a waking dream. I supposed I would return to Britain one day, but my spirit was not in it – not just yet, anyway. I recalled how any love I had ever had for the place had evaporated some time before I had left in the first instance. I realised that that was the negative reason for my need to travel, balanced out, as it were, by the positive of a desire to see the world.

Having travelled, and now being involved in a small way in making improvements to an entire industry, I had found something to assuage any subconscious desire to be rich and famous. I was involved in doing something interesting and useful, and with my appetite well and truly whetted, and with a whole lot more adventures ahead, I couldn't wait to get back.

THE END

POSTSCRIPTS

THE FATE OF THE
MV KIRIAKA ARO

Many years after these events, Joe Aroviri, who, as a young Bougainvillean boy was a frequent passenger on the boat, and Stewart Gibson, one of my colleagues at Kuraio, gave the following account of the fate of the *Kiriaka Aro*.

Part of Stewart's brief from VSO was for him to be Master of the *Kiriaka Aro* for the year he was to be in Kuraio. On his arrival in September 1970, Bill Mentzer, the Catholic Priest who had started the West Coast Development Society (WCDS), handed Stewart a copy of the *Admiralty Manual of Seamanship* in preparation for a visit to the Harbour Master in Kieta.

When the day came, Stewart, in being questioned about his experience with boats, answered truthfully that for the previous three years he had been owner and Master of a converted 24-foot steel hulled ship's lifeboat. As a result, he was awarded a

50 Ton Master's Ticket restricted to operating in Bougainville waters and Rabaul. Thus armed, he relieved the Australian who, with Jacob, had been running the *Kiriaka Aro* between Buka and Rabaul for some time.

Later, after having made forty or so round trips between Buka and Rabaul, Stewart had gained enough expertise to take the written exam and passing this, earned his 250 HP Engineer's Ticket. Eventually, Mark Roberts replaced Bill Mentzer who, by now had left Kuraio. Stewart then decided to help Mark run the WCDS and run the *Kiriaka*. Luckily VSO provided two more volunteers, Chris Powell to look after the cattle and Martin DeVries, who was able to get his 250 HP Engineer's Ticket. Martin and Jacob continued to run the boat until the annual dry-dock survey, but Martin decided not to extend his one-year commitment and left after the 1972 survey. Nick (the author) then came along in September 1972, but not willing, or able, to risk managing the boat, he left in mid-January 1973. Then, as he said he would, Jacob left. Surprisingly, after all the previous concerns, the WCDS managed to find someone else to captain her. Following on from this, Chris and Stewart left, and Mark (who had originally left in 1972) returned to Kuraio late in 1973.

While Mark found the local crew with the necessary Tickets, the Maritime Authorities advised the WCDS that it was too dangerous for the local crew to make the crossing from Buka to Rabaul and recommended instead the *Kiriaka Aro* be restricted to Bougainville coastal waters. Consequently, they ended up shipping produce to Kieta, on the east coast of Bougainville, rather than taking it up to Rabaul.

On one occasion in late 1974, while returning from Kieta to Buka Passage at night, they apparently failed to make a 'running fix' correctly. The *Kiriaka Aro* went up on a reef near the shores of Hantoa, a few 100 km's out of Buka and was lost. Joe and the many others who depended on the boat were devastated, as were we volunteers who had helped run her.

MINING BOUGAINVILLE

"There is enough on earth for everybody's need,
but not for everyone's greed."
- Mahatma Gandhi

Bougainville's problems[84] were simmering away for a few years before I lived briefly on that island. At the heart of the matter, but by no means the sole cause[85], was the 1967 agreement giving Australia's CRA mining company more than half the ownership and much of the profits from the mine at Panguna. But there was also an issue over how they achieved the agreement. There was a huge imbalance in power and understanding over the deal and after a while, Bougainvillean's felt they were being short-changed over the value of the mine. It did not help that they could not, or would not, see Papua New Guinea as being one nation, or recognise the virtue of spreading the wealth to benefit the entire country.

The underlying cause of the crisis can be tied back to greed. Greed on the part of the CRA and the Bougainvillean's alike, but with ethnic differences and ignorance also playing a part.

Even after renegotiation of the original agreement in 1974, Bougainvillean's still felt they were being cheated, and there were concerns of a revival of a secessionist movement that had been dormant since the early 1970s.

Later, in 1976, a compromise agreement resulted in the granting of provincial status for the island, but this did not resolve a great deal either. In 1988, after realising there was little chance of an acceptable resolution, a group of people labelled as rebels, but in reality, people fighting for an outcome they saw as more just, shut the mine down.

The resulting state of emergency and civil conflict lasted until 1997. Between 10,000 and 15,000 people lost their lives, economic activity virtually stopped, schools closed, health services declined, and much of the island's infrastructure destroyed. Then in 2000, after all that anger and sadness, the various parties signed a peace agreement, and established the Autonomous Region of Bougainville. But by the 21st century, after so many years, life had still not returned to the stage that it was in the 1970's. The mine remained closed, the wealth locked in the ground; the result was a 'lose-lose' situation for all concerned, then and for the foreseeable future.

In fundamental terms, one could argue that wealth for a few Bougainvillean's overrode the virtue of justice for the many in the rest of the country. Similarly, the possibly excessive value for CRA and its shareholders resulted in lesser value for either Bougainville or Papua New Guinea. Contrary to the common understanding of Western democratic, capitalist society, the basic tenet of justice (espoused by some[86]) does not allow for the sacrifices of a few to be outweighed by the larger sum of advantages enjoyed by the many. One can see the reality in this in the change of mind of (the few) landowners ceding the very thing upon which they depend for their livelihood to (the many) other Papua New Guineans despite the financial incentives provided.

Or, the few Bougainvillean's ceding the wealth of 'their' mine to the rest of the country.

However, ignoring the philosophical arguments for or against concepts of justice, it does appear that allowing the contemporary order of things to prevail (i.e. mining of minerals and use of royalty payments to provide social infrastructure) would result in a better outcome for a greater number of people.

The on-going fundamental issue over what is equitable distribution of wealth is one continuing to challenge the whole of society today.

CARGO CULT REVISITED!

Back in 1978, while we were having a heart-to-heart chat on the lawn at East Hill, my dear old Aunt Mary told me it was unfortunate that although the welfare system in Britain had done so much for society, it had also resulted in too many people expecting too much for far too little effort. Now, forty years on, greed through laziness continues. Abuse of welfare is higher than ever before in the West and the powerful, greedy and immoral continue to work the system, to be spoilers, paid for by the virtuous and at the expense of the genuinely needy.

I saw similar expectations, entitlement if you like, among the followers of the so-called cargo cult in Papua New Guinea. While admittedly based on a different premise of ignorance (with perhaps a shade of sorcery for good measure) rather than guile, it produced (and still is producing) the same problem – expectation of something for nothing.

"No one is entitled to take out of life more than they put into it." That is what my aunt said then, and it holds true today. This goes for a nation, for family and for the individual alike. The world does not owe anyone a living. As the King James 2000 Bible asserts, one should work to earn one's living; "By the sweat of their brow they shall earn their bread" etc. However, this does not mean anyone should be disenfranchised of basic human needs.

The reality is that because of greed, those honest, (virtuous) people who have worked hard and paid taxes, part of which were supposedly to help them in later years, can now only expect miserly support from the State later in life. Where is the justice in that?

Significant shifts in thinking are needed to counter this problem and to develop a system providing a more equitable way forward. The provision of welfare from society must be linked more effectively to an agreement on the part of the recipient to change effort.

An embryonic form of this can be seen in the cashless debit card[87]. This provides welfare assistance in the form of goods and services only for members of the Australian indigenous community, designed to overcome the misuse of cash, which is all too frequently, squandered on drugs or alcohol. Although introduced at certain pilot projects, sadly, some in society believe the card to be demeaning and have attempted to thwart its wider adoption.

Ultimately, however, the adage of 'Give a man a fish and he will feed for a day and teach him to fish, and he will feed for life' suggests the best way. Able-bodied people have a moral responsibility to work as hard and efficiently as they can and, if possible, share any excess with others less fortunate, to help improve the quality of their lives also.

Compassion!

Thanks for reading.

BIBLIOGRAPHY

The following books and on-line sources have all provided valuable information:

Elizabeth Bonshek: *Revaluing Pots: Wanigela Women and Regional Exchange*

Rachel Carson: *Silent Spring*, 1962

D.J. Clancy: *Native Affairs – Kiriaka and South Kunua. Mission Agricultural Societies*, 19 February 1964. TPNG, 13914-51/1/13

Donald Denoon: *A Trial Separation: Australia and the Decolonisation of Papua New Guinea*, 2012. ISBN: 92186292

Irwin B. Firchow and Jacqueline Firchow: *The Rotokas People of Bougainville Island*

Michael J. Field: *Chronology of Bougainville Civil War*, 30 January 1998

Errol Flynn: *My Wicked, Wicked Ways: The Autobiography of Errol Flynn*

Arthur Grimble: *A Pattern of Islands*, John Murray (Publishers) Ltd, Albemarle Street

G. Holden: *Papua New Guinea Village Studies of the early 1970s: History and Reflections*

Graham Hassan: 'Religion and Nation-State Formation in Melanesia: 1945 To Independence', a thesis submitted for the degree of Doctor of Philosophy of the Australian National University, October 1989

Hasa: *Difference Between Value and Virtue*, 2017, Pedia.com

Maryanne Hanette: *The tale of how Buka got its modern name*

James Joyce: *Dubliners*, Grant Richards Ltd. 1914

Hugh M. Laracy: 'Catholic Missions in The Solomon Islands', thesis submitted in partial fulfilment of the requirements for the Degree of Doctor of Philosophy in the Australian National University. November 1969

Mark Lightbody and Tony Wheeler: *World's Wild Places – Papua New Guinea*, Lonely Planet

Malinowski: *The Sexual Life of Savages*, based on fieldwork in Papua New Guinea's Trobriand Islands

Patricia May and Margaret Tuckson: *The Traditional Pottery of Papua New Guinea*

R. J. May: *Political Parties in Papua New Guinea*, ANU Press

Roy Mackay: *New Guinea*, Time-Life Books

Riall Nolan: *Bushwalking in Papua New Guinea*

Paul Oates: *Tropical matters medical*, PNGAA Library

Chris Peter: *The tradition of the pig killing ceremony*, Sina Sina, Simbu Province.

John Rawls, Professor Emeritus at Harvard University: *A Theory of Justice*

John Ryan *The Hot Land: Focus on New Guinea*

James Sinclair: *Kiap*, Pacific Publications, 1981

Suwa, J (2005), *The Abandonment of Yabob Island 1942-1975 and the Memory of Cultural Continuity*. Hirosaki University, Hirosaki, Japan. Refereed papers from The 1st International Small Island Cultures Conference Kagoshima University Centre for the Pacific Islands, February 7th-10th 2005

G. W. Trompf: *Payback: The Logic of Retribution in Melanesian Religions*, University of Sydney 1994 ISBN: 9780521416917

Rev. Neville Threlfall: *Mangroves, Coconuts and Frangipani*

Christopher Winch and John Gingell: *Philosophy of Education: The Key Concepts* (2nd edition). London: Routledge, 2008.

Other Books

The author prepared guides to Papua New Guinea crafts on behalf of the government in the 1970s, and copies of these can be found by searching the Internet.

A sequel to this book, to be entitled Fortuity: Of Virtue and Reality, is under way. If you would like to be informed as to when it is available please contact the author via the publisher of this book.

ACKNOWLEDGEMENTS

Great thanks go to my dear wife Selma and daughter Kavita, who both allowed me to indulge myself over the years in telling my stories ad nauseam.

Thanks also to Graham Richard (Dick) Bird OBE, the VSO Field Officer who did a remarkable job in caring for us volunteers (and me in particular) in PNG during those wonderful years. Dick went on to become the Director of Voluntary Service Overseas and was awarded the Order of the British Empire for voluntary services in 1995.

Kind thanks also to Stewart Gibson and Christopher Powell, my colleagues at Kuraio, who did so much to help the Kereaka and who corrected my memory of events and added many important details.

Thanks also to Joe Aroviri, who, as a young boy, travelled on the *MV Kiriaka Aro*, and who kindly related the story of her fate.

Sister Margaret Ryan AO, who, having lived in the Highlands of PNG, was well qualified to draw my attention to many facts and events I had missed, and at the same time patiently edited my early drafts and improved my prose.

Robert Allen LLB (Hons) (Melbourne) who also kept me on the straight and narrow and checked that I had not written anything defamatory or offended anyone!

Posthumous thanks again also to my dear mother, who dutifully kept all the aerogrammes I had written to her during my travels and which provided foundation material for this book.

My diaries and my letters were not that detailed. I also owe enormous gratitude to both the valuable resources of a multitude of websites provided through the Internet (credited as accurately and comprehensively as possible at the End Notes) and particularly to Wikipedia, all of which enabled me to fill in many missing facts.

If I have missed out anyone or failed to acknowledge a source of information, I apologise, and put it down to a memory challenged by the passing of the years!

E&OE and note on terms used

This narrative is true, although after a period of some forty years between events and my writing about them I trust I will be forgiven for any errors and omissions.

I have often used terms such as 'native', 'local', 'meri' etc. Unless explained to the contrary, none of these terms are intended to be derogatory. 'Raskol' however, is an understated name, commonly used in PNG for petty, and not so petty, criminals.

Also, I have changed the names of some individuals, and I have used a little poetic licence to elaborate here and there, where it is justified.

Lastly, I recognise that my story skims over many of the extremely important cultural aspects of what I was dealing with in assisting in the development of the handcrafts sector. I have referenced some material here but there is a plethora of other excellent reporting on the cultural aspects of the crafts that can be readily found on the Internet.

Endnotes

1 An aeroplane with a reputation for high fuel consumption and noise levels and at least a few significant crashes under its belt!

2 'Kiriaka' is more accurately spelt 'Kereaka'; a mistake made by the foreigners who first made contact.

3 Now known as *Tok Pisin*. See http://www.everyculture.com/knowledge/Tok_Pisin.html

4 Shortly after this I was learn there was a rarely used airstrip at the next Mission station at Sipai, north of Kuraio, but at this stage there was still no road to Sipai.

5 Stewart obtained an Explosives Licence after undertaking a course by the local Public Works Department.

6 The name Buka originates from the indigenous word 'boka'. When the local people first saw explorers and traders in 1768, they were amazed and started shouting 'Boka', which translates into *'What is it?'* Source: *'The tale of how Buka got its modern name'*. By Maryanne Hanette http://www.bougainville24.com/page/4/

7 Fr. Leo Le May, (born Sep. 23, 1909, died: Sep. 9, 1983). Appointed Bishop of Bougainville on November 15th, 1966 and resigned July 1st, 1974.

8 Probably *Physalia physalis* – with a helmet (float), 12 in long, 5 in wide; with tentacles, up to 165 feet long

9 Father Roger J. Bourgea, S.M., (born May 29th, 1932 died July 23rd, 2015). Sent as a missionary to Bougainville and served in parishes there from 1961 to 1975.

10 Commercial development was backed, somewhat reluctantly it transpired, by the Catholic Marist organisation with grants from the 'Freedom from Hunger' campaign, again, as with Sipai, under Father Leo Le May.

11 '...Fr. William Mentzer, Dr William (Bill, Willy) Francis Mentzer - Born in Monongahela, PA, May 22, 1924, died January 29, 2005. *'...He had climbed up the Kuraio cliff in August 1961 with a loaded revolver in his hand. He was taking religion and law and order back among the people Bougainville calls the Kiriaka. His priestly predecessor had been run out of Kuraio, fleeing an apparent threat of death. Mentzer is a determined American who believes that among the Kiriaka; he is fighting to keep out a local brand of Communism spreading....'*: The Hot Land: Focus on New Guinea – John Ryan.

12 Source: *'Catholic Missions in The Solomon Islands'* - 1966 by Hugh M. Laracy - Thesis submitted in partial fulfilment of the requirements for the Degree of Doctor of Philosophy in the Australian National University. November 1969

13 Source: *'Religion and Nation-State Formation in Melanesia: 1945 To Independence'* - Graham Hassan. A thesis submitted for the degree of Doctor of Philosophy of the Australian National University October 1989

14 Wantok i.e. "one talk" refers to belonging to a tribe or clan that talks the same language but may also refer to a close friendship to which one may share allegiance.

15 Alternatively known as the Tauri River

16 Included amongst whom were Kakapitai, Raphael and Ropiri.

17 It was eventually realised that cattle were unsuitable for smallholder projects in PNG.

18 *Colocasia esculenta.*

19 A tractor with hydraulically operated loading bucket on the front and narrow digging bucket at the rear.

20   Bob Dylan – *'All Along the Watchtower'* lyrics © Sony/ATV Music Publishing LLC

21   A civil engineering firm that started road and bridge construction in 1968, a year before the start of Bougainville copper mine.

22   The Government contributed $40,000 to start the first stage of road in the 1968/69 Budget, in response to Fathers Brosnan (Fr. Bourgea's predecessor at Sipai) and Mentzer's demands to support their work and halt the return of 'cargo cult'. In June 1968 the Territory's Parliament decided it was politically urgent to build a road through the Kiriaka, Kunua and Hahon areas to help market the crops from Kuraio and Sipai missions. Source: John Ryan *'The Hot Land'*

23   *Pteropus alecto.* Black flying fox, See pidgin English: http://www.june29.com/hlp/lang/pidgin.html

24   These were difficult times and some of Bougainville's priests including Bill Mentzer and Bernard Brosnan up at Sipai and others were feeling frustrations. They all had their opinions on the start up of mining at Panguna. Indeed, Bishop Leo Le May *'...had a difficult two years until 1967, trying to keep his priests out of politics...'* Source: The Hot Land, John Ryan

25   *Spik poison* is a form of black magic that, as I discovered later, was practiced by a variety of other Papua New Guinean clans.

26   It wasn't until many years later and after I left Bougainville, that I realised the implications of what we were doing at Kuraio and the underlying dislike, by a few people in the broader community, for us *'whity'*.

27   After having been on the island for too long, in *pidgin* English the condition was rather aptly referred to as being *'long long'*.

28   The Bed Dryer comprised a layer of stainless mesh resting on carbon steel Arc Mesh, which in turn was supported by timber beams. The Bed is ~1.2m above ground, supported all round on a stone wall.

29   There were more than thirty bulls.

30   The *kovokovo*, or Jews harp, (a bamboo mouth harp) produces music from its own elastic constituent material.

31   The idea is to take the bearing of a known lighthouse or beacon from the boat, hold one's course and speed; wait a fixed time, then take a new bearing. After plotting both bearings, you then use dividers, the parallel rule and the chart to find your location at the time the second bearing was taken.

32   Tim Blake was an English salvage diver who worked for the owner of the scrapping rights on the Japanese war wrecks. Sadly, he drowned while diving in Rabaul harbour in 1979.

33   I later learned that while most of us only know the event as the Chinese Dragon dance, it is correctly called *wŭ long* and is part of a tradition going back over a thousand years.

34   Later on, Chris was involved in training High School children in the accounts and managing the record keeping of the Society.

35   The start up by CRA of mining at Panguna, just two years earlier (1969) had been directly linked to an increase in the activities of the Hahalis Welfare Society in Buka which had grown from a modest Kibbutz-like operation to *'.... a successful enterprise covering livestock, copra, cacao, dressmaking and trade stores. All money was collectively pooled and doled out according to need...'*

However, both the mine at Panguna and the Hahalis were to become very serious issues for the Catholic Mission and the people of Bougainville generally.

They used these events as a driver for secession from the soon to be established newly independent state of Papua New Guinea of which they were supposedly a part. Source: *The Rotokas People of Bougainville Island, Irwin B. Firchow and Jacqueline Firchow AND* http://en.wikipedia.org/wiki/History_of_Bougainville.

36 Steamships, along with Burns Philp and Carpenters, were the three main trading companies in PNG.

37 PMV's were trucks converted by the addition of metal benches either side of the interior and leaving open sided windows, making a very basic bus.

38 *Payback: The Logic of Retribution in Melanesian Religions.* Author: G. W. Trompf, University of Sydney. 1994 ISBN: 9780521416917

39 Originally a makeshift or temporary dwelling but a term commonly used in PNG to refer to basic, but more permanent, usually cement sheet walled, accommodation.

40 A decidedly derogatory name for the natives!

41 Surprisingly I found I was being paid more in PNG than I'd been earning as a Commercial Trainee in private enterprise in the UK! So, with the lower living costs, I was far better off financially as a volunteer in PNG than in the U.K., even on local wages!

42 The common term for indigenization of all positions within government

43 The push to self government started much earlier with the 1962 visit of Sir Hugh Foot (Lord Caradon) chair of UN Trusteeship Councils to New Guinea where he effectively forced the pace for Australia to consider it as part of their responsibilities under the UN, to grant self government. Source: *'The Hot Land'* J Ryan, pp110-114

44 The Administrator had representational responsibilities as head of the government of the Territory; in this capacity, he represented the Commonwealth Government and did not directly represent the Sovereign.

45 Johnson, Sir Leslie Wilson (Les) (1916–2000). Johnson's formal role as Administrator ended in 1973; after which he became High Commissioner when PNG became self-governing.

46 The dark blue Short Wheel Base, Four Wheel Drive Toyota Land Cruiser was the standard Administration issue transport in the provinces and surprisingly hard to handle on gravel roads!

47 Not her real name.

48 The Anga people, also known as the 'dreaded' Kukukuku

49 Sometime referred to as a 'Yipwon' and more precisely: A standing wooden anthropomorphic figure carved in profile. Head with pierced nose, perforated cheek and painted beard; torso consisting of symmetrical series of opposed hooks, usually from the Karawari River Area, Middle Sepik, New Guinea.

50 http://www.png-tourism.com/png-tours/mt-hagen-cultural-show/13.html

51 With thanks for additional material from: *'New Guinea'* by Roy Mackay in the Time-Life Books World's Wild Places; *'Lonely Planet - Papua New Guinea'* - a travel survival kit by Mark Lightbody and Tony Wheeler, and *'Bushwalking in Papua New Guinea'* by Riall Nolan

52 Many claim Mount Wilhelm, 4,509 m (14,793 ft.) as the highest mountain in Oceania (or Australia) on account of Indonesia being part of Southeast Asia. However Wilhelm is surpassed in height by Puncak Jaya, 4,884 m (16,024 ft.) and several other peaks in Indonesian Papua

53   This is in the Chimbu, the smallest but most densely populated of all provinces in PNG; bordered by Madang to the north and the Gulf country to the south.

54   Sergeant Christopher Donnan died in 1971

55   The Wahgi River runs along one side of Kundiawa, and the Chimbu River (which eventually joins the Wahgi) flows along the other.

56   Indeed, there were some examples in the shops that were of significant cultural value, the sale and export of which I, and many others, thought needed to be controlled.

57   http://www.dfat.gov.au/geo/png/png_brief.html - ultimately called the National Cultural Council

58   On a broader level, as far as I knew, Business Development never really had a debate over whether it was sensible to encourage locals to earn money (in any activity) and participate in the economy, it was assumed that this was our raison d'être.

59   Source: https://pngaa.net/Library/CoastwatcherMemorial.html

60   Sourced, with thanks: Suwa, J (2005) The Abandonment of Yabob Island 1942-1975 and the Memory of Cultural Continuity, Hirosaki University, Japan. Refereed papers from The 1st International Small Island Cultures Conference Kagoshima University Centre for the Pacific Islands, February 7th-10th 2005 http://www.sicri.org

61   One of the worst riots in PNG's history. Source: Standish in NT 30th July-4th August 1973: 8 in *"Payback: The Logic of Retribution in Melanesian Religions"* By G. W. Trompf

62   As Secretary of the Department of Business Development (later renamed as the Department of Commerce) from 1971 to 1975, he was the first Papua New Guinean appointed as the head of any government department. He later became Sir Paulias Nguna Matane GCL, GCMG, OBE, KStJ, (born 21 September 1931 -) and was the eighth Governor-General of Papua New Guinea, serving from June 2004 to December 2010.

63   South Pacific, the most popular local beer.

64   Wirz's collection of PNG artefacts can be seen in the *Museum der Kulturen* in Basel, Switzerland.

65   A horizontal signal drum made of a hollowed out, two to three-metre long, tree trunk.

66   *'Political Parties in Papua New Guinea'* R. J. May - ANU Press - press-files.anu. edu.au/downloads/press/p77961/pdf/ch0564.pdf

67   LP 'Led Zeppelin IV', by Jimmy Page and Robert Plant

68   "A mischievous young person, an uncultivated, rowdy but good hearted person", or "a person who acts with apparent disregard for social or political conventions" Source: Oxford Modern Australian English Dictionary

69   Led Zeppelin, the progenitors of heavy metal and hard rock; crazy Frank Zappa, avant-garde Kraftwerk, weird Pink Floyd, and sensational Hendrix, as well as 'underground' singers like Lou Reed.

70   Thanks for background information from: *'The tradition of the pig killing ceremony'*. Chris Peter, Sina Sina, Simbu Province. At Keith Jackson and Friends. http://asopa.typepad.com/asopa_people/2012/06/the-tradition-of-the-pig-killing-ceremony.html

71   *'My Wicked, Wicked Ways: The Autobiography of Errol Flynn'*

72 Commercial development began around 1969, with the establishment of the Hargy Oil Palms Ltd (HOPL) in West New Britain, a joint venture between the PNG Government and Shin Asahigawa Pty Ltd.

73 Simply, a dinghy powered by an outboard motor.

74 For a more deserving, in-depth description of tapa cloth see: *Painting The Past And The Future. Bark cloth of The Maisin People In Papua New Guinea.* © Anna-Karina Hermkens - Research financed by The Netherlands Foundation for the Advancement of Tropical Research (NWO-WOTRO), and the Radboud University of Nijmegen, Netherlands. Circa 2005

75 Thanks for detail provided by *'Revaluing Pots: Wanigela Women and Regional Exchange'* - Elizabeth Bonshek - http://press-files.anu.edu.au/downloads/press/n2571/html/ch05.xhtml?referer=2571&page=12

76 Sister Helen Roberts, a trained triple certificated nurse, joined the Mission in 1947 and had been posted to Wanigela, in the Collingwood Bay area of Oro Province in 1949. She was awarded the MBE for service to nursing and community in the 1987 New Years Honours.

77 2.73 million people in 1973

78 These trucks could carry 105 tonnes of ore. The biggest trucks on the roads in England at the time carried around 35 tonnes.

79 Kabiu (The Mother), Tovanumbatir (The North Daughter), Turagunan (The South Daughter), Tavurvur (Matupit Crater), Rabalanakaia (literally The Heart of the Volcano) and Kalamanagunan (Vulcan Crater). Source: *'Mangroves, Coconuts and Frangipani'* Rev Neville Threlfall. See also here: https://sites.google.com/site/simpsonhafen/ Tavurvur is one of the most active and most dangerous volcanoes in Papua New Guinea. It was this one that exploded violently in 1994, devastating Rabaul. http://www.volcanodiscovery.com/rabaul-tavurvur.html.

80 The town was evacuated in 1937, and the Australian administration moved to Lae after the volcano erupted killing 500 people.

81 Source: *'Mangroves, Coconuts and Frangipani'* Rev Neville Threlfall.

82 *'Silent Spring'*, the metaphorical title for the book by Rachel Carson published in 1962. As one of the original environmentalists, before the term was coined, she was suggesting a bleak future for the whole natural world unless something was done to stop the indiscriminate use of pesticides. Ms Carson's endeavours in this and other areas eventually lead to the establishment of the U.S. Environmental Protection Agency.

83 Source: https://www.duomomilano.it/en/infopage/sculpture/cd479ca7-3571-48f4-b8f7-31ce72d45b67/

84 Source: *'Chronology of Bougainville Civil War'* By Michael J. Field, AFP 30 January 1998.

85 There were many other issues associated with social unease, amongst them, being the *'cargo cult'* and Hahalis Welfare Society. One can read about these in, for example, *'The Hot Land'*, by John Ryan.

86 Justice is the first virtue of social institutions, (as truth is of systems of thought) and justice denies that the loss of freedom for some is made right by a greater good shared by others. It does not allow that the sacrifices imposed on a few are outweighed by the larger sum of advantages enjoyed by many. Source: *A Theory of Justice (Excerpts) - John Rawls - Professor Emeritus at Harvard University.*

87 *'Cashless debit cards protect Aboriginal women and children'* - Jacinta Nampijinpa Price - The Australian - December 26, 2017.